T0079885

BISHOP BURGESS

Bishop Burgess and his World

Culture, Religion and Society in Britain, Europe and North America in the Eighteenth and Nineteenth Centuries

edited by

NIGEL YATES

UNIVERSITY OF WALES PRESS
CARDIFF
2007

British Library Cataloguing-in-Publication Data
A catalogue record for this book is available from the British Library.

ISBN 978–0–7083–2075–4

Typeset by Columns Design Ltd, Reading
Printed in Great Britain by Antony Rowe Ltd, Wiltshire

Contents

CONTENTS

List of Illustrations

List of Contributors

Dom Aidan Bellinger, Abbot of Downside.

A. J. Brothers, Department of Classics, University of Wales, Lampeter.

Joris van Eijnatten, Department of History, VU University of Amsterdam.

Anders Jarlert, Professor of Church History, University of Lund.

Julie Lethaby, Project Development Officer, The Leprosy Mission.

Peter Miles, Department of English, University of Wales, Lampeter.

Peter Nockles, Methodist Church Archivist, John Rylands University Library, Manchester.

Keith Robbins, Honorary Professor and former Vice-Chancellor, University of Wales, Lampeter.

Mark Smith, Lecturer in English Local History, University of Oxford.

Eryn White, Department of History and Welsh History, University of Wales, Aberystwyth.

Nigel Yates, Professor of Ecclesiastical History, University of Wales, Lampeter.

Paula Yates, Department of Theology and Religious Studies, University of Wales, Lampeter.

Introduction

This volume comprises nine of the keynote addresses and shorter communications delivered at a conference on 'Bishop Burgess and his World' held at the University of Wales, Lampeter, in June 2003; the two addresses from the conference session on 'Church, State and Ecclesiastical Reform in the Long Nineteenth Century' held as part of the proceedings of the Commission Internationale d'Histoire Ecclésiastique Comparée at the University of Exeter in July 2003; and the text of the St David's Day lecture delivered at the University of Wales, Lampeter in March 2004. The editor and contributors acknowledge their gratitude to the University of Wales Press for undertaking the publication of this volume to their usual high standards, and to the Department of Theology and Religious Studies at the University of Wales, Lampeter, and the University Research Committee for making generous grants towards the cost of publication.

This volume is part of a much wider project launched by the University of Wales, Lampeter, in collaboration with the Free University of Amsterdam and the University of Lund, to investigate comparative developments in church–state relations and the impact of these on programmes of ecclesiastical reform during the 'long nineteenth century', between roughly 1780 and 1920, across the British Isles (including Ireland), the Low Countries, Germany and Scandinavia. The purpose of this project is to see to what extent there were common trends in religious developments across a wide geographical area, as well as the extent to which such developments were constrained by local factors, religious, political and social, in this period. Work on this project involves teams of scholars in several British and European universities collaborating on different aspects of this topic. The conference at Lampeter and the CIHEC session at Exeter in 2003 were designed to offer members of these teams, as well as colleagues not involved in the project, an opportunity to explore important themes in the cultural, religious and social history of the eighteenth and nineteenth centuries, some of which will form a major part of the project now being undertaken. Work on the project is scheduled for completion in 2010, with publication of the final volume shortly thereafter.

Bishop Thomas Burgess of St David's and Salisbury (Illus. 1), who founded the institution now known as the University of Wales, Lampeter, was a key figure in the cultural, religious and social history of the late eighteenth and early nineteenth centuries. He was, as Mark Smith outlines in the first essay in this volume, one of the promoters of ecclesiastical reform in the Church of England. Although he wrote theological works, his major contribution to international scholarship was in the field of classical studies, as revealed in the interesting correspondence discussed in the essay by A. J. Brothers. Burgess's own theological concerns are reflected in four essays. The Church of England in the years before the Oxford Movement saw itself very firmly as being an integral part of European Protestantism. Joris van Eijnatten has looked at what this meant in terms of theological scholarship in the Netherlands in Burgess's lifetime. Burgess was one of those High Churchmen who tried to take a tolerant view of the evangelical revival, which had an impact on all the Protestant churches of Europe in the late eighteenth century. Eryn White looks at the impact of the evangelical revival in Wales, and Nigel Yates sets this aspect of the revival in the wider context of its manifestations in other Celtic parts of the British Isles. Whilst Burgess endeavoured to befriend evangelicals, despite his opposition to some of their beliefs, he was strongly hostile to Roman Catholicism, which was beginning to experience a revival in parts of England, not unconnected with the presence of French exiles, from about 1790, as documented in the study by Dom Aidan Bellinger.

One of Burgess's major concerns was with education at every level. The beginnings of the movement for the establishment of elementary schools in one part of Wales by Burgess's episcopal contemporary, Bishop Majendie of Bangor, are explored in the essay by Paula Yates. Burgess's most notable

achievement, however, was his establishment of St David's College at Lampeter, and his example was followed by other Anglican bishops outside the British Isles, a topic examined in the essay by Peter Miles. Keith Robbins and Anders Jarlert discuss another topic close to Burgess's heart, the relationship between church and state, and examine the changes that took place in this relationship during the nineteenth century in the British Isles and Scandinavia. The final two essays, by Peter

3

Nockles and Julie Lethaby, look at the more specifically Anglican aspects of religious change in the early nineteenth century, and in particular the impact of the Oxford Movement on Anglicanism. Burgess was dead within four years of Keble's Assize Sermon, and he would have deplored many of the developments in Anglicanism in the years after his death. He was, however, a man who in his own generation was at the heart of cultural, religious and social developments in the world that he knew, and he provides a useful focus for a series of studies that endeavour to illustrate both the complexity of that society and the wide measure of common ground that united its leaders and opinion-formers across national boundaries, and even across the Atlantic Ocean.

Nigel Yates
University of Wales, Lampeter
June 2004

1

Burgess, Churchman and Reformer

MARK SMITH

His Lordship . . . laboured zealously to improve the means of Divine worship – to correct every approach to neglect or irregularity – and, in a word, to increase and nurture the flock committed to his charge . . . and while his loss is deplored, not only as a local bereavement, but as a national deprivation, we may find consolation in the reflection, that the accumulated fruits of his many years' labour remain a bright beacon and example to all.[1]

His name, even were all his other claims to public gratitude forgotten – were his Biblical labours, his profound and elegant learning; his zeal for the circulation of the Word of God; his exertions for the defence of our revered Church . . . his benevolent efforts . . . his aimiable deportment; his personal piety to lapse from remembrance – would still live . . . so long as the invaluable institution of St David's College shall remain to testify his enlightened munificence . . . he was a man of the primitive type; a man of peace, of prayer of study, of humility, and of mortification; a man such as is not often seen in these days of secularity and moral rail-road innovation.[2]

When placed side by side, these quotations, the first from the orthodox High Church *Christian Remembrancer* and the second from the moderate evangelical *Christian Observer*, provide an ideal point of departure for an exploration of what we might, perhaps, describe as the enigma of Bishop Burgess. It is not at all unusual, of course, for obituaries, to speak well of the dead. But it was Burgess's fate to be spoken of, not just well, but with affection and enthusiasm, in many quarters and from many points of view. High Church encomia of an essentially orthodox bishop who numbered Archdeacons Churton and Daubeny among his correspondents are hardly surprising,[3] but the fondest recollections seem to have come from evangelicals. Indeed, so glowing was the *Christian Observer*'s preliminary account[4] that several correspondents accused the periodical of partiality in not adverting to the Bishop's careless manner of conducting business.[5] The editor, S. C. Wilks, did incorporate in a further eulogy of Burgess a couple of anecdotes to this effect, but then printed no fewer than eleven letters from the late Bishop, for the sole purpose of illustrating the extremely efficient way in which he had conducted business with the *Christian Observer*![6] Had any doubts remained about the official attitude of the periodical, these were definitively laid to rest by its review of Harford's biography of the Bishop, which described him as:

> a man of profound and varied learning, of deep and saint-like devotion, of the most amiable manners and the most guileless and charitable heart, combined with an extraordinary simplicity of character, which gave to his deportment an air of great originality, and sometimes even excited a smile, though never unmingled with respect and reverence.[7]

The consequence of this widespread approbation has been to cause some confusion among historians used to analysing the later Hanoverian Church in terms of party divisions. Arthur Burns, for example, reviewing this party-based literature, has pointed out that, 'men such as . . . Thomas Burgess . . . can be encountered in the character of both moderate evangelical and high churchman'.[8] Similarly, Peter Nockles, in his perceptive essay on church parties in the pre-Tractarian Church of England, includes Burgess among a list of bishops 'who cannot readily be categorized in an exclusive way', and who 'could be claimed by the Evangelical and Orthodox parties alike'.[9]

The modern view of Burgess, like that of the *Christian Observer* in 1840, has of course largely been shaped by a single source – the work of the Bishop's first and only substantial biographer, John Scandrett Harford.[10] Harford was a man of

considerable fortune, inheriting from his father both a prosper-
ous banking business and several landed estates. He was, from
1820, closely associated with Burgess and became the most
important supporter of the Bishop's favourite project. He gave
the site for the college at Lampeter, together with a considerable donation from his own resources, and in addition lent the
influence of his family connections to secure royal support for
the scheme.[11] He was also a man of considerable literary
pretensions who had, in 1808, already completed a first essay
in biography,[12] and who later went on to write several more,
including works on Michelangelo and William Wilberforce.[13]
Given this profile, it is perhaps not surprising that Burgess
should have selected Harford as his literary executor and,
therefore, also as his potential biographer.[14] In one important
respect, however, the biographer differed from his subject, for
Harford was a decided, if moderate, *evangelical* churchman, of
a somewhat romantic turn of mind, sometimes identified as the
original of the hero in Hannah More's *Coelebs in Search of a
Wife*.[15]

Harford's biography of Burgess was addressed to the general
reader, who was assured that it was written 'from personal
knowledge and authentic data'. Its declared object was 'to
trace the formation and development of his character, and its
practical influence in the exalted station which he filled in the
Church'.[16] However, rather like the picture of William Wilberforce created by his High Church sons,[17] the impression of
Burgess's character, work and theology which Harford created
from this 'personal knowledge and authentic data' was also the
product of considerable artifice. Closely resembling the
engraved portrait which peers short-sightedly at the reader
from the frontispiece of the work, Harford's Burgess is first and
foremost a scholar – a man who, had a vocation to the pastoral
ministry not intervened, might have emerged as a great critic of
classical Greek literature. Along with the scholarship went a
characteristic shyness and modesty, which Harford illustrates
by telling a story that Burgess had turned down the offer of a
valuable prebend at Salisbury because it would have required
him to sit in one of the most conspicuous stalls in the cathedral.[18] The remainder of his character, which is introduced in

the opening chapter, seems to have been fixed from his early days at Winchester College:

> Manly and independent in his disposition, but at the same time mild and inoffensive, he steadfastly pursued a course of good conduct. . . . That calm self-possession, that love of books, that taste for a studious life, which characterised the Bishop to the end of his career, were not only thus early developed, but had even stamped a thoughtful expression on his countenance.[19]

This line is maintained consistently through the volume; as Bishop Barrington's chaplain, for example, he is described as:

> tall, erect, and dignified, and there was a cast of pleasing, not repulsive gravity over the calm expression of his intellectual features. His smile was peculiarly winning. The Reverend Mr Smelt, . . . who often met him at Durham used to say, 'Of all the sweet things I can think of there is nothing quite equal to Burgess's smile.'[20]

Similarly, as Bishop of St David's, Burgess was 'habitually amiable, gentle, humble, affectionate; but firm and inflexible in the maintenance of principle and the discharge of duty'.[21]

Alongside a continuing devotion to scholarship, Harford traces, from the early 1790s, a second mainspring of Burgess's life and career: 'The religious principle had been silently deepening in his mind, and he felt anxious to employ his talents for the promotion of the glory of God and the salvation of souls, in the active discharge of pastoral and parochial duties.'[22] This pastoral vocation is followed through his work as incumbent of a rural parish at Winston, and his episcopates at St David's and Salisbury, with a particular stress on his concern for clerical education, his support for religious societies, and his careful use of diocesan pastoral machinery, such as visitations and the reinvigorated office of rural dean.[23]

Significantly, it is in this *pastoral* context that Harford introduces the serious discussion of Burgess's theology. As incumbent of Winston, we discover that Burgess's sermons bore 'the impress of a heart truly devout, and of a judgement which clearly apprehended the great scope and aim of the Gospel of Christ',[24] and also that,

> Deeply attached to the Church of England, convinced that its doctrines are scriptural, its mode of government apostolic, and its formularies impregnated with the elevated yet chastened devotion of the purest ages of Christianity, he was among the most devoted of her sons. But although, in this sense, a high churchman, there was no bitterness in his orthodoxy. However uncompromising in his opinions, charity and kindness influenced his whole mode of communicating them to others; nor could a Dissenter, after personal conference with him, fail to bear away the impression that he was one in whom the love of God was predominant, and who had a smile for real goodness, wherever it was to be found.[25]

In the final appendix to the biography, Harford gave a list of works published by Burgess prior to the year 1823. Given that almost 75 per cent of the forty works appearing in the second half of the list (those published from 1814–23) were controversial in form,[26] Harford could hardly deny that the retiring, charitable, pastoral and, above all, sweet-smiling Burgess of the remainder of the biography was also a persistent, not to say perennial, controversialist. However, here the biographer organized his material with particular care. All Burgess's controversial writings, especially his work on the ancient British church, on the works of Milton and on the authenticity of 1 John 5: 7, were grouped around two major themes – a defence of Protestantism against Romanism and a defence of Trinitarian orthodoxy against Unitarianism.[27] Burgess is thus represented primarily as a champion of the Established Church against *external* and, especially, heterodox opponents. The impression given by the extensive treatment of these themes in the text of the biography is reinforced by the choice of material in the appendices. In addition to the list of published works, these comprised Burgess's piece on Granville Sharp's Rule on uses of the definite article in New Testament Greek, which was a key text in the Unitarian controversy, his letter to Lord Melbourne on the 'Idolatry and apostasy of Rome', and, finally, a text which indicated Burgess's relatively favourable approach to orthodox Dissenters, describing the circumstances under which he would admit former Dissenting ministers to Orders in the Church of England.[28] Moreover, for Harford, just as important as the themes of Burgess's controversial writings was the spirit in which he engaged in them. It might have been the case that Burgess's 'conclusions were sometimes drawn in stronger terms than the premises warranted', but, nevertheless,

> As a controversialist, he was a rare instance of tenacious earnestness and zeal in maintaining and defending his own opinions, or challenging those of others, without the slightest admixture of polemical bitterness. Controversy was always carried on by him in a courteous and Christian spirit, and he gave no advantage to an opponent by want of temper, or by any ebullitions of spleen or impatience.[29]

Here, then, we have the foundation of Burgess's subsequent reputation: the courteous and scholarly, if sometimes also obstinate and tedious, controversialist, who, according to the *Dictionary of National Biography*, 'for, several years in succession . . . exhausted the patience of the Royal Society of Literature by a demonstration that the newly discovered treatise "De Doctrina Christiana" could not be written by Milton';[30] the moderate High Church or even cross-bench bishop who readily associated with evangelicals, and, above all, the modest and committed clergyman – the 'gentle and unassuming man, much more of a pastor than a prelate' of D. T. W. Price's *Bishop Burgess and Lampeter College*.[31]

A somewhat different picture begins to emerge, however, if we examine Burgess's role in the controversy which gave rise to one of the rarest of his printed works, *Reflections on the Judgment delivered by Sir John Nicholl, against the Rev. T. W. Wickes* – a controversy which Harford excluded altogether from the biography, despite its being the subject of an extensive correspondence surviving among the Bishop's papers. The case of Kemp versus Wickes, which centred on the issue of the right of Dissenters to seek burial according to the rites of the Established Church, can be briefly stated. John Wickes, the rector of Wardley cum Belton in Rutland, had, in 1808, refused to bury the child of two of his parishioners, John and Hannah

Swingler, who were Calvinistic Dissenters, contending, as he later explained in a tract addressed to the Bishop of Peterborough, 'that baptism performed by any other than the acknowledged, legal, and established clergy is invalid', and that the child was therefore excluded from burial by the Prayer Book rubric.[32] The case was taken up by a local Independent minister, John Green, who brought it to the attention of the Dissenting Deputies in London. They decided to turn it into a test case and arranged for another local Dissenter, William Kemp, to act as plaintiff. In December 1809, the case was heard by Sir John Nicholl, the Official Principal of the Court of Arches (the senior ecclesiastical court of the province of Canterbury), who found in favour of Kemp. The judgment, though long and complex, rested on three main points:

> First, that the 68th canon required ministers to bury any corpse (except that of an excommunicate) according to the form in the Book of Common Prayer;
> Second, that the rubric for the Prayer Book burial service excepted only persons who had died unbaptized, excommunicate or by suicide;
> and third, that 'unbaptized' meant persons not validly initiated into the Christian Church in general.

Nicholl went on to note that the child concerned had been baptized using water and the Trinitarian formula, which the ancient church had regarded as the two things necessary for valid baptism. Moreover, the Church of England, since the Reformation, while considering it to be irregular had, nevertheless, acknowledged the validity of *lay* baptism, and therefore had not regarded the services of an episcopally ordained minister as essential to the validity of the rite. Consequently, since Dissenting baptisms were to be regarded as Christian baptisms, Dissenters and their children could not be excluded from burial as unbaptized, as had been maintained by Wickes.[33]

Having gained their victory, the Dissenting Deputies sought to ensure that it was publicized as widely as possible. They had employed their own shorthand writer to make a verbatim record of the judgment and they published it, somewhat to the consternation of Sir John Nicholl, early in the following year.[34]

Encroachment on Anglican churchyards was not the only issue exciting concern about the advance of religious dissent in this period, and the years 1809–11 also saw, for example, the origination, promotion and eventual defeat of Lord Sidmouth's proposed legislation to limit Dissenting itinerancy.[35] In this somewhat febrile atmosphere, the publication of the judgment in Kemp versus Wickes was bound to create a furore. Clerical controversialists reached for their pens, and so did the editors of the *Reviews*. Hard on the heels of the judgment came a critical *Letter to Sir John Nicholl*, published anonymously by 'A Clergyman',[36] and in the April number of the *Anti-Jacobin* the editor took advantage of a review of the *Letter* to launch a scathing attack on the judgment, and a vitriolic and abusive assault on Sir John Nicholl himself.[37] First in the field, with a piece printed under his *own* name, however, was the redoubtable Charles Daubeny, the far-from-moderate High Church Archdeacon of Sarum, who devoted to the judgment a considerable portion of his archidiaconal Charge for 1810.[38] By the beginning of 1811, Burgess, who regarded the judgment as tending 'directly to the subversion of the Established Church',[39] seems to have concluded that it was incumbent on him, as Bishop of St David's, a diocese with a significant number of Calvinist Dissenters[40], to make his own position clear. He chose to do so, however, not by the publication of a pamphlet on the subject, the course Daubeny would follow in the same year,[41] but by printing a circular letter addressed to the clergy of his diocese.

In undertaking this task, Burgess followed a method which he had adopted for a number of his more widely circulated works and which was described to Harford by G. S. Faber, from whom Harford had solicited correspondence which might help in the compilation of the biography:

The Bishop never wrote to me more than half a dozen lines, merely saying, that he had inclosed some <u>printed</u> thoughts of his which were intended for publication, and asking me to give my opinion or to suggest any ideas which might be useful for his purpose. Thus you will perceive, my letters were not answers to <u>letters</u> of the Bishop, but to the <u>printed</u> <u>sheets</u> which he had sent down to me … Such was the mode in which our <u>correspondence</u>, if it may be so called, was carried on: and I do not recollect that I <u>ever</u> received a <u>letter</u>, in the common acceptation of the word, from the Bishop.[42]

In the case of Kemp versus Wickes, Burgess seems to have sent out the work in March or April 1811 while he was still in the process of composition. It was consequently delivered, a few pages at a time, to a small circle of correspondents. Some of these men had local connections, including Ralph Churton, the Archdeacon of St David's, and Charles Prichett, Rural Dean of Castle Martin. Others were more far-flung, including Bishops Barrington and Huntingford, Johnson Grant, the High Church historian, A. L. Luders, the lawyer, and last, but certainly not least, the Archdeacon of Sarum. Although Burgess's original drafts do not survive, it is possible, by comparing the letters of his correspondents with the final version of the printed circular, both to infer what his first thoughts must have been and to trace their development. We should note at the outset, however, that in selecting this particular group as his sounding board, Burgess was hardly likely to be pulled towards a moderate or cross-bench position. Barrington was certainly a moderate High Churchman, but Huntingford, who owed his preferment to Sidmouth,[43] was unlikely to wish to conciliate Dissenters, and the remaining three most significant correspondents, Johnson Grant, Ralph Churton, intimate of the Hackney Phalanx,[44] and Charles Daubeny, darling of the *Anti-Jacobin*,[45] are generally identified with a much more definite form of High Churchmanship. The letters, therefore have an additional value in permitting us to overhear some significant leaders of this school thinking aloud about an issue which was to become increasingly controverted over the next four decades.[46]

Wickes and his early defenders, as Johnson Grant pointed out, justified the refusal of burial to the child, 'on so high grounds, as that baptism out of the church is no baptism at all'.[47] Judging by the correspondence, it would appear that this was Burgess's first thought, too. Bishop Barrington immediately suspected that a malign influence had been at work on his friend and wrote, on 17 April,

We do not often differ in opinion, and when we do, I suspect myself to be in the wrong. In the present instance however I conceive the opinion which you have adopted has arisen from your judgement having been warped by the unfounded opinions of Mr Daubeny.[48]

While Barrington may have been unusually forthright, Burgess's other correspondents also seem to have responded unfavourably to his line of argument, and a number of objections emerged, which might be classified as pragmatic, legal, theological and ecclesiological.

The pragmatic and legal arguments were, as might have been expected, most often voiced by the bishops and lawyers. Barrington's initial response, for example, went on to stress the pastoral problems that would be caused by following Daubeny:

> The good effects of the decree are peace and union; the bad ones resulting from Mr Daubeny's principles would be perpetual animosities and lawsuits in every parish. On his principles how large a proportion of the inhabitants of this island must be considered as not being Christians, and treated as such, at a moment the most interesting to their surviving friends.[49]

Later in the month Barrington pointed out that Burgess could not seriously expect the substance of his circular letter not to get into the provincial press, and from there to be drawn to national attention. He further explained the consequences in a letter written at the end of May:

> You ask me my Dear lord what I apprehend are likely to be the effects resulting from the discussion of Sir John Nicholls's judgement. They lie in a narrow compass ... I knew from personal experience the Dissenters were warm and determined and had a common purse to prosecute ... Should they learn that you or any other of the bishops are employed in controverting the judgement, while they are holding their meetings on the rejection of Lord Sidmouth's bill, they will not fail to come to some strong resolution on the subject which at the moment will produce very general irritation.[50]

The Bishop of Gloucester's views were similar in character,

> I was of opinion more injury would be done to the Church by keeping alive Dissension, than benefit could be derived from animadverting on the sentence, erroneous though it was. That persuasion had not left me when Mr Archdeacon Daubeny published. Nor has it now.[51]

Johnson Grant's pragmatic concerns, on the other hand, were less about peace in the parishes or the potential political problems arising from controverting the judgment than about the use that opponents might make of the argument that only an episcopally ordained priest could perform a valid baptism, and, in particular,

> the imputation it is likely to draw from the pens of adversaries, of preferring identity in form of government, to affinity in vital principles, as the criterion of unity in the visible church. Thus do we stretch out a more cordial right hand of fellowship to Papists than to some of our own sects, who have comparatively fewer errors in doctrine, to some who pretend even, I say not with what truth, that they differ from us in nothing but in form.[52]

The legal argument was stated baldly by Barrington in his first letter:

> The Law by Sir J. Nicholl's sentence is now established, and must be regarded as Law till altered by a superior jurisdiction. The line of conduct therefore at present is clear both to the clergy who ask the opinion of their Bishops and the Bishops who give it.[53]

This sort of conclusion could also be linked to pragmatic considerations, as in the legal historian Alexander Luders's suggestion that, on the question of 'expediency and propriety', it might be better to express views privately to the judge or try an appeal, rather than to address them

> publicly to the Clergy under you, who in respectful duty to you, must be taught to disrespect the lawful authority to which they are bound to submit. The <u>consequences injurious</u>

to <u>religion</u>, the fear of which your Lordship justly states to be the motive, may be alleged also on the other side.[54]

The theological arguments centred, not on the validity of Dissenting Orders, which naturally none of Burgess's High Church correspondents was prepared to admit, but on the question of whether lay baptism with water and using the Trinitarian formula might be considered valid. Perhaps the first correspondent to argue this case was the historian Johnson Grant, who wrote on 9 April to argue that while baptisms unauthorized by the Church did not admit their recipients to membership of the Church of England, they did admit to membership of the universal church. Thus, lay baptism 'cannot be said to be altogether not valid, <u>to be no baptism at all</u>'.[55] However, this was clearly not a fixed position for Grant, who having slept on the matter, wrote again the following day to say that he had changed his mind and now thought all baptisms outside the Church were invalid, and that if other professing Christians were to be regarded as participating in salvation, 'we do not intend it from a belief in the virtue of their baptism, which is nothing at all, but of their faith, and of the compassion of God'.[56] By 26 April, Grant had clearly had time to consider the matter in much greater detail, and had changed his mind yet again. He wrote a third, much longer, letter, saying that he was now undecided on the issue, though he thought that baptisms outside the forms of the English Church could not be denied all validity.[57] Charles Pritchett also had doubts, but expressed them more succinctly, informing the Bishop that, 'The more I ponder on this subject, the greater difficulties overwhelm me.'[58]

Rather more decisive was the response Burgess received from his archdeacon, Ralph Churton. Churton began by invoking the authority of other leading High Churchmen, assuring Burgess that, 'Mr Norris, his brother in law Mr Sikes and others are decidedly <u>against</u> the judgement of Sir J. Nicholl. I incline to that side of the question, which seems to have clear and cogent arguments in its favour.'[59] But he then went on to argue from the example of the early church that lay baptism had been considered valid and might be still, even in the present state of the Church in England.[60]

Churton and Johnson Grant were equally exercised by the ecclesiological consequences of a hard-line position on lay baptism, 'If Lay Baptism is invalid', noted Churton, 'it will . . . unchristianize the Kirk of Scotland, and all the Calvinian Christians abroad.'[61] In his third letter, Grant put the issue in even starker terms,

> If a person not episcopally baptized is not baptized – is no member of Christ's visible church, then all members of all sects, the whole of the church of Scotland and several churches abroad, are not baptized, no one person belonging to them is admitted into Christ's visible church; nay, since, by analogy, a person not baptized, and an excommunicated person . . . stand on the same grounds; and since an excommunicated person is to be regarded as an heathen and a publican, the whole church of Scotland, and all the bodies above alluded to, are to be regarded as Heathens and Publicans.[62]

He then went on to raise the awkward case of Thomas Secker, who, having been born and brought up as a Dissenter, had become Archbishop of Canterbury without receiving episcopal baptism. 'There seems to me then', Grant continued,

> no way of escaping the inferences, that Secker was no member of Christ's church, although nominally at the head of it; that the burial service of that church might have been refused him; that all ordinations conferred by him were null, and that he is to be held as having been a heathen and a publican.[63]

Burgess was clearly under pressure from a range of correspondents to moderate his initial line, and Grant concluded his lengthy epistle of 26 April with such an appeal: 'Why not bring the matter then into a narrower compass? Why bring the question about "the true church", " the visible church", and "the catholic church", upon the carpet at all?'[64] In the final printed version of his circular Burgess did opt for the more moderate argument that the Prayer Book rubric used the term 'unbaptized', not in a general or abstract sense, but in the particular sense of not being baptized according to the forms of the Church of England, that is, by a lawful minister with water and the Trinitarian formula. This allowed Burgess to defend

Wickes's conduct and to deny to Dissenters a right of burial using the Prayer Book service, while sidestepping the issue of the general validity of baptism not conducted by episcopally ordained ministers.[65] Indeed, he took care to emphasize, in a lengthy preface to the document, that this 'interpretation of the Rubrick does not *unchristianize* Dissenters; it does not declare them to be *not baptized at all*, and *not Christians*; but, not baptized by a lawful minister; and forbids the use of the burial service for persons so baptized'.[66]

On other issues, however, Burgess proved to be rather less conciliatory. Once Daubeny had pointed out the error in his preliminary draft, the Bishop immediately substituted the word 'congregation' or 'Society' for 'Church' in describing Protestant Dissenters.[67] Here, he was simply following standard High Church usage, but he went rather further when, against the cautions of Churton, he included in the final version of the circular an argument that it was wrong that a minister who,

> believes, that they are at least in an unsafe state, who live and die in schism; – should yet be compellable to bury ... a Dissenter not only as a *dear brother*, but with the *express* and *declared* hope that 'this our brother doth rest in the Lord'.[68]

What conclusions can be drawn from this discussion of Burgess's circular? Perhaps the most striking feature of the correspondence is the range of opinion manifested by professed members of the High Church school. Peter Nockles has already pointed out that there was 'no one monolithic viewpoint'[69] among this body, but it is worth emphasizing that in the early nineteenth century such diversity could extend even to apparently central issues, such the conditions of the validity of baptism. Indeed, in this correspondence can be perceived a reflection of the process by which the orthodox school was evolving its position, and thus by which its members were learning to be High Churchmen, just as in the notes of meetings of the Eclectic Society we can see a process of evangelicals evolving and learning evangelicalism.[70] The process also reveals some interesting overlaps. When, for example, Churton, a man described by Nockles as 'an exemplar of

Orthodox churchmanship',[71] sought to persuade Burgess to drop his argument relating to the burial service, he did so by contending that,

> Hope goes, and goes willingly even to the very brink of despair; and I can honestly say of any Christian, as I could even of a Jew or a Turk or a Heathen, I <u>hope</u> he 'rests' in peace, unless I was absolutely certain, as no man can be, of the contrary. But 'sure and certain hope' (even if I could say so of any man) has no reference at all to the <u>individual interred</u>; it is merely the <u>general ground</u> or <u>reason</u> for using such a solemn service.[72]

This was language more usually associated with moderate evangelicals defending the use of the service for the ostensibly unregenerate than with the Hackney Phalanx.[73]

Perhaps equally striking is what the correspondence reveals about Burgess's own position on the spectrum. Here, he appears not as a moderate or cross-bench figure, but as a man whose first instinct was to adopt a relatively extreme position, from which he was gradually hauled back by more moderate voices like Barrington, Churton and Grant. Indeed, there seems to be a straightforward line of development from Burgess's initial thoughts about the indispensability of an episcopally ordained clergyman to the validity of baptism through to Mant's preoccupation, a few years later, with the proper administration rather than the right reception of the sacrament.[74] Moreover, we should be wary of overemphasizing the extent to which Burgess's arguments were eventually moderated. The version of the *Reflections* which finally came into circulation was closest, in terms of the line that it took, to Daubeny's *Respectful Examination*, which was published probably around April 1811 and recommended by Burgess to his readers.[75]

The consistency of Burgess as a relatively hard-line, rather than moderate, High Churchman and the lack of theological convergence between the Bishop and contemporary evangelicals can be further illustrated by a review of his intervention in the controversy of the later 1820s over the doctrine of justification. In his visitation Charge of 1826, J. H. Browne, the

Evangelical Archdeacon of Ely, chose to expound, in contradistinction to doctrines of justification by works alone or by a mixture of faith and works, what he understood as the Anglican reformed doctrine of 'justification by faith only'.[76] In an appendix to the published version of the Charge Browne noted that,

> The most subtle acute, and elaborate work which has ever appeared in opposition to this doctrine, from the pen of any divine of the Church of England, is the celebrated 'Harmonia Apostolica' of Bishop Bull. As this doctrine has not unfrequently been assailed by arguments which, in all probability, were originally borrowed from that work; and as it may fairly be presumed, that these arguments are the strongest which can be adduced against it, I will take this opportunity of noticing some of them, and, at the same time of pointing out the remarkable coincidence which may be detected between the Bishop and the Romanists.[77]

He then proceeded to undertake this task in over forty pages of small type. It is possible that Browne's Charge would have passed relatively unremarked, had it not been for the appendix, but an attack on the seventeenth-century Bishop Bull, one of the sacred cows of Hanoverian High Churchmanship, was clearly a step too far.[78] It provoked a rapid and angry response from hard-line High Churchmen, with two replies being published in the following year: one by Charles Mount, the incumbent of Christ Church, Walcot (the church founded by Daubeny in Bath),[79] and the other by the Archdeacon of Sarum himself.[80] Daubeny's work, which comprised both a hostile review of Browne's charge and a lengthy vindication of Bull, revealed a distinctive view of the English Reformation and a characteristic High Church account of the doctrine of justification. For Daubeny, the English Reformation was, in its first phases (until the reign of Mary I), essentially free from Calvinist influence, which had been intruded on the Church by the returning Marian exiles.[81] The Church of England's formularies in general and its understanding of justification, as reflected in the Articles and Homilies, in particular, could not, therefore, legitimately be interpreted in a Calvinist sense. Daubeny was able thus to represent Bishop Bull and contemporary High

Churchmen as the true heirs of the Reformation and to contrast their views with those of Browne, noting 'that no compe-
tent Divine will go through his charge with attention, without
discovering a strong taint of the Calvinian Heresy, more or less
pervading the whole of it'.[82] Browne had set out an evangelical
understanding of justification by grace through faith, in which
the righteousness of Christ was imputed to the faithful believer,
with good works necessarily following under the sanctifying
influence of the Holy Spirit. Daubeny, following Bull, agreed
that the formal cause of justification was to be found in the
grace of God, which he regarded as being primarily conveyed
through baptism, but contended that good works were then
required as a condition of final justification,

> though man, in his present fallen state, must be justified by the
> merits of another, if justified at all, still he will not be justified
> by those merits, unless by a renewal unto holiness he has been
> brought into a fit condition to be benefited by them. Thus,
> whilst fallen man can in no sense be justified *by* his own
> works, still, in a certain sense, he will not be justified *without*
> *them*, that is, without those works which, under the Gospel
> covenant, the grace of God would, had he not been wanting to
> himself, have enabled him to perform. The distinction between
> *meritorious title* to salvation, and the *due qualification* for its
> possession, being, it may be presumed, too clear to be
> necessarily pointed out.[83]

Browne's initial response was contained in his *Strictures* on
Daubeny's *Vindication*, also published in 1827.[84] He confronted Daubeny directly, denying both that Calvin could be
regarded as a heretic and that his own doctrine of justification
was distinctively Calvinist.[85] He contended that his own views
were those of the vast majority of English divines prior to the
mid seventeenth century, and on this basis was able to argue
that the understanding of justification espoused by Bull (in the
Harmonia Apostolica) and, by implication, that of contemporary High Churchmen of the stamp of Daubeny, was not in
accordance with the formularies of the Church of England.[86]

Although Burgess was a relatively late entrant into this
battle for the Reformation legacy of the Church of England, his
intervention, when it finally came in December 1827, was

characteristically weighty. He chose to publish his thoughts, not, as in the Wickes case, in a privately circulated pamphlet, but in an episcopal Charge – and one published with all the interest attendant on a primary visitation. It was a clear statement of his position in his first public pronouncement to the clergy in his new diocese of Salisbury. In its published version, Burgess's intervention stretched to a total of 183 pages and comprised an introductory letter to the clergy, a preface to the Charge, the Charge itself (43 pages, of which 7 related to the Bishop's understanding of justification and regeneration) and a 93-page appendix, which Burgess described as a separate tract, entitled *Justification by Faith Only: In what it consists, to what institution it belongs and what relation it bears to Final Justification.*[87] Cumulatively, this work represented what was probably Burgess's most complete published statement on the doctrine of justification, and it took the form, not of an eirenicon, but of a point-by-point defence of Daubeny's position. Like Daubeny, he espoused firmly a doctrine of double justification:

> The remission of sin through faith only is our first justification, and is confined to this life; and is as distinct from the *final justification* of the last day, as pardon is from reward . . . For the judgement of the last day will be not to *pardon*, but to *reward* or *punish* every man according to his works.[88]

For Burgess, as for Daubeny the first justification – by faith – was conveyed by baptism – a view that he regarded as enshrined in the Articles and Homilies of the Church[89] – while its liturgy clearly taught a gospel covenant of faith and works:

> In these Collects our Church has founded the hope of obtaining salvation, and therefore final justification, not on *faith only*, but on Christ's own promises that he would, in the day of judgement, reward every man *according to his works*, – not works only, but faith and works, as means and conditions of salvation.[90]

Burgess's argument was bolstered, not just by appeals to Scripture, patristic sources,[91] and the Anglican formularies, but also by an appeal to the theology of the Anglican reformers (especially Cranmer and Hooker) as a guide to the authoritative interpretation of the formularies.[92] In contrast, the doctrine of imputed righteousness, upheld by Browne, was to be rejected as both unscriptural and foreign to the Anglican tradition represented by those divines and formularies.[93]

The surviving correspondence surrounding the *Charge* is much sparser than that relating to the *Reflections*, but the survival of one cautionary letter from G. W. Marriott (the High Church lawyer) tends to confirm that on this occasion, too, Burgess did not represent the more conciliatory section of the High Church school but, rather, the relatively extremist position associated with Daubeny.[94] Indeed, so complete was Burgess's identification with the Archdeacon of Sarum that he even made a spirited attempt to defend one of the latter's more outré claims – that justification by faith alone was one of the five points of Calvinism.[95]

The nature of Burgess's argument did leave him open to refutation, and one final round of controversy ensued when Browne responded to the Bishop in the appendix to his next archidiaconal Charge, in 1828. Browne again defended his position on the basis of Scripture and the Anglican formularies, and explicitly criticized Burgess's interpretation of the theology of the Anglican reformers. In particular, he argued that the *Necessary Erudition of a Christian Man*, from which Burgess had culled Cranmer's doctrine of double justification, did not represent the authentic voice of Cranmer at all but, rather, that of much more conservative figures who had overruled the reformers – especially Stephen Gardiner, the Bishop of Winchester. He was, moreover, able to cite in support of his position the testimony of Bishop Ridley and the opinion of Jeremy Collier, the High Church historian.[96] Browne was also able to argue that his understanding of the doctrine of imputed righteousness, far from being foreign to the Anglican tradition, had in fact represented its mainstream teaching before the era of Bishop Bull. Here he chose to cite another external authority, the late seventeenth-century Bishop of Lincoln, Thomas Barlow, who in his *Letters on Justification*, addressed to one of his diocesan clergy, had asserted:

Sure I am that all the learned divines and dutiful sons of the church of England, who have writ of our justification *coram Deo*, before the late unhappy rebellion; at least, all I have yet met with, such as Bishop Jewell, Hooker, Reynolds, Whittaker, Davenant, Field, Downham, John White &c.; do constantly prove and vindicate the imputation of our blessed Saviour's righteousness against the contrary doctrines of Racovia and Rome. So, that in truth, it is only you and some neoterics who, since the year 1640, deny such imputation, *cum veritatis damno et ecclesiae scandalo.*[97]

Burgess had an opportunity to defend his position in the Charge accompanying his second visitation of Salisbury, in 1829. However, by this date he seems to have become preoccupied with the Catholic question, which, for Burgess, tended to relativize what was essentially a domestic dispute within the Church of England. In this context, while not willing to concede any ground on the substance of Browne's case, the Bishop was prepared to adopt a more conciliatory position on its consequences:

If then any one have this faith, and it be 'the faith that worketh by love,' – that 'love which fulfilleth the law,' – he need not disturb himself by the apparent contradictions, which verbally divide the disputants on the subject of justification among the members of our Church.

The dispute assumes a different form, when the comparison is between the doctrines of Rome, of Geneva, and England; – between different branches of the Reformed Church, or between any one of them and the Church of Rome; – between Congregations, which differ from each other only, or chiefly in form and discipline, or between them and a Church which assumes to itself the title of *the Church*, and denies it to all others, holding them to be excluded altogether from the communion of the Christian Church, and from the pale of salvation.'[98]

From a post-Tractarian perspective, this dispute might be considered notable more for the ground which the participants held in common than for that over which they contended. Both High Churchmen and evangelicals displayed a commitment to

the supremacy of Scripture in determining doctrine, a determined loyalty to the public formularies of the Established
Church and a desire to show that their own theology was in
continuity with the Anglican reformers – a series of positions
that was to be precipitately abandoned by the Oxford radicals
over the next decade.[99] However, in the mid 1820s, the dispute
served mainly to underline the fundamental theological differences between the emerging evangelical school and an influential group of High Churchmen. When considering Burgess's
own position in relation to this theological spectrum it is
illuminating to note that in the Browne controversy the Bishop
yet again found himself operating in tandem with Charles
Daubeny, and very publicly taking a line which was to cause
considerable embarrassment to his evangelical biographer.[100]

Nevertheless, Burgess the hard-line orthodox controversialist was still at the same time the Burgess who preferred men of
the evangelical school within his diocese, sought the aid and
counsel of leading evangelical clergy and laymen, and not only
supported bodies like the British and Foreign Bible Society, but
defended them when they were assailed by other High Churchmen.[101] If we abandon the traditional explanation – that this
was the product of Burgess's moderation, that there was a
tendency towards theological convergence between the Bishop
and the evangelicals – then how should we account for the
affinity?

Three possible answers suggest themselves. The first relates
to the structure of relationships within the Established Church
in the period between the 1780s and the later 1820s, for while
there were certainly differing schools of thought within the
Church at this time, it is arguably inappropriate to label them
as parties or to assume that the most important alignments and
divisions within the Church were created by theological affinities alone. This is especially the case if we are meant to
understand the word 'party' by analogy with the political
groupings that came to shape parliamentary activity or with
the hard-edged theological parties within the Church that also
crystallized in the middle decades of the nineteenth century.
Particularly suggestive, in this context, is the way in which
networks of sociability and of common interest could, in the
small world of the later Hanoverian Church, cut across lines of

theological divergence, bringing together individuals of rather different or even opposed theological positions. At least partly as a consequence of the patronage of Shute Barrington, Burgess was linked to this kind of network. Barrington seems to have combined an eye for talent with a striking lack of party consciousness, and so at Durham, for example, he promoted High Churchmen like Henry Phillpotts, latitudinarians like William Paley, and evangelicals like Thomas Gisborne.[102] It was also through Barrington that Burgess was drawn directly into perhaps the most important of the theologically diverse social networks – the one that might best be labelled the 'Friends of Hannah More'. Their acquaintance began when More and Burgess were both staying at Barrington's palace in Salisbury in 1785; one evening Burgess elected to stay behind to keep More company when she was prevented by a violent toothache from attending a concert. Despite these unpromising circumstances the pair seem to have hit it off, and began a friendship which lasted until More's death, almost fifty years later.[103] The core of the social network centred on More included prominent High Churchmen, especially bishops like Porteus, Barrington and, later, Burgess, as well as leading evangelicals, including William Wilberforce, Thomas Gisborne and Henry Ryder (from 1815 Bishop of Gloucester).[104] In addition to substantial networks like this, we should also note a multiplicity of individual connections, like the 'glowing friendship' between Isaac Milner, the moderate Calvinist President of Queens' College, Cambridge, and George Pretyman, Bishop of Lincoln and author of the *Refutation of Calvinism*.[105]

Such networks and friendships, in addition to providing a context for sociability between churchmen of different schools, could also have practical consequences. Anne Stott has recently shown how, in the case of More, the network could operate to moderate and ultimately defuse ecclesiastical controversy in the Blagdon affair.[106] They could also promote the use of influence and patronage across theological lines, of the kind usually associated with party groups. Pretyman, for example, deployed his influence with William Pitt to have Milner appointed as Dean of Carlisle.[107] Perhaps more importantly, personal contacts could help to bring High Churchmen and evangelicals together to work for various causes of reform and Church extension. These causes themselves then became further bridges between men of different styles of churchmanship. Thus, even the leaders of the Hackney Phalanx, who were among the most suspicious of evangelical influence in the Church, could, as Joanna Innes has demonstrated, be drawn into cooperation with evangelicals through organizations like the Proclamation Society.[108] Indeed, it is arguable that, whatever the noise made by conflict, cooperative action may have been the normal way in which business was conducted, at least until sharper divisions began to emerge in the later 1820s and 1830s. This was certainly the experience of Burgess. It is possible that Burgess first met Henry Ryder through Hannah More, and it was certainly through Ryder that he met his most important evangelical collaborator, John Scandrett Harford.[109] Lampeter, jointly promoted by Burgess and Harford, was a notably collaborative project, and its subscription lists indicate substantial support from evangelicals, like Ryder, Thornton, Wilberforce and Lewis Way, and High Churchmen, like Van Mildert, Daubeny and Joshua Watson.[110]

The second suggestion relates to the area of spirituality. The close links between High Church spirituality in the first half of the eighteenth century and that of the emerging evangelical revival are now well known to historians.[111] Little work has been done on the spiritual affinities between pre-Tractarian High Churchmen and evangelicals in the later Hanoverian period. A careful look at the evangelical correspondence with, and commentary on, Burgess, however, reveals that it was at precisely this point that they felt closest to him. Charles Simeon, for example, in the course of a letter on the subject of spiritual resignation, remarked, 'It is your own kindness and condescension that embolden me . . . to divulge the secrets of my heart; and . . . because I feel assured that there is a responsive chord in your heart, that will vibrate to the touch.'[112] Harford, meanwhile, recalled that in one of his last conversations the Bishop had affirmed that 'the most sustaining words to me are these: "Being justified by faith, we have peace with God"' and that justifying faith was 'something far beyond the mere assent of the understanding'.[113]

Burgess seems to have been sufficiently impressed with evangelical piety to recommend the devotional use of works by William Wilberforce and Hannah More because of 'their truly scriptural principles of vital and spiritual religion'.[114] Similarly, he reproduced, for the instruction of candidates for Holy Orders, lengthy extracts from Thomas Scott's *Force of Truth*, cautioning against Scott's Calvinistic theology but at the same time asserting that, 'whatever were his errors in doctrine, his painful compunctions on the recollection of his want of moral preparation for the Ministry of the Church, may afford a very salutary lesson to future Candidates for the same holy Ministry'.[115] Burgess also evidently felt spiritually close to a number of his evangelical friends, and was willing to confide in Lewis Way, for example, that

> it often distressed him to feel that his personal conviction of sin was not what it should be, or what he desired to attain. And that in the Communion service, the expression 'The burden of sin is intolerable' was one he lamented he felt a deficiency in using in its full sense.[116]

On the evangelical side, too, this perceived spiritual affinity was frequently contrasted with acknowledged theological difference. The *Christian Observer*, for example, noted that, 'We did not concur with him in every opinion, even upon matters of importance; but we rejoice to bear this unfeigned testimony to his Christian virtues.'[117] Harford, meanwhile, almost certainly with the 1826 Charge in mind, noted that,

> the whole tenor of the Bishop's sentiments . . . proves how entirely he rested on the merits of Christ as the sole ground of our justification. We are the more particular in drawing attention to this point, because we are aware, that though from first to last he never built on any other foundation, there are statements in some of his printed works which have been censured as defective with respect to this vitally important doctrine.[118]

Sentiments of this kind should draw our attention to the fact that both orthodox High Churchmanship and evangelicalism exercised an influence that spread far beyond the confines of the fully paid-up members of the two schools, and that a reciprocal impact on their respective spiritualities was part of this broader cultural influence. Clearly, in the case of Burgess, at least, evangelicals were confident that they had found a man in whom the spirit was willing, even if the doctrine was weak.

The third and final suggested affinity between Burgess and evangelicals relates to issues of Church Order and the legitimacy of certain kinds of participation in the public sphere. While Burgess held an exalted view of the position and prerogatives of the Established Church, he also seems to have had a creative view of Church Order which encouraged innovation and even perhaps minor irregularities, if they might further its pastoral mission. He was, for example, following his patron Shute Barrington, an early and enthusiastic supporter of Sunday schools, when they were still controversial.[119] Similarly, as incumbent of Winston, Burgess pioneered cottage lectures in two different locations of his parish, despite the strictures of the 71st canon against preaching in private houses. Later, as Bishop of Salisbury, he recommended to his clergy the introduction of prayer meetings in the houses of the poor, at which the minister could read, in addition to the prayers, 'some short discourse suited to their age and necessities'.[120] Perhaps the best illustration of Burgess's zest for innovation, however, can be found in the subscription books of the diocese of St David's. On his arrival in the see, Burgess inherited a situation in which incumbents were required, in addition to the usual subscriptions, to swear that they would be resident on their vicarages.[121] At some point after 1810, however, it appears that Burgess had the oath struck through and replaced with,

> I AB do solemnly promise that I will be resident on my . . . of . . . in the Diocese of St David's unless I shall be otherwise dispensed withal by my Diocesan. I also solemnly promise That if there be no parsonage House on the benefice [or benefices] to which I am now going to be instituted or if the House be unfit for Residence I will use my utmost endeavours for the erecting of a New House or for repairing the present house sufficiently for the residence of a minister And I further solemnly promise That I will to the utmost of my power promote among my parishioners the duty of Family Prayer, by

my example as well as by my Instructions and that, for this purpose, I will not fail to have daily Prayer in my own family.[122]

This bold use of the subscription process to impose an obligation, not just to improve the prospects of residence on a benefice, but also to observe a particular devotional practice with a view to its encouragement among the people at large appears to have been unique to St David's, and represented a considerable innovation in episcopal practice. The particular focus on family prayer is also a further reflection of the potential affinity between devout High Church and evangelical spirituality.

If a willingness to contemplate modest pastoral innovation placed Burgess closer to regular evangelicals than to most conservative High Churchmen, his attitude to participation in the public sphere represented an even more dramatic departure. An attempt to address and appeal directly to the public in general was the chief characteristic of one of Burgess's earliest publications – *Considerations on the Abolition of Slavery and the Slave Trade, upon grounds of natural, religious, and political duty*, published in 1789. Here, Burgess, at the start of his career, was both choosing to intervene in a contentious political issue on the basis of Christian principle and rational argument, and appealing consciously above sectional interests to the 'deliberate judgement of a whole people'.[123] He also mounted an explicit defence of the right and, indeed, duty of the clergy, 'to excite the attention of the public to the moral turpitude, and commercial impolicy of Slavery, and to second the appeals of disinterested humanity, by inculcating the duty and necessity of abolishing it'.[124] This stands in contrast to a more cautious High Church tradition of limiting such pronouncements to a clerical audience or eschewing them altogether. Even the pugnacious Daubeny, for example, seems to have felt obliged to shelter behind a language of professional obligation and the duties of his office as archdeacon when intervening in the Wickes controversy.[125]

Moreover, even as a bishop, Burgess was willing not only to appeal to the public but also to embrace one of the public sphere's most characteristic forms – the voluntary association. One of his first actions, for example, on becoming Bishop of St David's and again as Bishop of Salisbury was to organize a Church Union society, in the first instance to support the distribution of Bibles and other religious literature and to promote education, and in the second to provide relief for infirm clergy.[126] Although in some respects these societies were impeccably High Church in their objectives – the St David's society, for example, intended to distribute only tracts approved by the SPCK – they were also in some respects evangelical in form. They were mixed bodies, including both clergy and laity, and at Salisbury, while the offices of president and vice-presidents of the society were reserved for the clergy, any subscriber of one guinea or more annually could be a member of the committee. Burgess's enthusiasm for the voluntary association as an eligible means of pursuing desirable objectives represented a clear affinity with evangelical methodologies and made it natural for him to support sometimes-controversial organizations, like the Bible Society and the Jews' Society.[127] In this respect, Burgess's attitude contrasted strongly with many of the conservative High Churchmen whose theology he shared, but who retained a strong attachment to hierarchical forms. Their position was summarized by Churton, who added the following caution to an otherwise favourable response to Burgess's suggestion, during the Wickes controversy, that an association to protect the Established Church might be formed,

> The society . . . would be a noble and I hope a highly beneficial institution; but it requires mature consideration, It should, I presume, be concerted first of all with the Archbishop, or rather with both of them, and your Brother Bishops; nor perhaps should anything further than private consultation and conference be done without still higher approbation and authority . . .Our excellent Constitution and our truly Apostolical Church are so wisely framed and so sufficient for all true Christianlike unostentatious excellence, that I am a very unwilling advocate for all voluntary and uncommanded acts and instances of obedience, all vows, clubs, societies and institutions whatsoever.[128]

The conservative reluctance about entry into the public sphere in general, and the use of the voluntary association in particular, potentially put the Church at a disadvantage when confronted by rather nimbler Dissenting and radical opponents, as even Churton recognized, and this attitude was to wane in the nineteenth century.[129] However, it is noteworthy how often High Church concerns about evangelicalism between 1790 and the 1820s focused on issues of methodology,[130] and it is probable that one of the key dividing lines between those High Churchmen who, like Burgess, generally supported evangelical initiatives and those who generally attacked them was less a matter of theological identity than of a differing degree of willingness to accept methodological innovation, in the face of looming pastoral crisis.

This then, we might suggest, is the solution to the enigma of Thomas Burgess: neither a cross-bencher nor a moderate but a man with a high orthodox theology, combined with a wide acquaintance, a warm spirituality and, in particular, a willingness to embrace innovation in order to defend and extend the Establishment to which he was devoted, Thomas Burgess was both a Churchman *and* a Reformer.

Notes

1   *Christian Remembrancer*, 19 (1837), 322–3.
2   *Christian Observer*, 1 (Jan. 1838), 64. It is noteworthy that in the late 1830s evangelicals could still be comfortable with the deployment of 'Apostolic' and 'Primitive' as terms of approbation. They had not yet gained an exclusive association with Tractarian churchmanship. Such language is, however, notably absent from the *Observer*'s review of Harford's biography of Burgess only two years later. *Christian Observer*, n.s., 38 (Sept. 1840), 549–71.
3   Bodleian Library, MS Eng. Lett. c.134, Burgess MSS.
4   *Christian Observer*, 1 (Jan. 1838), 64–8.
5   *Christian Observer*, 1 (Dec. 1838), 786.
6   Ibid., 786–8. For Wilks, see D. M. Lewis (ed.), *Dictionary of Evangelical Biography* (Oxford, 1995).
7   *Christian Observer*, n.s., 33 (Sept. 1840), 550. The reviewer also drew attention to Burgess's own famous 'benignant smile'. Ibid., 549.

8   R. A. Burns, 'W. J. Conybeare: "Church parties"', in S. Taylor (ed.), *From Cranmer to Davidson: A Miscellany*, Church of England Record Society, vol. 7 (Woodbridge, 1999), p. 229.

9   P. B. Nockles, 'Church parties in the pre-Tractarian Church of England 1750–1833: the 'Orthodox', some problems of definition and identity', in J. Walsh, C. Haydon and S. Taylor (eds), *The Church of England c.1689–c.1833 From Toleration to Tractarianism* (Cambridge, 1993), p. 347.

10   J. S. Harford, *The Life of Thomas Burgess D.D.* (London, 1840).

11   Ibid., pp. 302, 310–12, 318–21; University of Wales Lampeter, Archives H/2/45, St David's College, Lampeter, Prospectus and List of Benefactors.

12   J. S. Harford, *An Account of the Latter Days of R. V. Pryor, to which is Prefixed a Brief Sketch of his Life and Character* (1808). He had also written a rather less friendly biography of Paine, *Some Account of the Life, Death, and Principles of Thomas Paine* (Bristol, 1819).

13   J. S. Harford, *The Life of Michelangelo Buonarotti*, 2 vols (London, 1857); J. S. Harford *Recollections of William Wilberforce Esq.* (London, 1864).

14   Harford, *Burgess*, p. vi.

15   For Harford's romanticism see, for example, Bristol Record Office, 28048/P72, Diary of J. S. Harford, February 1824–1825; Lewis (ed.), *Dictionary of Evangelical Biography*.

16   Harford, *Burgess*, p. vi.

17   R. I. Wilberforce and S. Wilberforce, *The Life of William Wilberforce*, 5 vols (London, 1838). The work is generally regarded as applying a High Church gloss to its evangelical subject.

18   Harford, *Burgess*, pp. 119–20.

19   Ibid., p. 6.

20   Ibid., p. 200.

21   Ibid., p. 220.

22   Ibid., p. 174.

23   Ibid., pp. 175–8, 226–47, 271–8, 432–5. For the revival of diocesan structures in the early nineteenth century see A. Burns, *The Diocesan Revival in the Church of England c.1800–1870* (Oxford, 1999), *passim*.

24   Harford, *Burgess*, p. 178.

25   Ibid., pp. 179–80.

26   Ibid., pp. 551–7.

27   See, for example, ibid., pp. 249–270, 279–291, 403–23.

28 Ibid., pp. 531–50.
29 Ibid., p. 529.
30 The *Oxford Dictionary of National Biography* (hereafter *ODNB*).
31 D. T. W. Price, *Bishop Burgess and Lampeter College* (Cardiff, 1987), p. 33.
32 J. W. Wickes, *Perlege Si Vis A Letter Addressed to the Right Reverend Spencer, Lord Bishop of Peterborough in Answer to an Appeal made to the 'Society for defending the Civil Rights of Dissenters Relative to the Important Question of Church Burial by the Established Clergy'* (Stamford, 1808), p. 12. Wickes's pamphlet treated his opponents with thinly veiled contempt and identified Swingler 'as a deluded, infatuated, and ignorant disciple of the lowest description of Methodists . . . sometimes developing his own mystical lucubrations upon the new birth; and at others stretching out his itching ears to the bagpipe melody of Huntingdonian stanzas'. Ibid., pp. 26–35. The latter comment may have been a tactical error, since the Bishop's elder brother, Martin Madan, had been associated with the Countess of Huntingdon. For further details of the case see the short account in B. Manning, *The Protestant Dissenting Deputies* (Cambridge, 1952), pp. 293–9.
33 *The Judgment, delivered, December 11ᵗʰ, 1809, by the Right Honourable Sir John Nicholl, Official Principal of the Arches Court of Canterbury; Upon the Admission of Articles Exhibited in a Cause of Office prompted by Kemp, against Wickes* (London, 1810), *passim*.
34 Ibid.; Bod. MS Eng. Lett. c.137, Burgess MSS, fos 202–3, J. Nicholl to Burgess, 12 September 1811.
35 For the Sidmouth proposals, see, for example, D. Hempton, 'Thomas Allen and Methodist politics', in D. Hempton, *The Religion of the People* (London, 1996), pp. 109–129.
36 'A Clergyman', *A Letter to Sir John Nicholl on his Late Decision in the Ecclesiastical Court, against a Clergyman, for Refusing to Bury the Child of a Dissenter* (London, 1810).
37 *Anti-Jacobin Review and Magazine* (April 1810), 374–86. For a review of the dispute rather more favourable to Nicholl and critical of Daubeny, see the *Quarterly Review*, 7 (1812), 200–23.
38 C. Daubeny, *A Charge Delivered to the Clergy of the Archdeaconry of Sarum* (London, 1810).
39 Bod. MS Eng. Lett. c.137, Burgess MSS, fos 202–3, J. Nicholl to Burgess, 12 September 1811.
40 Baptists and Independents were both strong in south Wales but the issue was becoming more acute at this very time, as the

Welsh Calvinistic Methodists were beginning their final disengagement from the Established Church with the ordinations of 1811. Some of Burgess's concern, therefore, may have been related to a sense of growing crisis.

41 C. Daubeny, *A Respectful Examination of the Judgment Delivered December 11, 1809 by the Right hon. Sir J. Nicholl, Official Principal of the Arches Court of Canterbury Against The Rev. John Wight Wickes . . . in A Letter to Sir John Nicholl* (Bath, 1811). The pamphlet is 144 pages long – more than three times the length of the transcript of the original judgment.

42 Bod. MS Eng. Lett. c.140, Papers relating to Thomas Burgess, fos 4–5, G. S. Faber to J. S. Harford, 4 May 1838.

43 *DNB.*

44 For Grant and Churton see P. B. Nockles, *The Oxford Movement in Context* (Cambridge, 1994).

45 In its number for September to December 1809, for example, the *Anti-Jacobin* noted, with respect to Daubeny, that 'We never sit down to read any production of this learned and zealous divine without deriving, from the perusal of it, an equal portion of mental delight, and of mental improvement. He is a guide whom we follow with pleasure, with confidence, and with a certainty of pursuing the right path', and proceeded to call for his immediate elevation to the bench. *Anti-Jacobin Review and Magazine*, 34, Sept.–Dec. 1809 (1810), 23, 156–7.

46 Controversy surrounding the conditions and effects of valid baptism continued with the publication of parts of Richard Mant's Bampton Lectures in 1815 and rumbled on until the Gorham dispute of 1847–50.

47 Bod. MS Eng. Lett c.135, Burgess MSS, fos 89–98, J. Grant to Burgess, 26 April 1811. For an example, see C. Daubeny, *A Charge Delivered to the Clergy of the Archdeaconry of Sarum* (London, 1810), 25–7.

48 Bod. MS Eng. Lett. c.133, Burgess MSS., fos 69–70, S. Barrington to Burgess, 17 April 1811.

49 Ibid.

50 Bod. MS Eng. Lett. c.133, Burgess MSS, fos 77–8, S. Barrington to Burgess, 31 May 1811.

51 Bod. MS Eng. Lett. c.136, Burgess MSS, fos 88–9, G. Huntingford to Burgess, n.d.

52 Bod. MS Eng. Lett. c.135, Burgess MSS, fos 102–3, J. Grant to Burgess, 10 May 1811.

53 Bod. MS Eng. Lett. c.133, Burgess MSS, fos. 69–70, S. Barrington to Burgess. 17 April 1811.

54 Bod. MS Eng. Lett. c.137, Burgess MSS, fos 56–6, A. L. Luders to Burgess, 15 May 1811. For Luders see *DNB*. This opinion was also shared by that other eminent ecclesiastical lawyer Sir William Scott. National Library of Wales, SD/Let/1223, Luders to Burgess, 7 October 1811.

55 Bod. MS Eng. Lett. c.135, Burgess MSS, fos 81–4, J. Grant to Burgess, 9 April 1811.

56 Bod. MS Eng. Lett. c.135, Burgess MSS, fos 85–6, J. Grant to Burgess, 10 April 1811.

57 Bod. MS Eng. Lett. c.135, Burgess MSS, fos 89–98, J. Grant to Burgess, 26 April 1811.

58 Bod. MS Eng. Lett. c.138, Burgess MSS, fos 13–14, C. P. Pritchett to Burgess, 4 May 1811.

59 Bod. MS Eng. Lett. c.134, Burgess MSS, fos 9–12, R. Churton to Burgess, 16 April 1811.

60 Ibid.

61 Ibid.

62 Bod. MS Eng. Lett. c.135, Burgess MSS, fos 89–98, J. Grant to Burgess, 26 April 1811.

63 Ibid. William Coxe also drew attention to the anomalous position of the children of English colonists, who might well have received lay baptism from necessity, with no schismatic intention, and yet who would be denied Anglican burial if Burgess's position were implemented consistently. Bod. MS Eng. Lett. c.134, Burgess MSS, fos 91–2, W. Coxe to Burgess, 29 April 11.

64 Bod. MS Eng. Lett. c.135 Burgess MSS, fos 89–98, J. Grant to Burgess, 26 April 1811.

65 T. Burgess, *Reflections on the Judgment delivered by Sir John Nicholl against the Rev. J. W. Wickes* (1811), *passim*. Burgess did, however, allow that persons could be admitted to the Church by confirmation or ordination, and thereby be entitled to church burial.

66 Ibid., p. xiv.

67 For example, ibid. pp. ix, 19; Bod. MS Eng. Lett. c.134, Burgess MSS, fos 153–4, C. Daubeny to Burgess, 9 May 1811.

68 Burgess, pp. 77–8.

69 Nockles, 'Church parties', 341.

70 J. H. Pratt (ed.), *Eclectic Notes; Or, Notes of Discussions on Religious Topics at the Meetings of the Eclectic Society, London During the Years 1798–1814* (London, 1856).

71 Nockles, *Oxford Movement*, p. 17.

72 Bod. MS Eng. Lett. c.134, Burgess MSS, fos 17–18, R. Churton to Burgess, 25 June 1811.

73 See, for example, G. Carter, *Anglican Evangelicals Protestant Secessions from the Via Media, c.1800–1850* (Oxford, 2001), p. 15.

74 See, for example, R. Mant, *Two Tracts Intended to Convey Correct Notions of Regeneration and Conversion According to the Sense of Holy Scripture and of the Church of England Extracted from the Bampton Lecture of 1812* (London, 1815), p. 11.

75 Burgess, *Reflections*, p. 2.

76 J. H. Browne, *On Justification. A Charge delivered to the Clergy of the Archdeaconry of Ely at a Visitation held in the Parish Church of St Michael's Cambridge on Monday April 24 1826, With an Appendi.* (London, 1826), *passim*.

77 Ibid., p. 43.

78 For Bull, see J. Spurr, *The Restoration Church of England* (New Haven and London, 1991), pp. 312–16. For his influence on later generations of High Churchmen, see P. B. Nockles, *The Oxford Movement in Context* (Cambridge, 1994), pp. 256–9.

79 C. M. Mount, *The Doctrine of Justification by Faith Only as Held by the Church of England and Explained by Bishop Bull Vindicated against a Charge lately Published by the Venerable J. H. Browne, A. M. Archdeacon of Ely* (Bath, 1827). The pamphlet is dated May 1827. For Christ Church, see 'Charles Daubeny', in ODNB.

80 C. Daubeny, *A Vindication of the Character of the Pious and Learned Bishop Bull from the Unqualified Accusations Brought Against it by the Archdeacon of Ely in his Charge Delivered in the Year 1826* (London, 1827).

81 See, for example, ibid., pp. 122ff.

82 Ibid., p. 10.

83 Ibid., p. 111. See also his reference to '*evangelical* works of righteousness under the new covenant, which are expected to be found in every redeemed sinner; not indeed as the *meritorious* cause of his justification, but that *sine qua non*, without which, according to the conditions of the new covenant, no Christian professor must expect to be completely and finally justified'. Ibid., p. 26.

84 J. H. Browne, *Strictures on a Work Entitled A Vindication &c in a Letter to the Reverend Charles Daubeney LLD Archdeacon of Sarum* (London, 1827).

85 Ibid., pp. 1–15.

86 Ibid., p. 42. See also the analysis in A. E. McGrath, *Iustitia Dei A History of the Christian Doctrine of Justification*, 2nd edn (Cambridge, 1998), pp. 285–98.

87   T. Burgess, *A Charge Delivered to the Clergy of the Diocese of Salisbury, at the Primary Visitation of the Diocese in August MDCCCXXVI* (London, 1828).

88   Ibid., p. 80.

89   Ibid., p. 83.

90   Ibid., p. 120. The reference here was to the collects for the first Sunday in Advent, Ash Wednesday, the Sunday before Easter, and the 11th, 13th, 14th and 25th Sundays after Trinity.

91   Ibid., p. 69.

92   Burgess argued, for example, that Cranmer had held a similar doctrine of first and final justification, and cited the *Necessary Erudition of a Christian Man* as his source for Cranmer's theology. Ibid., p. 74.

93   Ibid., pp. 90–5. Burgess was prepared to allow a limited understanding of the imputation of Christ's passive righteousness in the first justification as the means by which men are pardoned, but not of Christ's active righteousness as the basis on which men might be accounted holy. He was particularly concerned to acquit Hooker of holding the latter doctrine.

94   Bod. MS Eng. Lett. c.137, Burgess MSS, fos 167–9, G. W. Marriott to Burgess, n.d.

95   Ibid., xxx–xxxvii. What High Churchmen meant when they accused evangelicals of Calvinism is a subject which I intend to explore further in M. Smith, *Churchmen and Reformers: Reshaping the Church of England 1790–1830* (forthcoming). It is noteworthy, however, that in this context at least Daubeny was using the term primarily to denote the doctrine of 'Salvation by Faith alone', as opposed to a preoccupation with election or the scope of the atonement.

96   J. H. Browne, *On the Connexion between Faith and Works. A Charge delivered to the Clergy of the Archdeaconry of Ely at a Visitation held in the Parish Church of St Michael's Cambridge on Tuesday April 29, 1828* (London, 1828), pp. 117–19. A similar point had been made two decades earlier in the *Christian Observer*'s review of the second edition of Daubeny's *Guide to the Church. Christian Observer*, 4 (1805), 165.

97   Ibid., 111–12. Barlow, appointed as Bishop of Lincoln in 1675, was a Calvinist and an opponent of the theological school represented by Bull. See *ODNB*.

98   T. Burgess, *A Charge delivered to the Clergy of the Diocese of Salisbury in the summer of 1829 at the Triennial Visitation of the Diocese* (Salisbury, 1829), p. 36.

99 For an extended discussion of this process and an earlier dispute between Daubeny and Overton see P. B. Nockles, 'A disputed legacy: Anglican historiographies of the Reformation from the era of the Caroline divines to that of the Oxford Movement', *Bulletin of the John Rylands University Library of Manchester*, 83, i (Spring 2001), 121–67.

100 Harford, *Burgess*, pp. 505–3.

101 Ibid., pp. 271–8, 341.

102 *ODNB*; *Christian Observer*, n.s. 38 (Sept. 1840), 552.

103 Harford, *Burgess* pp. 110–12.

104 The network around Hannah More is particularly well documented. See, for example, M. J. Crossley Evans, 'The curtain parted: or four conversations with Hannah More, 1817–1818', in *Transactions of the Bristol and Gloucestershire Archaeological Society*, 110 (1992), 181–211; A. Stott, *Hannah More The First Victorian* (Oxford, 2003).

105 M. Milner, *The Life of Isaac Milner* (London, 1842), p. 71.

106 Stott, *Hannah More*, pp. 232–57.

107 Milner, *Isaac Milner*, p. 71.

108 J. Innes, 'Politics and morals; the reformation of manners movement in later eighteenth-century England', in E. Helmuth (ed.), *The Transformation of Political Culture in England and Germany in the Late Eighteenth Century* (Oxford, 1990), pp. 57–118.

109 Harford, *Burgess*, p. 302.

110 University of Wales Lampeter Archives H/2/45, St David's College, Lampeter, Prospectus and List of Benefactors.

111 See, for example, J. D. Walsh, 'Religious societies: Methodist and Evangelical 1738–1800,' in W. J. Sheils and D. Wood (eds), *Voluntary Religion, Studies in Church History*, 23 (1986), pp. 279–302.

112 Bod. MS Eng. Lett. c.138, Burgess MSS, fos 79–80, C. Simeon to Burgess, 4 April 1835.

113 Harford, *Burgess*, p. 503.

114 *Christian Observer*, 4 (1805), 38. These included Wilberforce's *Practical View*, which had been given a rather less friendly reception by Daubeny. See C. Daubeny, *A Guide to the Church in Several Discourses Addressed to William Wilberforce Esq. M.P.* (London, 1798).

115 T. Burgess, *An Exhortation to Students in Divinity from Arrian's Discourses of Epictetus in Greek Latin and English for the Use of Candidates for Orders in the Diocese of Salisbury* (Salisbury, 1832), p. 26.

[116] Bod. MS Eng. Lett. c.140, Burgess MSS, fos 16–17, Drusilla Way to J. S. Harford, 12 March 1840.

[117] *Christian Observer* (1838), 64.

[118] Harford, *Burgess*, pp. 503–4. The point was repeated with considerable emphasis in the *Christian Observer*'s review of Harford's biography. *Christian Observer*, n.s., 38 (Sept. 1840), pp. 558–9.

[119] Ibid., pp. 103–6.

[120] Harford, *Burgess*, p. 177; Burgess, *Charge* (1827), pp. 41–2.

[121] Similar oaths were also required of incumbents in the dioceses of Llandaff and St Asaph, but not Bangor. National Library of Wales, SD/SB/7 Diocese of St David's Subscription Book, 1793–1810; LL/SB/12, Llandaff Subscription Book, 1802–15; SA/SB/10, St Asaph Subscription Book, 1805–18; B/SB/6, Bangor Subscription Book, 1815–33.

[122] NLW, SD/SB/8, Diocese of St David's Subscription Book, 1810–22.

[123] Harford, *Burgess*, pp. 133–6.

[124] T. Burgess, *Considerations on the Abolition of Slavery and the Slave Trade upon Grounds of Natural, Religious and Political Duty* (Oxford, 1789), pp. 143–6.

[125] See, for example, C. Daubeny, *A Charge Delivered to the Clergy of the Archdeaconry of Sarum: On the 26th, 27th, 28th and 29th of June 1810* (London, 1810), pp. 1–9.

[126] *An Account of the Society For Promoting Christian Knowledge and Church Union in the Diocese of St David's* (1811); T. Burgess, *Charge* (1828), pp. 162–4.

[127] Harford, *Burgess*, pp. 271–8.

[128] Bod. MS Eng. Lett. c.134, Burgess MSS, fos 9–12, R. Churton to Burgess, 16 April 1811.

[129] See, for example, Bod. MS Eng. Lett. c.134, Burgess MSS, fos 17–18, R. Churton to Burgess, 25 June 1811.

[130] See the examples given in W. J. C. Ervine, 'Doctrine and diplomacy: some aspects of the life and thought of the Anglican evangelical clergy, 1797–1837', unpublished Ph.D thesis (University of Cambridge, 1979), pp. 217–27.

2

Burgess and the Classics:
A Letter of April 1792

A. J. BROTHERS

In the autumn of 2001 Mr Peter Miles, of the Department of English at University of Wales, Lampeter, noticed in a London antiquarian bookseller's catalogue a manuscript letter by the Founder of the original St David's College at Lampeter, Bishop Thomas Burgess. The letter was purchased personally by Lampeter's then Vice-Chancellor, Professor Keith Robbins, and presented by him as a gift to the University Archives early in January 2002, in anticipation of the 175th anniversary commemoration of the opening of Burgess's College, events for which were planned to begin on St David's Day (1 March) of that year.

The letter was written from Oxford on 6 April 1792 to Professor Daniel Wyttenbach in Amsterdam. This was some months after Burgess had resigned his Fellowship at Corpus Christi College, Oxford, in order to follow Bishop Shute Barrington of Salisbury (whose chaplain he had been since 1785) when the latter was translated to the wealthy diocese of Durham in 1791.[1] In form, the letter is a single sheet of quarto, folded once, and the text fills the first side and part of the second in the resulting four-side octavo (p. 42). The letter is then folded again several times, and addressed on the outside 'A Monsieur / Monsieur Professeur Wyttenbach / à Amsterdam / (Holland)' (p. 42). It was despatched from Oxford the day after it was written, on 7 April 1792: beside the address is a stamp in blue-black ink with the single word 'OXFORD', and above the address is a red circular date-stamp with 'PA[ID]' at

41

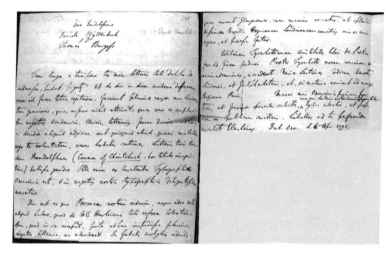

Text of letter from Thomas Burgess to Daniel Wyttenbach, 6 April 1792

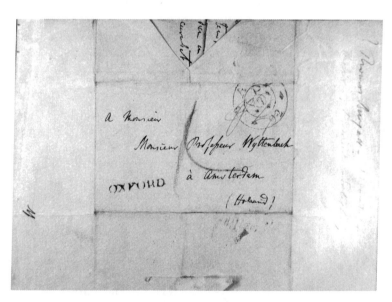

Address and postmark of Burgess – Wyttenbach letter, 7 April 1792

the top of its outer ring and '92' at the bottom of it, and with
'AP' at the top of the inner ring and '7' in the central circle.[2]
The letter is written in Latin, which was the customary language for correspondence between classical scholars who
spoke differing native tongues.

Burgess's correspondent, Daniel Wyttenbach (1746–1820),
was at this time at the *Athenaeum Illustre* in Amsterdam. Born
in Berne, Switzerland, he was Professor of Greek, of Philosophy
and of History at Amsterdam from 1779 to 1799, before
moving to the University of Leiden.[3] His great reputation as a
classical scholar was based on his edition of the works of
Plutarch, starting with the *Moralia* of 1795–6 (four volumes in
two, Oxford, Clarendon Press), plans for which are mentioned
in the letter, and a copy of which is in the Founders' Library at
Lampeter.[4]

That Wyttenbach and Burgess not only corresponded but
had met is clear from Wyttenbach's biography of another great
classical scholar in Holland, David Ruhnken (1723–98), *Vita
Davidis Ruhnkenii* (Leiden and Amsterdam, 1799), also in the
Founders' Library. In 1784 Burgess had travelled to Holland
and Paris in pursuit of his classical researches, and Wyttenbach
(p. 189) describes his visit to Ruhnken and himself:

> mox gratissimus advenit hospes Thomas Burgessius, Britannus;
> cujus excellentem literarum scientiam, rara ornabat animi probi-
> tas, morumque modestia: unde amicitia cum praesente nobis
> conciliata, deinde cum absente epistolis officiisque viguit.

[Later a most agreeable guest, Thomas Burgess, a Briton,
arrived; his outstanding knowledge of literature was adorned
by a rare integrity of mind and modesty of character: as a
result, the friendship forged between us when he was here
flourished afterwards through letters and mutual services when
he was gone.][5]

Burgess again visited Holland – and also Paris – in 1787. It is
in connection with this later visit that Burgess's biographer
John Scandrett Harford[6] mentions his subject's acquaintance
with Wyttenbach and Ruhnken (as well as with Heyne and
Villoison), and quotes Wyttenbach's recollection of their meeting in 1784. He adds that Burgess 'kept up with them for

several years an occasional correspondence', and that Wyttenbach's plans for the printing of his Plutarch in Oxford formed
the chief subject of their subsequent letters. Our letter confirms
the truth of these facts.

The letter is presented here in the form of a mini-edition: the
Latin text is followed by an English translation, and it is to the
latter that most of the notes are tied.

Text

Viro Eruditissimo
Danieli Wyttenbach
S. D.
Thomas Burgess

Tam longo a tempore te meas litteras tibi debitas desid-
erasse, pudet pigetq[ue]. Ut de die in diem scribere differrem,
cum id facere toties cogitarem, fecerunt plurimae causae cum
leviores, tum graviores, quas referre nihil attinet; quas vero ex
compluribus negotiis academicis, clericis, litterariis forsan
divines: ad haec si desidiae aliquid adjicias, aut quicquid aliud,
quam mutatam erga te voluntatem, veras habebis rationes.
Litteris tuis tandem Randolphum (*Cannon of Christchurch*,
hoc titulo insequitur,) petiisse gaudeo. Ille enim ex Curatoribus
Typographiae Oxoniensis est, & in negotiis nostris typographi-
cis diligentissime versatur.

Diu est ex quo Porsonum nostrum viderim, neque adeo certi
aliquid habeo, quod de MSS. Harleianis tibi referam. Colla-
tionis opus, quod in se recepit, puto adhuc impediisse plurima
negotia litteraria, ne absolveret. In fabulis Aeschyleis edendis
quas curant Glasguenses, cum maxime versatur: et splendidis-
simam Vergilii Heginanam Londinensem consiliis suis ac curis
regere, et praeesse fertur.

Editionem Tyrwhittianam Aristotelis libri de Poetica fere ad
finem perduxi. Praeter Tyrwhitti novam versionem, & animad-
versiones, accedent variae lectiones codicum Veneti, Leidensis,
et Gulpherbitani, et, si mature veniant ad manus, Regiorum
Paris[inorum]. Musei mei Oxoniensis primam partem, et
Gravinae opuscula selecta, una cum Santenii nostri Carmina

ab Juvenilibus,[7] typis absolvi, et propediem in publicum mit-
tam. Libellos ad te perferendos curabit Elmsleius. Dab. Oxon.
d. 6. Apr. 1792.

Translation

Thomas Burgess
to the most learned gentleman
Daniel Wyttenbach
greetings

I am ashamed and upset that you have for so long a time felt
the absence of a letter of mine which I owe you. Very many
reasons, both fairly trivial and more serious, which it is not
important to mention, have meant that I put off writing from
day to day, when I was so often thinking of doing so; these, you
may perhaps guess, have arisen from numerous matters of
academic, clerical and literary business. If you add to this a
certain amount of laziness, or anything else other than a
change in my feelings towards you, you will have good reason.
I am glad to have at long last sought out Randolph[8] ('Cannon
of Christchurch', this is the title he uses[9]) with your letter. For
he is one of the Curators of the Oxford Press, and involves
himself with every care in my own printing concerns.

It is a long time since I have seen our friend Porson,[10] and I
do not have any definite news to tell you about the Harleian
manuscripts.[11] I think that up to now a very great number of
literary tasks have prevented him from finishing the work of
collation which he has taken upon himself. He is engaged at the
moment in the editing of the plays of Aeschylus, which the
Glasgow men are undertaking:[12] and he is said to be directing
with his advice and attention the very splendid London edition
of Heyne's Vergil,[13] and to be in charge of it.

I have almost completed Tyrwhitt's edition of Aristotle's
book on Poetry.[14] Besides Tyrwhitt's version[15] and notes, there
will in addition be variant readings of the Venice, Leiden and
Wolfenbüttel manuscripts, and, if they come to hand in time, of
the Royal Paris ones.[16] I have completed for the press the first
part of my *Museum Oxoniense*,[17] and selected minor works of

Gravina,[18] together with our friend Santen's *Carmina ab Juvenilibus*,[19] and I shall shortly publish them. Elmsley[20] will see to it that these short works are delivered to you. Written at Oxford on the 6th day of April 1792.

Burgess's letter demonstrates his friendly, even familiar, relations with many eminent classical scholars in Britain and in continental Europe towards the end of the eighteenth century. It also gives a clear picture of his own academic work at the critical turning-point of his life, when he had just moved to Durham and had exchanged the life of an Oxford teacher and researcher in the classics for that of a cleric who was soon to become a parish priest and, eventually, a diocesan bishop, and whose published work was soon to concentrate more and more on Theology and Hebrew. It further proves, in general terms, the correctness of Harford's account of this period in his life, while revealing a number of inaccuracies of detail in that account.[21] And it reminds the members of his Welsh foundation, where Classics has been taught since its opening and where Classics teaching still flourishes today, that in the earlier part of his career their founder was a Classical scholar, not yet primarily a theologian.

Notes

1   Since the letter is addressed only from 'Oxford', there is no way of knowing whether Burgess wrote it while staying at his old college, or from some other address in the city.

2   There are, of course, no postage stamps, since they did not appear until 1840.

3   I am indebted to my Lampeter colleague Dr Mirjam Plantinga and, through her, to Professor Jan Maarten Bremer of the University of Amsterdam, for providing help and information here.

4   It is not surprising that this work, and many of the others mentioned in the letter, are in Lampeter's Founders' Library, since they were all owned by Burgess, and on his death in 1837 the Bishop left his personal library of some 10,000 volumes to his Welsh foundation. For the *Moralia*, see further n. 8 below.

5   J. S. Harford, *The Life of Thomas Burgess, D.D., F.R.S., F. A. S. &c &c &c, Late Lord Bishop of Salisbury*, 1st ed (London, 1840), p. 85, places this visit in 1785. But he does so solely on the evidence of a letter to Burgess from Thomas Tyrwhitt dated 26 November 1785, which refers to 'some MSS. in Spain, probably those of which you saw copies at Leyden'. However, this mention need not necessarily be taken as referring to the current year, but could equally be taken as referring to an earlier one. Since Wyttenbach's statement in his *Life of Ruhnken* is firmly tied to the year 1784, that date should prevail.

6   Harford, *Burgess*, p. 114.

7   The phrase *una . . . Juvenilibus* is squeezed in between the lines as an afterthought, above a *caret* mark.

8   John Randolph (1749–1813) had been a very prominent member of Oxford University for several years. As well as his association with the Press and with Christchurch, mentioned here, he was Professor of Poetry 1776–82, Proctor 1781, Regius Professor of Greek 1782–3, Regius Professor of Divinity 1783–1807 and Bishop of Oxford 1799–1807. In the latter year he became Bishop of Bangor, but in 1809 was translated to London, where he was Bishop until his death four years later.

     Burgess's dealings with the Press on Wyttenbach's behalf – obviously, from the mention of 'your letter', at Wyttenbach's prompting – are further attested in Harford, *Burgess*, pp. 114–15. The negotiations were clearly successful, since the Clarendon Press did indeed publish the edition of Plutarch's *Moralia* a few years later (see n. 4 above), and Wyttenbach dedicated the work to Oxford University.

9   'Cannon' was the usual spelling at this time. Why Burgess does not call Randolph 'Professor' is not clear. Perhaps his carefully chosen words imply that Wyttenbach had referred to him as such, but that Randolph preferred the other title.

10   Richard Porson (1759–1808), the renowned classical scholar and textual critic, and discoverer of 'Porson's Law' about the third metron in the iambic trimeters of Greek tragedy. The year 1792 was eventful for Porson: in July, some four months after Burgess's letter was written, he was forced to resign his Fellowship at Trinity College, Cambridge, because he would not take Holy Orders, and he was refused permission to apply for a vacancy in one of the only two Lay Fellowships (which was shortly afterwards awarded to the Master's nephew); but in November of the same year he was appointed Regius Professor of Greek. He hardly ever lectured to undergraduates, living for

most of the time in London, where he devoted himself to research. His published works are, however, comparatively few.

11 Porson collated the Harleian manuscript of Homer's *Odyssey* (Harl. MS 5674) for the 'Grenville Homer', an edition of Homer printed privately by the statesman William Wyndham, Baron Grenville (1759–1834), and his brothers, and published by the Clarendon Press in 1801.

12 A folio Aeschylus was published by the Foulis Press, Glasgow, in 1795, containing some corrections in the text by Porson; but it appeared without his name and without his knowledge. He is said to have sent his corrected text to Glasgow in order for a text to be printed from it in London; this edition was printed in 1794, but not published until 1806 – still without Porson's name. This partly corrected text was the first step to an intended edition of Aeschylus, which he never completed.

13 Christian Gottlieb Heyne (1729–1812) was Professor at Göttingen from 1763. He had made his reputation with his Tibullus of 1755, and this was followed by his four-volume Vergil (Leipzig, 1767); the London edition of the latter was published in four volumes in 1793. The Founders' Library possesses a first edition of both Vergils, and the second (1777) edition of the Tibullus. Harford (*Burgess*, p. 114) says that Heyne and Burgess met on the latter's 1787 visit to Europe.

14 Thomas Tyrwhitt (1730–86) was one of the greatest textual critics of the eighteenth century; he was also Burgess's mentor, inspiration and close friend. His acceptance of Burgess's request to dedicate his new (1781) edition of Dawes's *Miscellanea Critica* to him was the start of a long and, for Burgess, most fruitful relationship between the two men, which was ended only by Tyrwhitt's death five years later. The most important of Tyrwhitt's many kindnesses was his payment to Burgess, from 1781 to 1783, of a salary equivalent to that of a curate to enable him to stay in Oxford rather than take Holy Orders, leave the city and take a country curacy (Harford, *Burgess*, pp. 23–4, 56–7, 88–9). Burgess did, of course, eventually take Orders, but not until 1784, after his election to a Fellowship at Corpus Christi College, Oxford.

After Tyrwhitt's death, Burgess saw his late friend's unpublished edition of Aristotle's *Poetics* through the press – almost, one imagines, as an act of *pietas* – while he was a prebendary of Durham Cathedral. The work appeared in 1794, and two (different) copies are in the Founders' Library. Also in the Library is Tyrwhitt's own copy of the Aldine Press edition of the *Poetics* (Venice, 1536). This was later owned by Burgess, who has written inside: 'Thomas Burgess Dec. 7. 1797. This book belonging to my late dear friend Thomas Tyrwhitt Esq was given to me by his brother the Revd. Rob. Tyrwhitt.'

15 An accompanying Latin translation of the original Greek text, such as it was customary to supply in eighteenth-century editions, not a translation into English.

16 Burgess's principal work included the provision of these additional readings, as is made clear on pp. xiii–xiv in the publisher's introductory address to the reader: 'appendix continet Varias Lectiones ... quas in usum hujusce Editionis auctarii loco comparavit BURGESSIUS' ('The appendix contains variant readings ... which Burgess has prepared for use in this edition in the place of a supplement'). The manuscripts from which the additional readings are taken are listed, and they include the Royal Paris ones, which, despite Burgess's doubts expressed here, clearly did arrive in time.

17 *Musei Oxoniensis Litterarii Conspectus* (Oxford, 1792). The work was dedicated to the second Earl of Guilford, Chancellor of Oxford University (better known as Prime Minister Lord North). It contains lists of variant readings for the texts of Hippocrates, Aristotle's *Poetics*, Quintus Curtius Rufus, Proclus' commentaries on Euclid, and the *Anecdota Graeca* of Proclus and of Johannes Tzetzes. The second part, *Musei Oxoniensis Litterarii Speciminum Fasciculus Secundus*, followed five years later (London, 1797), showing that Burgess kept up his classical studies for some time after his move to Durham. Both works are in the Founders' Library.

18 *Jani Vincentii Gravinae Opuscula ad Historiam Litterariam et Studiorum Rationem Pertinentia* (1792), which is also in the Founders' Library. Giovanni Vincenzio Gravina (1664–1718) was primarily a jurist. Born in Calabria, he was educated in Naples and in 1689 moved to Rome, where he held the Chair of Civil Law at the College of La Sapienza from 1699, and the Chair of Canon Law from 1703. The *opuscula* mentioned here are *Oratio de Sapientia Universa* (Rome, 1700), *Dialogus de Conversione Doctrinarum* (Rome, 1694), *Oratio de Instauratione Studiorum*, delivered before Pope Clement XI (reigned 1700–21), *Dialogus de Lingua Latina* and a letter, *De Poesi*, to Cardinal Scipio Maffei (Rome, 1712). These are preceded by a lengthy life of Gravina and a list of his works. It is interesting to note that, in his introductory address to the reader, Burgess writes that he had intended to include in the

volume some essays of his own, *De Initiis Studiorum*, *De Causis Linguae Graecae* and *De Hodiernis ad Perfecte Eam* [sc. *Linguam Graecam*] *Cognoscendam Impedimentis et Defectibus*, but that pressure of work had obliged him to postpone publishing them until later. They seem never to have appeared. The Founders' Library holds two copies of this work: a complete one which is still very largely uncut, and a second, lacking the title-page, the life and the list of works, but fully interleaved, which contains annotations in Burgess's hand.

19 Laurens van Santen (1746–98), Curator at Leiden, had a considerable reputation as a Latin poet in his own right. It is highly probable that these *Carmina ab Juvenilibus* ('Poems by the Young') are *L. Santenii Carmina Juvenilia, editio tertia* ('L. Santen's *Poems of Youth*, third edition'), which were printed privately in London in 1792. But the entry in the *British Museum Catalogue* makes no mention of Burgess's name in connection with the work as listed under 'Santenius', and nothing similar appears under the entry for Burgess; neither is there any comparable item in the list of publications given in Harford's *Life*. It would appear, then, that this was not an annotated edition of the poems, but a simple reprinting of the plain text, to which Burgess did not append his name.

20 This must surely be the Elmsley at whose London bookshop both parts of Burgess's *Museum Oxoniense* were sold (called 'Elmsly' in the 1792 first part) – see n. 17 above.

21 The confusion over the date of Burgess's first visit to Holland, and the attachment of Wyttenbach's tribute to the second visit, rather than the first, have already been mentioned. Another is Harford's statement (*Burgess*, p. 118) that Tyrwhitt's death occurred shortly after Burgess's return from the second continental trip in 1787. Tyrwhitt actually died on 15 August 1786.

3

The Burgess Generation: Dutch Academic Theologians and Religious Knowledge, 1760–1840

JORIS VAN EIJNATTEN

Introduction: How Sebald Fulco Rau became a professor

Sebald Fulco Johannes Rau was born in 1765 and died in 1807 as a Professor of Oriental Languages and Hebrew Antiquities. Unlike Thomas Burgess, who lived to be 81, Rau passed away at the early age of 42 years. Apart from holding various professorships at the theological faculty of the university at Leiden, Rau had also been a preacher of the Dutch Walloon (francophone) churches. His friends and pupils sorely regretted the abrupt termination of his promising career, and a Walloon minister and erstwhile pupil of Rau wrote a panegyric shortly after his demise.[1] This eulogy provides a useful contemporary overview of the determinants influencing the career of a Dutch theologian in the later eighteenth century; nine such determinants may be distinguished.

FAMILY RELATIONS

Rau was born into a family long famed for its learning, virtue and piety, and well known in both Germany and the Dutch Republic. His father was a theology professor at Utrecht, his grandfather a theology professor at Herborn in Germany, and his grandmother the daughter of another Herborn professor of theology. His mother belonged to a leading family from Frisia and Amsterdam.[2] These antecedents rather distinguish him from Thomas Burgess, who was the son of a grocer.

51

QUALITIES OF MIND AND BODY

Rau was possessed of a quick intellect, good judgement, a reliable memory and, above all, a rich, bold and limitless imagination, which contributed to his proficiency as a poet and his dexterity as a painter.[3] He was also exceedingly precocious in mastering languages. He spoke or read French, German, Latin, Greek, the oriental languages, and even English; he later also learned Italian.

QUALITIES OF THE SOUL

Rau's 'religious feeling' was strengthened by his innate feeling for beauty, for aesthetic perfection. According to his biographer, this resulted in a natural affection for Christianity.[4]

EDUCATION AND SOCIAL ABILITIES

Partly because of his excellent education, Rau displayed striking social abilities. He was able to socialize with cultivated people, both strangers and natives. He conversed easily, even with women and paupers, as his biographer informs us. He had made tours through Germany and Britain (travelling through Colchester, Cambridge, Manchester, Oxford, London and Windsor). In Paris, he was introduced to Cardinal Maury and to the minister of public worship Portalis, both of whom invited him to dinner. University staff had tutored him from the age of fourteen, so that he had become versed in history, Latin, Greek, mathematics, astronomy, logic, metaphysics and the experimental method. Naturally, he also successfully pursued his theological studies.[5]

PROOFS OF SCHOLARSHIP

Rau demonstrated his scholarly abilities in the thesis he defended at the university as an eighteen-year-old, as well as in several orations he held as a professor. Unfortunately, it was not given to him to publish more, apart from a few sermons. Before his death he suffered the profound misfortune of losing most of his personal manuscripts in the momentous explosion of a boat loaded with ammunition and anchored along a

Leiden canal. Rau's panegyrist hoped to publish his 'complete works' in the near future, as the *Opera philologica, oratorica et poëtica.*[6] He never did.

SIGNS OF SOCIAL DISTINCTION

Rau was made a member of a distinguished neo-Latinist poetry society at fourteen, and later in life was provided with member-ships of several academies of sciences, literary societies and a painting academy. The king of Holland, Louis Napoleon, gave him a knighthood and appointed him as National Orator.[7]

NETWORKS

Rau was related to the then-famous Leiden publishers Lucht-mans (taken over by Brill publishing house in the nineteenth century) and the life-long friend of a number of relatively prominent persons. He was married to a countess.

MARKS OF PROFESSIONAL EXCELLENCE

Rau was an outstanding professional, both as a Walloon preacher famed for his oratorical excellence and as a Professor of Oriental Languages, Sacred Poetry, Sacred Oratory and Theology.

PEER-GROUP STATUS

Rau's pastorship was exemplary and, according to his eulogist, a welcome antidote for the disrepute into which the office of pastor had fallen. He was an able teacher, loved by his stu-dents; he was orthodox by conviction and loyal to the church confessions. He excelled as a preacher, represented his church on different occasions and supervised the primary schools in the Leiden municipality. As an academic, he established a following of capable pupils. For these reasons he was held in esteem by persons of social and academic standing.[8]

Thus, according to Rau's panegyrist, the determinants of a successful career as an academic scholar of theology in the decades around 1800 may be categorized as follows: (1) family background, (2) intellectual and physical qualities, (3) spiritual qualities, (4) education and social abilities, (5) publication list, (6) signs of social distinction, (7) networks, (8) marks of professional excellence or career development, and (9) peer-group status.

A *divine population*

Social context of knowledge

These nine determinants may be construed as the criteria professors-to-be could be expected to meet. These divines offer an insight into the social context in which certain kinds of knowledge originate or evolve – in this case, the religious knowledge generated by academics. To put it briefly, one could say that contemporaries, apart from valuing the *kind* of theological scholarship the academies produced, also set great store by the reputation of the *producers*, as well as by the *manner* of production and the *social space* in which this took place. It is possible to work with a version of Harold Lasswell's definition of communication: 'who says what to whom with what effect?' What matters besides the actual content of theological knowledge is the social context in which it arises.[9] Thus, in the traditional academic system of the seventeenth and eighteenth centuries, what was regarded as the official theological knowledge normally arose in the context of ecclesiastical institutions. As institutional knowledge, it was therefore subject to evident limitations and restrictions as to content.

In this essay, I shall attempt to shed some light on the nature of the 'theological' or 'religious knowledge' for which Thomas Burgess's Dutch counterparts were responsible. In order to outline the nature of scholarship at the Dutch academies in the period between about 1780 and 1840, the determinants of Sebald Fulco Johannes Rau's career provide a useful point of departure. I will not elaborate here on family relations and networks, which require prosopographical data I do not have at hand. Neither will I discuss the physical, intellectual and spiritual qualities of Burgess's Dutch contemporaries, since the first are in most cases unknown, the second usually self-evident and the third a matter of often highly subjective appreciation.[10]

Instead, I shall look mainly at publication lists, and subsequently combine these with several other career determinants, particularly career development, signs of social distinction and peer-group status – what we would now call a 'track record'. In conclusion, I shall attempt to put the religious knowledge produced by the selected theologians into its historical context.[11] Given my emphasis on the context in which theology evolves, my definition of 'academic religious knowledge' is necessarily a broad one: it includes all forms of knowledge with which a professor of a theology-related discipline was concerned, both before and after his career as an academic. The aim is partly to allow a comparison with Thomas Burgess's British context, and partly to rehabilitate this generation of Dutch theologians. The latter have all too often been given short shrift by Dutch church historians, who still tend to regard them as complacent moralists and shallow supernaturalists.[12]

The academic theologian

First, however, we shall have to provide a definition of the academic scholar of theology. Whom may we reckon among the academic producers of theological scholarship in the northern Netherlands between 1760 and 1840? The group obviously includes the professors of theology, both the ordinary and the extraordinary, working at the five Dutch universities. It also logically includes lecturers and private tutors, although these were a comparatively rare species among the theologians. At the Leiden university, the supervisors of the States College and the Walloon College (institutions supporting certain theology students) were licensed to teach theology, so they, too, should be included.

The production of academic religious knowledge was not limited to the theological faculties or theology-related institutions alone. Prior to the early nineteenth-century reform of the academic curriculum, the faculty of arts provided the basic, propaedeutic course for all students. The faculty had always contained a relatively large number of academics who concerned themselves with subjects closely related to theology proper. This category includes the academic experts on the oriental languages and oriental literature, Hebrew, Arabic and/or Aramaic, Hebrew or Jewish antiquities, Greek, the exegesis of the Old and New Testaments, sacred poetry, sacred oratory and sacred hermeneutics, Christian antiquities, sacred or church history, the history of doctrine, and, not to be forgotten, moral philosophy and moral theology.

Apart from the teaching staff, students, too, contributed to increments in religious knowledge, if only through the large number of theses they defended over the years. In many cases, the *praeses* or supervisor (that is, the professor) wholly supplied the content of these *disputationes*, but even then, students should be taken into account as participants in the process of knowledge production. The same applies to the many others who were concerned with theology in its broader institutional setting, ranging from members of the board of directors and politicians to librarians and publishers. There were of course many 'amateurs' in the field, who had received a full academic education and were usually active as ministers in one of the various Protestant churches. They were active writers, usually but not exclusively on theological matters, and they sometimes corresponded with professional academics. I shall restrict myself here to the latter group, that is, to professors in the faculties of arts and theology.

As well as at the five universities, at Leiden (since 1575), Franeker (1585), Groningen (1614), Utrecht (1636) and Harderwijk (1648), theologians also worked at the so-called 'Illustrious Schools' (*Illustere Scholen*) and related institutions for higher education, in places such as Maastricht and Nijmegen. The Athenaeum in Amsterdam falls into this category. Then there were honorary professors (*professores honorarii*), urban clergymen held in such esteem by their town councils that they were furnished with unpaid positions as municipal 'professors'. Rotterdam, in particular, specialized in such academics.

The theologians mentioned thus far were all members of the Reformed or Calvinist Church, which before 1795 functioned more or less as the Dutch state Church. However, the Protestant Dissenters also possessed their own academies, Remonstrant, Mennonite and Lutheran, where they appointed their own professors of theology. I have included these Dissenters in the population of theologians examined for this article. By contrast, Roman Catholic theological scholarship was not formally practised at any institution in the northern Netherlands during the period under consideration. Dutch Catholic theologians mainly produced their scholarship in or via Louvain, in the southern or Austrian Netherlands, which later became part of the United Kingdom of the Netherlands before it was independently established as Belgium. For this reason, Catholics were not taken into consideration.

The Burgess generation

We shall also have to define the selected population of Dutch scholars in chronological terms, as a generation. To qualify as contemporaries of Thomas Burgess, this generation would have to include those theologians whose thought was moulded in the eighteenth century. If blessed with health as excellent as that of Bishop Burgess, they might live long enough to witness the revolt of the Belgians against the Dutch (in 1830), or perhaps to read about the accession of Queen Victoria (in 1837) in the newspapers. This generation, then, would conceivably include all Dutch academic theologians who were born between 1740 and 1770 and who died before 1850. I shall henceforth call them the Burgess generation (see Table 1). Although a bishop is obviously not quite the same as a university professor, it is nonetheless worthwhile to compare Burgess with the Dutch theologians of his age group. All were concerned to disseminate religious knowledge, all worked for a period of time at academic institutions, many were active as pastors in the field, and some played a significant role in political life or held influential social positions.

Table I. The Dutch 'Burgess generation' and years of birth and death.

name	year of birth	year of death
Bachiene, Philip Jan	1750	1797
Boers, Carolus	1746	1814
Broes, Brouerius	1757	1799
Brown, William Laurence	1755	1830

name	year of birth	year of death
Clarisse, Johannes	1770	1846
Eck, Cornelis Fransen van	1764	1830
Forsborgh, Pieter Haack	1740	1823
Fremery, Johannes de	1741	1819
Greve, Egbert Jan	1754	1811
Hamelsveld, IJsbrand van	1743	1812
Hemert, Paulus van	1756	1825
Heringa, Jodocus Ezn	1765	1840
Hesselink, Gerrit	1755	1811
Huisman, Ditmar	1764	1822
Konijnenburg, Jan	1758	1831
Koopmans, Rinse Klaasses	1770	1826
Laurillard dit Fallot, Georges Jacques	1746	1803
Lotze, Johannes Anthony	1769	1832
Muntinghe, Herman	1752	1824
Nuys Klinkenberg, Jacob van	1744	1817
Oever, Henricus Hieronymus ten	1746	1825
Oordt, Gabriël van	1757	1836
Palm, Johannes Hendrik van der	1763	1840
Pareau, Johannes Hendrik	1761	1833
Rau, Sebald Fulco Johannes	1765	1807
Regenbogen, Johannes Hendrik	1769	1814
Royaards, Herman	1753	1825
Sage ten Broek, Johannes Jacobus le	1742	1823
Scheidius, Everard	1742	1794
Schultens, Hendrik Albert	1749	1793
Smits, Dingeman Wouter	1747	1806
Suringar, Lucas	1770	1833
Tinga, Eelco	1762	1828
Voorst, Johannes van	1757	1833
Water, Jona Willem te	1740	1822
Willmet, Johannes	1750	1835
Ypeij, Annaeus	1760	1837

Let us take a brief look at some statistics concerning the Dutch academics of the Burgess generation. The group includes thirty-seven academics, who collectively reached an average age of almost 67 years. The oldest theologian of this group died at 85 years of age (compare with Burgess, who reached the age of 80), the youngest at 42. They obtained an academic position at the average age of 35.6; the oldest to be appointed was aged 64 (as 'honorary' professor), the youngest, 22 (none other than Rau). Their careers lasted on average twenty four years; some individual careers lasted more than forty years, the shortest barely three years. The group includes one extraordinary professor, fourteen professors working at the smaller town and Dissenting academies, and two honorary professors; four theologians at the illustrious schools went on to become full professors, and one full professor (specializing, of all things, in logic, metaphysics, hydraulics and hydro-statics)[13] ended up as an honorary professor. In other words, about two-thirds of the group (twenty-five) were ordinary, full professors. Of this group of twenty-five theology professors, nineteen ultimately worked as theologians, while six remained in the arts faculty as linguists (four) or moral philosophers (two). The provenance of these theologians was predominantly Dutch. Rau was from Heidelberg in Germany, while William Laurence Brown came from, and returned to, Scotland.

Professorial careers

The careers of this group are fairly typical. Most professors of theology began their careers as preachers (thirty out of thirty-seven). Among the minor professors, pastoral careers some-times lasted more than five decades, while the shortest career as a minister was three years.[14] Some academics had their careers terminated or interrupted due to political events, usually because they had the wrong political leanings. The first signifi-cant date in this respect is 1787–88, when two professors were removed for sympathizing with the revolutionaries known as the 'Patriots' (hence the 'Patriot Period', between 1780 and 1787). One of them, Van Hamelsveld, had his portrait removed from the chambers of the senate of the university at Utrecht in the wake of the counter-revolution of 1787, and subsequently had to devote himself to translating books for a living. The second important date is 1795, when the revolutionaries returned to power in the Batavian Revolution and ousted three academics who had sided with the conservatives.[15]

The careers of the group are typical in another respect, in that they demonstrate the existence of a hierarchy among the academies. The academy at Harderwijk was evidently not a place where self-respecting theologians wanted to remain for very long; each of the five theologians who began their career in Harderwijk ended up at another academy.[16] The same applied to Franeker and the minor academies.[17] On the other hand, an honorary professorship in one of the major towns was seen as the successful termination of a pastoral career. Leiden, of course, represented the summit of a career in theology, followed by Utrecht and Groningen.

Academic themes

The themes dealt with in academic addresses – the orations with which professors inaugurated or laid down their rectorates – offer an insight into the intellectual priorities of scholars. The significance of academic addresses lies in the fact that they were held publicly, before the academic community and its political sponsors, so that both content and wording were carefully chosen. Addresses therefore reflect the expectations of the university curators, the aspirations of the professor and the presumed potential of the academic community. Let me attempt to classify the orations. Of the eighty-four inaugural or rectoral orations held by the Burgess generation in the course of their careers, nineteen were concerned with theological studies or the social aspects of religion. No fewer than twenty-six were concerned with language, literature or Bible studies, eigthteen with pastoral theology and thirteen with historical issues; five were concerned with moral or social philosophy, two with doctrine and one with academic affairs. Several topics stand out.

STUDY OF THEOLOGY

Firstly, the theologians were apparently interested in drawing attention to the nature of the academic curriculum, and were particularly keen on defining and promoting the study of theology. They were also concerned to highlight the joys and burdens of the clerical office. They enlarged on such themes as the obstacles to studying theology,[18] the delights of theology, the curriculum devised by the Greek Church Fathers, the need to adapt the content of theological studies and the duty of theologians to study the Scriptures. There were also considerations of the 'perfect' theologian and the 'liberal' theologian.[19]

LITERARY ASPECTS

Secondly, many are devoted to the literary aspects of theology, including exegesis, biblical criticism and aesthetic issues. Sebastian Fulco Johann Rau compared the poetic qualities of Ossian, Homer and Job (1799) and expanded on the superiority of Hebrew over Arabic poetry (1794). Another orientalist discussed the aesthetics of Arabic literature.[20] An Arminian scholar, inaugurating in Amsterdam as Professor of Literature and Philosophy, praised the idea that Jesus had accommodated his message to the backward understandings of his Jewish contemporaries. One of his Reformed colleagues, on the other hand, warned against extreme interpretations of the sacred texts.[21]

APOLOGY

A third theme concerns apologetic theology. With a view to defending or recommending the Christian religion, Dutch professors held orations on the association between religion and philosophy and on current opportunities to spread the gospel.[22] Others talked about God's wisdom and goodness in establishing Christianity in the way he did, or about how Christendom had actually profited from the attacks on it by deists and 'naturalists'.[23] The apparent rise of unbelief in recent years was a subject of concern to all.[24]

Finally, a fourth characteristic theme may be qualified as both historical and nationalistic, in the sense that the speakers made a point of noting the specifically Dutch contributions to the study of theology. One theologian reflected on the significance of the Schultens dynasty: the gifted linguists Albert, Jan Jacob and Herman Alexander. The third member of that dynasty himself elaborated on the Arabic scholarship for which the Dutch were justly famed.[25] There was also praise for historical persons, such as Philip van Marnix and Simon Episcopius.[26] A member of the Burgess generation who became a professor of Dutch literary history inaugurated on the commendableness of studying the national literature.[27]

Four themes, then, are prevalent in these inaugural and rectoral orations: the practice of theology, the bible as literature, apologetics, and national self-esteem (church history as an independent field is not taken into consideration here). Their significance to Burgess's contemporaries is borne out by the fact that early nineteenth-century writers of overviews of the state of Dutch science and scholarship tended to underline similar themes. Discussion of Bible studies, for example, invariably provoked expressions of nationalist sentiment. One author focused on biblical criticism as an indispensable instrument in purifying the sacred texts from which theology itself is derived.[28] Unfortunately, the sensible ideas on biblical criticism developed by Desiderius Erasmus and Hugo Grotius (both evidently Dutch!) had been obscured by the rise of Protestant scholasticism. In the eighteenth century, however, the Dutch revived their tradition of moderate, careful criticism, following the revival of linguistic scholarship under Tiberius Hemsterhuis (1685–1766) and Albert Schultens (1686–1750).[29] Next to biblical criticism, scriptural exegesis should be accorded much more weight than in the past. Exegesis requires a balanced judgement; it requires, that is, interpreters trained to appreciate the poetry of the Old Testament and fully informed on the Hebrew antiquities. Johann Gottfried Herder (1744–1803) and Robert Lowth (1710–87) may first have drawn attention to the virtues of Hebrew poetry, but the study of Hebrew antiquities had long been a field in which the Dutch had excelled more than any other nation.[30] In fact, the Dutch had devoted themselves to interpreting the biblical texts ever since the establishment of Christianity in this region, a tradition epitomized, again, by Erasmus of Rotterdam and Hugo Grotius.[31] Another author similarly stressed the contribution to the revival of sound theological scholarship of eighteenth-century academics working within a much older Dutch tradition.[32] What Herman Boerhaave (1668–1738) and Jerome Gaubius (1705–80) were to the study of medicine, the three Schultenses (Albert, Jan Jacob and Herman Alexander) and Hemsterhuis were to the study of linguistics. They jointly turned Leiden into the most outstanding university in Europe, attracting students from Germany, Hungary, Russia, Sweden, Denmark, England, France, Italy, Greece, and even America and Arabia.

Publication lists

The Burgess generation as a whole produced 719 self-authored texts published independently: 509 as books or pamphlets, 210 as articles in periodicals or series (see Table 2). Together they wrote 42 forewords to books. They generated 94 translations (53 of which were translated by IJsbrand van Hamelsveld alone), 20 Bible translations, 7 commentaries on the Bible and 35 commentaries on other works, and edited 58 periodicals and monographs – and these figures include only the first volume of every first edition.[33] Johannes Hendrik van der Palm was the most prolific writer of this generation of Dutch theologians, accounting for 141 (132 + 9) published, self-authored writings. In the following, I shall take a closer look at each of the themes mentioned above (theological studies, the Bible as literature, apologetics, national self-esteem) as they emerge from the theologians' publication lists (see also Table 3).

Table 2. Number of publications per professor (first editions, and if applicable, first volumes only).

name	a	f	t	bt	c	bc	e	totals
Bachiene, Philip Jan	1							1
Boers, Carolus	9	1	2					12
Broes, Brouerius	15	1					1	17
Brown, William Laurence	34				1			35
Clarisse, Johannes	51	8	6	1	7		6	79
Eck, Cornelis Fransen van	11							11
Fremery, Johannes de	1							1
Greve, Egbert Jan	5			1				6
Hamelsveld, IJsbrand van	53	3	53	7	3		9	128
Hemert, Paulus van	36	1	2		1		1	41
Heringa, Jodocus Ezn	47	4	2		3		4	60
Hesselink, Gerrit	24							24
Konijnenburg, Jan	25		4	1			3	33
Koopmans, Rinse Klaasses	12	1						13
Laurillard dit Fallot, Georges Jacques	1		1					2
Lotze, Johannes Anthony	15		1			2	2	20
Muntinghe, Herman	23	9	4			1	3	40
Nuys Klinkenberg, Jacob van	11	1	2		2		1	17
Oever, Henricus Hieronymus ten	3							3
Oordt, Gabriël van	3							3
Palm, Johannes Hendrik van der	132	9	2	3		2	3	151
Pareau, Johannes Hendrik	16				1			17
Rau, Sebald Fulco Johannes	13	1						14
Regenbogen, Johannes Hendrik	13							13
Royaards, Herman	9							9
Sage ten Broek, Johannes Jacobus le	28	1			1		1	31
Scheidius, Everard	9		4		6	1	10	30
Schultens, Hendrik Albert	5		2	2	3	1	3	16
Smits, Dingeman Wouter	4							4
Suringar, Lucas	6							6

name	a	f	t	bt	c	bc	e	totals
Tinga, Eelco	11	1	7				2	21
Voorst, Johannes van	19				1		1	21
Water, Jona Willem te	45						4	49
Willmet, Johannes	7				3		3	13
Ypeij, Annaeus	22	1	7		3		1	34
totals	719	42	94	20	35	7	58	975

Codes: a = independently published, self-authored text (including publications in periodicals or series)
f = foreword
t = translation, other than bible translation
bt = bible translation (whole or in part)
c = commentary
bc = bible commentary
e = edited work.

Table 3. Categorical division of publications included in Table II.

Category	totals
occasional pieces	220
bible studies	165
education: religious	115
literature	81
language	60
church history	41
philosophy	41
secular history	39
religion: general	36
theology: dogmatic	35
theology: practical	33
theology: apologetic	25
classical scholarship	17
church matters	15
theology: auxiliaries	12
natural science	10
education: non-religious	9

Category	totals
theology: eschatology	6
general	4
secular law	4
world & people	3
medicine	2
theology: ecclesiastical law	2
totals	975

Note that sermons fall mainly under 'occasional pieces' and 'education: religious'.

The practice of theology

The first theme, the practice of theology, comprises several minor topics: (1) theology as an academic study, (2) the joys and burdens of the clerical office, and (3) popular religious instruction.

THEOLOGY AS ACADEMIC STUDY

Guidebooks for the best method of completing one's studies – the so-called *rationes studiorum* – had appeared irregularly since the sixteenth century. Everard Scheidius reissued one of these earlier essays on theological studies in 1790–92, a series of Latin tracts in two volumes by a seventeenth-century French Huguenot, Étienne Gaussen (1616–75). Apart from the essay on learning methods, the book covered such topics as the nature of theology, homiletics and the use of philosophy to theology.[34] Possibly because of its clarity and brevity, Gaussen's book had been very popular on the Continent during the eighteenth century. Six earlier editions, appearing in France, the Netherlands and Germany, had preceded the 1790–92 edition.[35] It is revealing, however, that the final edition of Gaussen's essays on theology was complemented by a third volume of essays, devoted to humanist studies in the arts faculty. This volume contained essays on learning methods by sixteenth- and seventeenth-century French and Dutch humanists, including Erasmus.[36]

Gaussen's outline of a five-year theology course, and his advice to students to range far beyond the study of theology proper, would probably have appealed to Burgess – who may have known one of the seven continental editions.[37] After all, in 1792 Burgess edited a volume of Gian Vincenzo Gravina's (1664–1718) writings on *historia litteraria* and *ratio studiorum*.[38] The latter combination – an overview of theological literature in conjunction with a manual on how to study – was popular among the Burgess generation as well. The first Dutch work on theological encyclopaedia, the *Encyclopaediae theologicae epitome* (1832, enlarged edition 1835), was basically a guide for theology students, a *ratio studiorum* in classical vein.[39] However, it included an immense bibliography of more than 800 pages. The book is actually not an encyclopaedia at all, since it contains no attempt to derive the structure of theological science from any clear principle. In contrast to accepted tradition, the sections on philology and history precede the section on systematic theology, and the book puts much emphasis on historical literature in general.[40] Both the Dutch theologians and Burgess apparently placed the study of theology in a broadly humanistic context, with a strong emphasis on history and bibliography.

THE CLERICAL OFFICE

The office of clergyman is a second theme with which Burgess and his Dutch colleagues were specifically concerned. In Wales, Burgess discussed the 'peculiar privileges of the Christian ministry' and 'the importance and difficulty of the pastoral office, and the danger of rashly undertaking it'.[41] In the Netherlands, professors, apart from addressing the subject in various academic orations, wrote handbooks for young ministers on how to cope with their office.[42] One even began a periodical on the subject, the *Ecclesiastical Advice-Taker and Advice-Giver* (1819–43).[43]

POPULAR RELIGIOUS INSTRUCTION

Religious education was hardly a new genre in the theological literature, but it was one taken most seriously by Burgess's

Dutch colleagues. Burgess himself wrote books of religious knowledge 'for the Christian instruction of the ignorant and simple'.[44] They include his *First Principles of Christian Knowledge*, an explanation of the catechism and the creeds.[45] His Dutch counterparts provided, among many other things, a commentary on the apocryphal writings for the 'unlearned'.[46] The Dutch tended to look especially towards Germany, where popular *Aufklärung* was in full swing.[47] They translated a rhymed course on the elements of Christianity for children, Johann Georg Rosenmüller's *Betrachtungen über die vornehmsten Wahrheiten der Religion* (1802) and Jochims's *Anleitung über die Religion überhaupt und über die geoffenbarte Religion insbesondere vernünftig und schriftmäßig zu denken* (1777), and writings by Lavater.[48] They discussed the parables of Jesus, wrote essays on contentedness (pointedly addressed to marginal social groups), or sermonized on the importance of not giving in to sensual pleasures.[49] One divine began a magazine called *Solomon* (1808–16), containing verse-by-verse explanations of, meditations on and applications of the book of Proverbs.[50] This 'moral weekly' – its aim was moral instruction – ran for no less than eight years.

The Bible as literature

One characteristic feature of the Burgess generation is a pronounced interest in literature and language. Burgess himself published an edition of Greek tragedies, wrote a book on spelling, and later became President of the Royal Society of Literature (1820). His Dutch counterparts published observations on medieval literature, commented on the sublime, wrote plays in five full acts on (for example) Constantine the Great,[51] and held membership of such poetry societies as 'Art is the Result of Labour'.[52]

BIBLE AS A LITERARY ARTEFACT

In the wake of literary scholars such as Lowth and Herder, the Dutch theologians of Burgess's generation showed increasing interest in the Bible as a collection of literary artefacts. The fact that they set forth their ideas mainly in essays and lectures held at literary and scholarly societies illustrates their new attitude to the sacred texts. In educated circles in Amsterdam, The Hague and Leiden, scriptural texts began to exert a distinct aesthetic appeal; the Bible became a source of refined pleasure. Johan Hendrik van der Palm, a highly celebrated writer and orator, discussed David as a poet of distinction and the excellence of Job as a painter of nature. Rau had compared Homer and Ossian, to their disadvantage, with the Hebrew poets.[53]

TRANSLATIONS

The new appreciation of the Bible as the cultural expression of ancient civilizations led also to a profound interest in the best way to interpret the Bible as a text wholly foreign to the culture of early nineteenth-century Europe. Burgess, too, was concerned with the issue, as testified by a pamphlet outlining the 'Reasons why a new translation of the Bible should not be published without a previous statement and examination of all the material passages, which may be supposed to be misinterpreted' (1816).[54] In the Netherlands, the old 'States translation' of 1637 (comparable to the King James Version) was considered obsolete, and there was a flurry of activity to produce a new translation of the Bible. Several theologians attempted a complete Bible translation. Contemporaries regarded at least one of these, appearing in three volumes between 1820 and 1830, as unparalleled. The translator's aim – and this characterizes the Burgess generation – was to ensure that his readers actually understood what they read, rather than offer them a literal rendering of the Hebrew and Greek originals, which they were bound to misinterpret. Hence, he often made use of descriptions rather than transcriptions, and assiduously attempted to convey the beauty of scriptural poetry and prose in the Dutch language.[55] Apart from the Bible as a whole, individual scriptural texts were also translated, with a specific preference for Ecclesiastes, Job, the Psalms and the apocryphal writings – that is, for what were considered the more literary texts.

PARAPHRASES

Paraphrases of the Bible were no less common among the theologians of Burgess's generation. Extremely popular was the *Bible for the Young*, which first appeared in twenty-four volumes between 1811 and 1834. It was not so much a children's Bible (although it was intended to be one) as a highly moralistic paraphrase of the Scriptures, catering for a broad, youthful public.[56] It was reissued eight times in the nineteenth century. A very popular paraphrase of the life of Jesus by the German Heinrich Christian Bergen (1747–1812), translated and prefaced by Dutch professors, was published four times.[57]

CRITICISM AND COMMENTARY

The attention paid to problems of interpretation and to historical contexts was, of course, connected with older traditions of humanistic biblical scholarship, as well as with one of the epoch-making changes in later eighteenth-century scholarship: the rise of historical criticism. Burgess, needless to say, also occupied himself with the subject, in his *Initia Paulina* (1804), his *Hebrew Etymology* (1813) and his *Observations on Mr. Sharp's Biblical Criticisms* (1820).[58] Likewise, Dutch writers of learned commentaries spent a great many hours poring over the minor and major prophets, as well as Paul's letters. 'Introductions' to the Old and New Testaments in particular were a new feature in the theological landscape.[59]

Apologetics

The third prominent theme in the academic theological scholarship of the Burgess generation, apologetics, is closely related to the first two: all-round clergymen were expected to be able to counter the claims of disbelievers and unbelievers, and they could do this only if their knowledge of the Bible was firm.

Apologetics was, again, a topic with which Bishop Burgess was closely concerned. He seems to have been Britain's expert on a single biblical verse – that of 1 John 5: 7 ('For there are three that bear record in heaven, the Father, the Word, and the Holy Ghost: and these three are one'). A reference to the verse appears in at least eight titles between 1820 and 1835. One learned Latin study edited by Burgess and wholly concerned with the passage from John's letter was *Adnotationes*, by John

Mill (1645–1707). It included commentaries by eight prominent British and continental scholars.[60] If ever there was a
testimony to the enduring international character of humanist
biblical scholarship, this was it.

Burgess was concerned throughout his life, from his Oxford
sermon of 1790 to his *Christian Theocracy* of 1834, to combat
Unitarianism and defend the divinity of Christ.[61] Unitarianism
did not pose as large a threat in the Netherlands as in England,
although there was some discussion on the subject (one of the
Arminian professors, Paulus van Hemert, was an Arian), partly
in response to Joseph Priestley.[62] A defence of the Trinity was
provoked by the so-called German neologians, who were also
responsible for rebuttals of a number of other larger and
smaller heresies.[63] Dutch professors defended the Resurrec-
tion,[64] the authority of the Apostles, the excellence of the
Gospel, the necessity of Revelation and the immortality of the
soul.[65] Soon after his return to Aberdeen, William Laurence
Brown, the Scottish erstwhile professor at Utrecht, wrote an
appendix to an edition of John Leland's well-known *View of
the Principal Deistical Writers* (1798).[66]

National self-esteem

The fourth theme, national self-esteem, is the most difficult to
identify. As far as Burgess is concerned, perhaps his nationalist
(all-British) feelings were best expressed in his writings against
the emancipation of Roman Catholics. Thus, he elaborated
among other things 'on the independence of the ancient British
Church of any foreign jurisdiction' (1812).[67] Incidentally, this
anti-Catholic, all-Protestant nationalism is a feature he shared
with most of his Dutch colleagues, who for this reason greatly
regretted the expulsion of the Dutch northerners from Belgium
in 1830. In addition, Burgess stimulated research into Welsh
culture, including Welsh antiquities, music and poetry. In the
Netherlands, orations held to commemorate important events
were particularly suffused with patriotic or nationalistic ideas.
Poems were recited, addresses declaimed and sermons
preached on topics related to national history, such as the
founding of Leiden University and the invention (by the Dutch
and *not* the Germans!) of the printing press in 1423 (rather

than 1450).[68] The arch-orator Van der Palm's celebrated account of the foundation of the Kingdom of the Netherlands in 1813, after the fall of Napoleon, was reproduced in eight editions between 1816 and 1889.[69]

The Burgess generation was much concerned with national history. They published on antiquities, numismatics and inscriptions,[70] as well as on major events in Dutch political history.[71] Most of all, they produced multi-volume works on the history of the Dutch Calvinist Church and wrote elegant essays on the heroes of the Dutch religious past, including Erasmus and Hugo Grotius.[72]

The formal context

Other themes than the four discussed in the previous section could have been broached, but it does seem that they were the most significant in the period under consideration. At this point it is possible to combine the information regarding the specific themes with which the academic theologians of Burgess's generation apparently were most concerned, with the kind of contextual data suggested by the panegyric upon Sebald Fulco Johannes Rau. A number of topics are pertinent here: society membership, essay competitions, lectures, sermons and periodicals.

MEMBERSHIPS

Practically all members of the Burgess generation were members, and often also directors or governors, of private or semi-private associations. These associations or societies (numbering at least thirty-nine) ranged from the Society for the Defence of the Christian Religion and the Dutch Missionary Society to provincial and national 'academies of sciences' and literary associations – and even the National Convention of 1796. Most theologians were members of various societies at the same time. Sebald Fulco Johannes Rau was a member of at least six, Jona Willem te Water of no fewer than seventeen. Burgess, of course, was made an honorary member of the Anti-Slavery Society, in 1804 founded a 'Society for promoting

Christian knowledge', and was active in various Bible and missionary societies.[73]

ESSAY COMPETITIONS

Some of these private or semi-private societies organized essay competitions and awarded first and second prizes (usually gold and silver medals) to the winners. The most important society – in terms of the quantity of prize-winning essays awarded to members of our group of Dutch theologians – was the Society for the Defence of the Christian Religion. This, of course underscores the importance of apologetics as a theme. The Burgess generation together contributed twenty-six times to the essay competitions of the Society for the Defence of the Christian Religion, most of them contributing (and winning) three or four times each. Interestingly, the majority of prize-winning essays were written during the term of professorship – rather than before, as might have been expected in connection with career opportunities.

LECTURES

Also connected with the literary, religious or political societies is the society lecture. Whilst Burgess held an address at the Royal Society of Literature (1827), Dutch theologians did so at, for example, the Society for Dutch Literature in Leiden. A substantial number of publications were conceived as a spoken text, as a lecture on self-knowledge, the true nature of rhetoric, or on Muhammad as the founder of the Islamic empire. These examples are all from the titles of lectures by one and the same theologian (Van der Palm), who was by far the most popular and the most famous orator in Dutch high society of the period.

SERMONS

It may be worthwhile to point out that one of the most common categories in terms of form was the sermon, published individually or as part of a larger collection (of 719 self-authored texts published independently, 114, or a little under 16 per cent, were single sermons or sermon collections). In the decades around 1800, the Dutch sermon had in fact begun to share the features of a society lecture. The Church itself was rapidly turning into a semi-private society with a (potentially) national rather than local membership; the new, so-called 'synthetic' method of preaching put strong emphasis on a thematic rather than analytic approach to Bible texts; and the sermon was seen primarily as a means of transferring practical information to the listeners and of transforming their behaviour. To all appearances, the sermon was simply a specific variety of society lecture.

PUBLICATIONS IN SERIES AND JOURNALS

A relatively large number of publications appeared in the form of essays or articles in series and journals. The Burgess generation alone published in at least fifty different journals or magazines, review periodicals, newspapers and society or academy series. Some contributed a single piece (which might be an essay, a poem or a review), others more than thirty. Periodicals on church history were obviously a new phenomenon to the Burgess generation. They collectively published eleven articles in the *Archief voor kerkelijke geschiedenis* (*Archive for Church History*, founded in 1829), which holds a sixth place after such literary periodicals as the *General Messenger of Art and Literature* (*Algemeene konst- en letter-bode*, established in 1801) or the *General Dutch Literary Exercises* (*Algemeene vaderlandsche letter-oefeningen*, founded in 1761). Exactly how many such smaller pieces were published is impossible to determine, if only because a substantial number appeared anonymously, especially in the earlier part of the period. We do not even know exactly which professors were connected as editors with which periodicals.

Religious knowledge 1760–1840

What do these data tell us about the nature of Dutch theological knowledge, and the social and intellectual context in which it evolved between 1780 and 1840? At least three points can be made.

SCHOLARSHIP AS A COLLECTIVE ENTERPRISE

Firstly, more than ever before, religious knowledge in the decades around 1800 was produced by a collective of scholars who did not necessarily know each other personally. In the traditional seventeenth- and eighteenth-century context of academic scholarship, the generation of theological knowledge had been a function of the specific mandate or field of the professor. Theology had originated in the broad context of the faculty, which imposed confessional or other restrictions on the content of theological knowledge. This applies also to the private lectures commonly held by university professors, despite the fact that there was more room here for innovation. Until well into the eighteenth century, scholarship was only a collective enterprise insofar as the professor acted as a supervisor (*praeses*), who generally wrote the theses his students were expected to defend.

The academic theologians of Burgess's generation were rapidly getting used to a wholly different context of knowledge production. They obviously remained members of the faculty, deriving part of their authority as such. At the same time, they participated in social groups that extended far beyond the universities. They made theology into a joint effort, by integrating the daily business of local theology faculties into the more anonymous concerns of supra-local organizations and institutions, including societies and associations, journals and magazines, and, of course, the book market itself. Not surprisingly, the better-known theologians were welcomed as writers of commendatory forewords.[74]

ANONYMOUS PUBLIC

This brings me to a second point. The transformation of early modern scholarship from an individual concern to a collective enterprise was closely related to the development of a larger and broader reading public. By the late eighteenth century, this public had become more self-aware, more critical and more demanding, but also more anonymous than before. On the one hand, writers acknowledged the importance of empathizing with, and adapting their discourse, to articulate and educated audiences. On the other hand, they regarded the increasingly anonymous reading public and its democratic habitus as a somewhat frightening phenomenon that needed instruction, education and guidance. Hence, among many other things, the large number of translations often addressed specifically to children, youths, the educated middle-class, to the uneducated, the poor and the ignorant. More than 75 per cent of the Burgess generation's publications were in Dutch, whilst less than 19 per cent were in Latin – although it must be added that the ability to write better Latin than foreign academics contributed to the theologians' self-image as custodians of the national spirit.[75]

NATIONAL INTEGRATION

The collective nature of scholarship and the growth of the reading public are in turn closely bound up with the development of new means of communication, and thus also with nation-building. The theologians of the Burgess generation regarded themselves as the moral leaders of the nation, bound to instruct the people in the religion best suited to its spirit. The explicit purpose or implicit effect of the many tract and missionary societies, of lectures and sermons, of popular textbooks and periodicals was to mould the new, anonymous public into a nation of responsible citizens.

Conclusion

Let me draw some conclusions from this discussion of the Burgess generation's concerns with religious knowledge and religious scholarship. The theological activity exhibited by this group was clearly well suited to the changing social context in which it took place. The emphasis on apologetics, the growth of national self-esteem, the attempt to reach broader audiences, and the attention paid to the cultural history of the Bible – all this was a kind of theological activity perfectly adapted to a context in which sociability, commerce and nation-building figured prominently. One might claim that this applies as much to academic theologians in the Netherlands as it does to

English bishops in Wales. Conversely, and on a somewhat broader scale, it may be concluded that the social context of the decades around 1800 itself generated the kind of religious knowledge with which the Burgess generation was evidently concerned. To put it another way, the content, the form and the plausibility itself of religious knowledge (or, for that matter, any other kind of knowledge) depend very much on who is concerned with which knowledge, and in which historical setting.

Notes

[1] J. Teissedre l'Ange, *Lofrede (. . .) op Sebald Fulco Johannes Rau* (Haarlem, 1808); Teissedre l'Ange had been a pupil of Rau's at Leiden in 1791.

[2] Ibid., pp. 6, 63–64.

[3] Ibid., pp. 6–9, 67–69.

[4] Ibid., pp. 19–20.

[5] Ibid., pp. 10–13, 48, 73, 132–3.

[6] Ibid., pp. 14–15; 71–72.

[7] Ibid., pp. 16–17, 72–3, 128.

[8] Ibid., pp. 24, 27, 96–7, 104, 124.

[9] Steven Shapin, *A Social History of Truth. Civility and Science in Seventeenth-Century England* (Chicago, 1994); Peter Burke, *A Social History of Knowledge. From Gutenberg to Diderot* (Cambridge etc, 2000).

[10] Such 'career determinants' were commonplace in pastoral handbooks that discussed clerical requirements; see Joris van Eijnatten, '*Theologus eruditus, theologus modestus*. The early modern pastor as communication worker', *Dutch Review of Church History*, 83 (2003), 309–18.

[11] In so doing, this article implicitly refers to Jürgen Habermas's notion of the 'public sphere' and Benedict Anderson's idea of 'imagined communities'; see Jürgen Habermas, *Strukturwandel der Öffentlichkeit. Untersuchungen zu einer Kategorie der bürgerlichen Gesellschaft* (Neuwied, 1962); Benedict Anderson, *Imagined Communities: Reflections on the Origin and Spread of Nationalism* (London, 1983). An extensive general treatment of Dutch religious history from this point of view may be found in Joris van Eijnatten, *Liberty, and Concord in the United Provinces. Religious Toleration and the Public in the*

Eighteenth-Century Netherlands, Brill's Studies in Intellectual History, 111 (Leiden, 2003).

12 Cf. Otto J. de Jong, *Nederlandse kerkgeschiedenis* (3rd ed; Nijkerk, 1986), pp. 307–9. Admittedly, the attitude towards this generation has become less dismissive than it was; for an older indictment, see e.g. C. W. Mönnich, in A. G. Weiler *et al.*, *Geschiedenis van de Kerk in Nederland* (Utrecht, Antwerpen, 1962), p. 244.

13 This was Le Sage ten Broek.

14 More than five decades: Le Sage ten Broek, Fremery and Nuys Klinkenberg; three years: Van der Palm.

15 These were Boers, Brown (who left of his own accord before things came to a head) and Nuys Klinkenberg.

16 Clarisse and Scheidius went to Leiden, Muntinghe and Ypeij to Groningen and Willmet to the Amsterdam Athenaeum.

17 Regenbogen and Van Voorst managed to get promoted from Franeker to Leiden, Tinga from Franeker to Groningen, Royaards from Middelburg to Utrecht and Schultens from Amsterdam to Leiden.

18 C. Boers, *Oratio de difficultatibus, disciplinae theologicae professionem prementibus; et de potissimis, quae illarum mitigationi inserviant, levamentis* (Leiden, 1779); S. F. J. Rau, *Oratio de eo quod jucundum est in studio theologico* (Leiden, 1788); J. A. Lotze, *Oratio, pro commendanda ratione, quam secuti sunt veteris ecclesiae Graecae doctores* (Leeuwarden, Amsterdam, 1804); J. Heringa Ezn, *Oratio, de theologiae in scholis institutione ad praesentem reipublicae christianae conditionem prudenter accommodanda* (Utrecht, 1794); B. Broes, *Oratio de literarum sacrarum studio, praecipuo theologi munere* (Leiden, 1784).

19 J. H. Regenbogen, *Oratio de theologo perfecto* (Leeuwarden, 1804); J. Clarisse, 'Oratio de theologo vere liberali' (1815), in Clarisse, *Orationes duae* (Leiden, 1815).

20 S. F. J. Rau, 'Oratio de poëticae facultatis excellentia et perfectione spectata in tribus poëtarum principibus, scriptore Jobi, Homero et Ossiano' (1794) and 'Oratio de poëseos Hebraicae prae Arabum poësi praestantia' (1799), both in Rau, *Orationes duae* (Leiden, 1800); J. Willmet, *Oratio de sensu pulcri Arabum* (Harderwijk, 1794).

21 P. van Hemert, *Oratio de prudenti Christi, Apostolorum, atque Evangelistarum consilio, sermones suos ac scripta, ad captum atque intellectum vulgi, quantum illud fieri potuit, accommodatium* (Amsterdam, 1791); J. H. Regenbogen, *Oratio*

de extremis in quae interpretes sacri codicis passim prolapsi sunt sedulo cavendis (Leeuwarden, 1799).

22 W. L. Brown, *Oratio, de religionis et philosophiae societate, et concordia maxime salutari* (Utrecht, 1788); J. van Voorst, *Oratio de temporum nostrorum ad promovendam religionis causam opportunitate* (Franeker, 1788).

23 H. Muntinghe, *Oratio de sapientia et bonitate divina, in antiquissima religionis patefactione conspicua* (Harderwijk, 1781); H. Royaards, *Oratio pro ordinis ratione, qua Deus in patefacienda religione, usus sit* (Utrecht, 1788); J. H. Pareau, *Oratio de conatibus incredulorum rei christianae plus emolumenti quam detrimenti afferentibus* (Deventer, 1790).

24 Cf. J. van Nuys Klinkenberg, *Oratio de incredulorum machinationibus reipublicae admodum perniciosis* (Amsterdam, 1784); IJ. van Hamelsveld, *Oratio inauguralis de statu rei christianae hodierno! Laeto an tristi? Quidque in posterum de eo sperare vel timere debeamus?* (Utrecht, 1784); G. Hesselink, *Oratio de causis cur doctrina evangelica, praesentia longe eminens, lucullentissimisque miraculis munita, a plurimus quidem licet protinus recepta, a multis tamen tam ex Judaeis quam ex gentibus rejecta fuerit* (Amsterdam, 1786).

25 E. Scheidius, *Oratio de eo, quod Schultensii, post immortalia erga literas orientales merita, posteris agendum reliquerint* (Leiden, 1793); H. A. Schultens, *Oratio de studio Belgarum in literis Arabicis excolendis* (Leiden, 1779); also J. Willmet, *Oratio de retinenda antiqua Batavorum in literis orientalibus gloria* (Amsterdam, 1805).

26 J. H. Regenbogen, 'Laudatio Philippi Marnixii, domini Montis Sanctae Aldegondae' (unpubl. oration, Franeker, 1810); J. Konijnenburg, *Laudatio Simonis Episcopii* (Amsterdam, 1790).

27 C. Fransen van Eck, *Over het aanbevelenswaardige van de beoefening der Nederlandsche letterkunde* (Deventer, 1817).

28 Hendrik baron Collot d'Escury, *Hollands roem in kunsten en wetenschappen, met aanteekeningen en bijdragen*, 7 vols ('s Gravenhage, Amsterdam, 1824–31).

29 Ibid., pp. 13–22; on moderate criticism, see Joris van Eijnatten, 'From modesty to mediocrity. Regulating public dispute, 1670–1840: the case of Dutch divines', in *Common Knowledge*, 8 (2002) (*Peace and Mind. Seriatim Symposium on Dispute, Conflict, and Enmity, part 2*), 310–32.

30 Collot d'Escury, *Hollands roem in kunsten en wetenschappen*, pp. 24–38.

31 Ibid., pp. 50–84, 108–30.

32 N. G. van Kampen, *Beknopte geschiedenis der letteren en wetenschappen in de Nederlanden, van de vroegste tijden af, tot op het begin der negentiende eeuw*, 3 vols ('s Gravenhage, 1821–6) II, pp. 85–6.

33 At least 170 titles were reissued as second editions.

34 S. Gaussenus, *Dissertationes I. De studii theologici ratione; II. De natura theologiae; III. De ratione concionandi*, ed. E. Scheidius (Leiden, 1792); and Gaussen, *Dissertationum pars posterior, continens diss. IV. De utilitate philosophae ad theologiam; V. De recto usu clavium; et VI. De verbo Dei*, ed. E. Scheidius (Leiden, 1792).

35 Editions were published in Saumur (1670), Utrecht (1678), Kassel (1697), Frankfurt (1707) and Halle (1723, 1727); apparently there was also an Amsterdam 1697 edition.

36 E. Scheidius (ed.), *Ioachimi Fortii Ringelbergii, Desiderii Erasmi, M. A. Mureti, G. J. Vossii, & C. Barlaei Commentationes de ratione studii* (Leiden, 1792).

37 See D. T. W. Price, *Bishop Burgess and Lampeter College* (s.l., 1987), 53.

38 T. Burgess (ed.), *Opuscula ad historiam litterariam, et studiorum rationem pertinentia* (Oxford, 1792).

39 J. Clarisse, *Encyclopaediae theologicae epitome, perpetua annotatione, literaria potissimum, illustrata. Futuris theologis scripsit* (Leiden, 1832; 2nd edn, 1835).

40 Cf. also A. Ypeij, *Beknopte letterkundige geschiedenis der systematische godgeleerdheid* (Haarlem, 1793), a *historia litteraria* of writings on dogma.

41 T. Burgess, *Peculiar Privileges of the Christian Ministry: Considered in a Charge Delivered to the Clergy of the Diocese of St. David's at the Primary Visitation of that Diocese in the Year 1804* (Durham, 1805); *On the Importance and Difficulty of the Pastoral Office, and the Danger of Rashly Undertaking it* (Carmarthen, 1811).

42 C. Boers, *Handboek voor jonge predikanten* (Leiden, 1807; 2nd edn, 1820); J. Konijnenburg, *Lessen over het leeraars-ambt in de christelijke kerk* (Utrecht, 1802).

43 J. Heringa Ezn, *Kerkelijke raadvrager en raadgever*, 4 vols (1819–43).

44 Quoted in Price, *Bishop Burgess*, p. 19.

45 T. Burgess, *First Principles of Christian Knowledge* (London, 1804).

46 IJ. van Hamelsveld, *Korte aanmerkingen over de Apokryfe Boeken voor ongeleerden* (Amsterdam, 1798).

47 See Joris van Eijnatten, 'History, reform, and *Aufklärung*. German theological writing and Dutch literary publicity in the eighteenth century', in *Zeitschrift für neuere Theologiegeschichte/Journal for the History of Modern Theology*, 7 (2000), 173–204.

48 Johann Georg Franck, *Digtkundige godgeleerdheid voor kinderen* (Utrecht, 1774; trans. C. Boers); Rosenmüller, *Christelijk huis- en handboek* (Amsterdam, 1806; trans. J. Clarisse); J. Jochims, *Handleiding, om over den godsdienst in 't algemeen, en over den geopenbaarden godsdienst in 't bijzonder, rede- en schriftmaatig te denken* (Amsterdam, Utrecht, 1789; trans. Van Hamelsveld); Johann Caspar Lavater, *Pontius Pilatus, of de Bijbel in 't klein en de mensch in 't groot* (Hoorn, 1805; trans. Clarisse of *Pontius Pilatus oder die Bibel im Kleinen*, 1782); Lavater, *Broederlyke brieven, aan verscheiden jonge heeren* (trans. by IJ. van Hamelsveld of *Brüderliche Schreiben an verschiedene Jünglinge*, 1782).

49 Johann Ludwig Ewald, *Jesus menschenkennis of overdenkingen over de gelijkenissen van onzen Heiland* (Utrecht, 1788; a third edn appeared in 1845; trans. by IJ. van Hamelsveld of *Blick Jesus auf Natur*, 1796); J. Clarisse, *Verhandeling over de vergenoegdheid, vooral voor minvermogenden en mingeoefenden* (Amsterdam, 1801); E. Tinga, *De jeugd aangespoord tot eene vroegtijdige godsvrucht, en gewaarschuwd tegen een onbetamelijk genot van zinnelijke vermaken* (Groningen, 1806).

50 A. de Groot, 'Johannes Henricus van der Palm', in *BL*, I, 242; it treated Prov. 10: 1 to 22: 16.

51 J. Clarisse, *Twee fragmenten, waarschijnlijk van eenen ridderroman* (Rotterdam, 1839); P. van Hemert, *Redevoering over het verhevene* (Amsterdam, 1804); J. Konijnenburg, *Konstantyn de Groote. Treurspel* (Amsterdam, 1818).

52 The Dutch name is 'Kunst Wordt Door Arbeid Verkregen'; members included Hamelsveld, Palm, Schultens, Konijnenburg and Broes. The 'Maatschappij der Nederlandsche Letterkunde' included eight theologians from the Burgess generation.

53 Van der Palm, 'Redevoering over David, voornamelijk als dichter beschouwd', in Van der Palm, *Redevoeringen en verhandelingen* (Amsterdam, 1810); Van der Palm, 'Verhandeling over den aanleg en de voortreffelijkheid van het boek Job', in Van der Palm *Verhandelingen, redevoeringen en losse geschriften* (Amsterdam, 1818). See also n. 18.

54 T. Burgess, *Reasons why a New Translation of the Bible Should*

Not be Published Without a Previous Statement and Examination of All the Material Passages, Which may be Supposed to be Misinterpreted (Durham, 1816).

55 De Groot, 'Johannes Henricus van der Palm', in: *BL*, I, 241; *Bijbel bevattende alle de boeken des Ouden en Nieuwen Verbonds*, 6 vols (Leiden, 1820–25).

56 A. de Groot, 'Johannes Henricus van der Palm', 241; Van der Palm, *Bijbel voor de jeugd*, 24 vols (Leiden, 1811–33).

57 Heinrich Christian Bergen, *Gedenkwaardigheden uit het openbaar leven van Jesus* (Leiden, 1793); trans. IJ. van Hamelsveld of *Denkwürdigkeiten aus dem Leben Jesu* (1791), with a preface by H. Muntinghe.

58 T. Burgess, *Initia Paulina; sive, Introductio ad lectionem Pauli Epistolarum* (London, 1804); *Hebrew Etymology, consisting of Select Passages of Scripture* (London, 1813); *Memoirs of Granville Sharp* (London, 1820).

59 J. A. Lotze, *Oordeelkundige inleiding tot de schriften des Nieuwen Verbonds* (Amsterdam, 1803); Johann Gottfried Eichhorn, *Inleiding in het Oude Testament* (Amsterdam, 1784–5; trans. of van IJ. Hamelsveld, *Einleitung in das alte Testament* (1780–3).

60 T. Burgess (ed.), *Adnotationes Millii, auctae et correctae ex prolegominis suis* (Carmarthen, 1822). The scholars are Johann Jacob Wetstein, Richard Bentley, Pierre Sabatier, John Selden, Christoph Matthæus Pfaff, Johann Albrecht Bengel, Joannes Franciscus Buddeus and Christian Friedrich Schmidt.

61 T. Burgess, *Christian Theocracy: Or, The Doctrine of the Trinity, and the Ministration of the Holy Spirit, the Leading and Pervading Doctrine of the New Testament* (Salisbury, 1834).

62 H. Royaards, *Diatribe de divinitate Iesu Christi vera* (Utrecht, 1791). Van Hemert had translated the *Versuch einer Geschichte des Arianismus* (1783–5) by Johann August Starck (1741–1816) as *Proeve eener geschiedenis van het arianismus* (1788).

63 Gottlob August Baumgarten-Crusius, *De leer der drieëenheid tegen de zogenaemde nieuwe hervormers verdeedigd* (Amsterdam, 1797; trans. of J. van Nuys Klinkenberg, *Schrift und Vernunft für denkende Christen*).

64 Gilbert West, *De geschiedenis en de bewijzen voor de zekerheid van de opstanding van onzen Heere Jezus Christus uit den dooden* (Utrecht, 1772; trans. of C. Boers, *Observations on the History of Jesus Christ* (1747)).

65 J. Clarisse, *Proeve over de waardij en het gezag van de leere der apostelen* (Hoorn, 1802); J. Clarisse, *Verhandeling, behelzende*

een kortbondig betoog en verdediging van de kracht van het bewijs voor den goddelijken oorsprong en verbindend gezag van het evangelie (Amsterdam, Den Haag, 1804); Archibald Campbell, *De noodzaekelykheid der Openbaering, of een onderzoek naer de uytgestrektheid der menschelyke vermoogens in 't stuk van godsdienst* (Utrecht, 1774; trans. of J. van Nuys Klinkenberg, *Necessity of Revelation* (1739)).

66   John Leland, *A View of the Principal Deistical Writers that have Appeared in England*, 5th edn (London 1798), appendix by W. L. Brown.

67   T. Burgess, *A Second Letter from the Bishop of St. David's to the Clergy of his Diocese; on the independence of the ancient British Church of any foreign jurisdiction* (Carmarthen, 1812).

68   B. Broes, *Eeuwzang op het twee honderdjaarig feest der Leidsche Hoogeschoole* (Leiden, 1775); J. H. van der Palm, *Redevoering op het vierde eeuwfeest van de uitvinding der boekdrukkunst binnen Haarlem* (Haarlem, 1823).

69   J. H. van der Palm, *Gedenkschrift van Nederlands herstelling* (Amsterdam, 1816).

70   A. Ypeij, *Nader onderzoek, betreffende de brug of het houten voetpad, ontdekt op de grenzen van Drenthe en Westerwolde* (Den Haag, 1821); J. W. te Water, 'Aanmerkingen over eenige Smyrnasche penningen', in: *Verhandelingen van het Zeeuws Genootschap*, IX (1782), 481–506; J. W. te Water, 'Antwoord op de vraag, betreffende de Dea Buronia, in een Latijnsch opschrift op een'ouden steen, te Domburg ontdekt', *Nieuwe verhandelingen van het Zeeuwsch Genootschap der Wetenschappen*, I (1807), pp. 255–78.

71   E.g. J. W. te Water, *Tweede eeuw-feest van de vryheid in den burgerstaat en godsdienst binnen (. . .) Vlissingen* (Middelburg, 1772).

72   A. Ypeij and Isaac Johannes Dermout, *Geschiedenis der Nederlandsche Hervormde Kerk*, 4 vols (Breda, 1819–27); A. Ypeij, *Leerrede ter gedachtenis van de groote verdiensten der Nederlandsche vaderen, betrekkelijk het werk der Kerkhervorming* (Groningen, 1817); C. Fransen van Eck, *De Desiderii Erasmi in doctrinam moralem meritis* (Deventer, 1831); J. van Voorst, *Verhandeling over de letterkundige verdiensten van Hugo de Groot* (Amsterdam, 1833).

73   Price, *Bishop Burgess*, p. 41.

74   J. H. van der Palm, H. Muntinghe and J. Clarisse are at the top of the list, each having written forewords to nine different works.

[75] The most prolific Latin-publishing theologian was E. Scheidius, with forty-five titles.

4

'A Breach in God's House':[1]
The Division in Welsh Calvinistic
Methodism 1750–63

ERYN WHITE

At the end of the eighteenth century Iolo Morganwg complained that north Wales had become as Methodistical as the south and that the south was as Methodistical as hell. Allowing for Iolo's anti-Methodist prejudices, that was the situation Thomas Burgess encountered when appointed to the diocese of St David's in 1803. By that time Calvinistic Methodism presented a real and present challenge to the Anglican Church in Wales. Indeed, it was during Thomas Burgess's incumbency that the Methodists finally split from the Church to form a separate denomination in 1811. The symbolic first ordination of Methodist ministers in south Wales took place within Burgess's own diocese, at Llandeilo in Carmarthenshire.[2] Burgess was, therefore, the first Bishop of St David's to be faced with Methodism as a Nonconformist denomination and a direct competitor. Yet the ultimate success of Methodism was by no means a foregone conclusion, and Burgess might well have been confronted instead with only the tattered remnants of the eighteenth-century revival.

As far as Welsh Calvinistic Methodism was concerned, the world Thomas Burgess was born into in 1756 was significantly different to that which he would encounter as a bishop in 1803. Welsh Methodism was going through what was surely one of its most difficult periods, in the wake of the split between Howel Harris and Daniel Rowland and their respective followers in 1750. The start of the revival in Wales is usually traced back to 1735, the year in which Rowland and Harris went through their conversion experiences. The beginning of the Methodist movement is more properly dated to 1737, the year in which Harris and Rowland first met and began to coordinate their efforts and the year which saw the establishment of the first permanent Methodist societies. The movement subsequently experienced several years of gradual growth, particularly in mid and south Wales, until progress slowed towards the end of the 1740s, as increasing internal tensions led to division. The causes of the separation centered on Howel Harris: the tension caused among the Methodist exhorters or preachers by his forceful personality, his perceived heretical tendencies and the question of his liaison with Madam Sidney Griffith. Harris had never been a conciliatory or accommodating figure within the Welsh Methodist Association. He was a stern critic of himself and others, who did not mince words when he saw a fault which he felt needed to be corrected, even if it concerned one of the leaders or clergymen in the Methodist ranks. Much of the tension in the Association probably arose from his sense of insecurity regarding his own lack of ordination. He was acutely aware that the other leaders of the movement – Daniel Rowland, William Williams and Howel Davies – were men in Holy Orders while he remained a mere layman, having been refused ordination on four occasions. He was, as a result, extremely sensitive about his status within the Methodist movement and constantly sought to reinforce the principle that he was Rowland's equal and not his subordinate. In addition, the issue of Harris's tendency towards Patripassionism, the suggestion that it was God who died on the Cross, had been a cause of contention in meetings of the Association from 1746 onwards. Harris quite clearly stated in his diary on more than one occasion that he had preached this heresy, so there were real grounds for his colleagues' concern. There was already a considerable degree of strain within the movement, therefore, before fuel was added to the flames by Harris's unwise liaison with Sidney Griffith, a married woman estranged from her husband. George Whitefield was among the friends who warned him that he was damaging the good name of the movement in persisting with a relationship that was widely suspected of being adulterous.

Harris, however, maintained Madam Griffith as his spiritual companion and prophetess, insisting that she was a Phoebe to his Paul and a Deborah to his Barak.[3] By April 1750, Harris realized the almost inevitable outcome of these tensions, although placing the blame squarely at the door of his opponents:

> I see ye Pride, Legality, Envy, Carnality and Childishness of ye Clergy and their not bearing me to be their father nor seeing ye glory of Christ nor honouring ye Exhorters will end, if ye Lord dont prevent, in Confusion, for I cant bow to their flesh and they cant come down except ye Lord bows them.[4]

The last united Association of the movement was held at Llanidloes on 9 May 1750, when Harris again stated that he did not accept that Rowland had authority over him. After departing from Llanidloes, both sides set about mustering their forces in separate meetings. On 23 June four clergymen and eleven exhorters met at Llantrisant and expelled Harris in his absence.[5] Harris dismissed the accusations against him with a clear conscience:

> on my having a Letter from Mr Whitefield charging me with Pride desiring Power and being Impatient of Reproof and acting and speaking unscriptural and cutting home about [Sidney Griffith] being att our association and giving my self to be ruled by a Woman &c I had freedom to go to ye Lord indeed and to lay all before Him and was cleared from each Charge.[6]

Harris himself attributed the split to years of plotting by the other leaders of the movement, Daniel Rowland, William Williams and Howel Davies, and their followers.[7] One of the most astute commentators on the separation and its causes at the time was Richard Tibbott, a Montgomeryshire exhorter who later became a Dissenting minister. He suggested that part of the problem was that Harris was too much inclined to believe ill of the others, too severe in his reproofs and too extreme in his opposition.[8] Tibbott urged Harris not to judge his former colleagues too harshly, since, he pointed out, Luther and Calvin had also failed to agree, but that had not meant that they had not both been blessed by God.[9] He had no doubt that those whom Harris now condemned would ultimately sit with him at God's right hand.[10] The appeal for moderation, however, came far too late to prevent a separation that would last for thirteen years.

When writing about the division some of the earliest historians of Welsh Methodism, such as John Hughes, in *Methodistiaeth Cymru*,[11] and John Morgan Jones and William Morgan, in *Y Tadau Methodistaidd*,[12] tended to emphasize theological differences as the primary cause of separation. Their aim seems to have been to move on swiftly to the reinvigorated movement of the 1760s, paying as little attention as possible to Sidney Griffith. The division was regarded as an unfortunate temporary restriction on the expansion of the movement, accounted for by John Hughes as the Devil's attempt to hamper the growth of religion by fomenting internal strife. By 1931, however, John Roberts, in his history, *Methodistiaeth Galfinaidd Cymru*, acknowledged that the 1750s had a much greater significance than being merely a brief interruption before normal service was resumed. He speaks of Harris's experience on returning to the movement in 1763:

Yr oedd craith yn aros ar ôl y rhwyg yn rhywle, a iâs hen atgofion yn oeri tipyn ar wres y gariadwledd. Ond y mae sŵn rhywbeth arall ym mhrofiad Harris ar ôl 1762. Ar ambell drawiad, y mae yn debyg i deimlad dyn a fu oddi cartref yn hir, a adawodd dwr o blant, ac a ddychwelodd yn ôl a chael y plant wedi troi yn llanciau ac yn wŷr. Yr oedd Rowland a'i bobol wedi tyfu ar hyd llinellau oedd yn newydd iddo fe, ac wedi magu cymeriad nad adwaenai mohono yn llawn. Yr oeddynt fel pe byddent wedi dod i'w hadnabod eu hunain yn well, a thrwy hynny yn sicrach ohonynt eu hunain. Gresyn bod blynyddoedd y sefydlogi hwn mor dywyll i ni.

[A scar remained somewhere after the division, and the shiver of old memories cooled the heat of the love-feast. But there is the sound of something else in Harris's experience after 1762. On occasion, it is like the feeling of a man who has been away from home for a long time, who left behind a crowd of children, and who returned to find the children had turned into youths and men. Rowland and his people had grown

along lines that were new to him, and had developed a
character that he did not completely recognize. It was as if
they had come to know themselves better, and through that
had become surer of themselves. It is a shame that the years of
this settling are so dark to us.][13]

It is indeed a shame that we do not know more about this
period, but to a large extent this is inevitable. The tendency of
historians of Welsh Methodism to come to a halt in 1750 is
wholly understandable, given the nature of the sources. This is
one of the most difficult periods to study in depth in Methodist
history, as it was Howel Harris who had been chiefly responsible for collecting and preserving Methodist records prior to the
division. He was almost obsessive about keeping copies of
letters he sent and preserving letters he received, in some cases
showing scant regard for the author's request that they be
destroyed.[14] The only letters obviously missing from the collection are those sent to Harris by Sidney Griffith. He kept copies
of his letters to her and also her last note, written shortly before
her death in May 1752,[15] but it seems that he must at some
point have destroyed her correspondence. He also kept records
of the minutes of the Association meetings, along with the
reports on the various societies. Every historian of the Methodist movement before 1750 owes Harris an incalculable debt as
a result. The same range of sources are simply not available for
the period of the division. The Countess of Huntingdon, the
aristocratic patron of English Calvinistic Methodism, ultimately did historians a great disservice by requesting that
Rowland's papers be sent to her so that she might arrange for a
biography to be written. The biography never emerged and the
papers could not be found after the Countess's death. They
must surely have included some valuable information about
this crucial period in Methodist history. The result is that there
is no firm evidence regarding numbers of societies and members during the division. There is not much help to be had from
other quarters, either. The church visitation returns, for
instance, regularly required parish clergy to estimate the
number of Dissenters in their parish, but, of course, the
Methodists were not Dissenters in this period. Most of them
were members of the Church and continued to attend church

services in addition to Methodist meetings, so were often not accounted for in visitation returns.

The sources available in the Calvinistic Methodist Archive do show that for a while from the summer of 1750 there were a Rowland party and a Harris party contending for support from Welsh Methodists. However, it soon became clear that it was Rowland and the Methodist clergy who commanded the most widespread support and who would emerge as the 'official' branch of Welsh Calvinistic Methodism. There were probably a number of members who felt that Rowland had a certain orthodoxy and authority as an ordained clergyman. The majority of the most prominent exhorters – as the Methodist preachers were usually called – also sided with Daniel Rowland. Since many of these were local superintendents with several societies under their care, they tended to carry the allegiance of those societies with them. Harris seemed to realize from the beginning of separation that some regions were stony ground as far as his cause was concerned. Cardiganshire and Carmarthenshire in the south-west, in particular, were strong-holds for Daniel Rowland, with their superintendents – William Richard, William John, James William and Morgan John Lewis – among his most loyal lieutenants. Harris encountered dwindling support in Pembrokeshire, where loyalty to Howel Davies may well have been a crucial factor, although Harris's rather high-handed attitude may also have played a part. In July 1750, during his first visit to the county after the separation, he reproved local exhorters who questioned Sidney Griffith's role in the movement, condemned Howel Davies and made it plain that he 'did not come to consult with them but to tell them ye Rent is made and to open ye Whole Truth to them that they may choose what side to take'.[16] Most of them chose the opposing side. Of the Pembrokeshire exhorters, the young John Sparks, for whom Harris had been something of a mentor, seemed the most receptive to Harris's arguments, but by 1752 he had departed without warning to join the Moravians. Although there were not a large number of societies or exhorters in mid and north Wales, most of these also sided with Rowland. There was, however, greater confusion and uncertainty in other areas, especially Glamorgan, where exhorters and societies were divided.[17] Some backed Howel Harris;

many of them, indeed, had initially been drawn to the movement by his influence and felt an abiding sense of loyalty to him as their spiritual father. Some supported Daniel Rowland, feeling deep unease regarding the influences working on Harris, including his so-called 'prophetess', Sidney Griffith. Others were torn, bewildered and grieved by the prospect of being forced to choose between the major leaders of their movement. In the prevailing atmosphere of uncertainty, rumours abounded and both sides cast aspersions on the other. Harris's right-hand man in Glamorgan was Thomas William, and his reports from the county between 1750 and 1751 demonstrate quite clearly the gradual erosion of support for Harris, as prominent exhorters such as John Richard withdrew their allegiance.[18] John Richard had been responsible for the societies in west Glamorgan and south-east Carmarthenshire, in the vicinity of his home in Llansamlet. At the initial separation he had sided with Harris, despite showing signs of wavering from the start. On 6 December 1750 Harris's party held a select association at John Richard's home at Llansamlet, demonstrating his continued loyalty at that point.[19] However, he wrote to Harris in January 1751 explaining that in all conscience he felt bound to stay away because that seemed to be God's design for him, and his first duty had to be to Harris's master, God, and not to Harris himself. He suggested that many of the exhorters who deserted did so for the same reason.[20] For some months, Harris and Thomas William cherished hopes of John Richard's return to their ranks, but by September 1751 they feared that his mind had been poisoned by Daniel Rowland and that he was lost to them.[21] This was an important defection, and Harris's supporters faced continued competition for the Glamorgan societies. Thomas William reported to Harris in April 1751 that attempts had been made to drum up support in the county by a visit from Daniel Rowland himself, or, as Thomas William described him, 'the Devil in his white robes like a little lamb'.[22] By October 1751, Thomas William himself was the only Glamorgan exhorter left in Harris's camp, although in February 1752 even he was excluded from the Harrisian associations until, it was stated, his spirit was restored.

In this atmosphere of uncertainty it is not surprising that several societies decayed or transferred their allegiances to

Dissenting groups. After all, the worst the Dissenters were accused of during this period was of being 'dry',[23] so they were unlikely to be rocked by scandal, heresy and division. Gradually, many of those who had initially supported Harris distanced themselves from him. Several letters from this period show leading figures who had sided with Harris attempting to extricate themselves as tactfully as possible. On 4 and 5 October 1751, Harris wrote a series of letters to some of his erstwhile colleagues – John Sparks, James Relly, Thomas Bowen, John Richard and William Powell – challenging them regarding their desertion of his cause and urging them to return to the work.[24] His efforts were in vain, and July 1752 saw the last meeting of the association of Harris's supporters. Harris, exhausted after years of evangelical activity, had decided to retreat and regroup at Trefeca, where he established his 'Family', a religious community over which he was able to exercise all his talents for discipline and organization. He ordered his remaining exhorters to go where they felt called to preach and labour, and abandoned the old practice of appointing each to a locality or circuit. His emphasis from then on would be on drawing suitable converts to the Family, rather than on establishing and maintaining societies.[25]

At this point, the future of Welsh Methodism seemed precarious. There was even a danger that the revival would fracture and fragment beyond all hope of repair, as other factions emerged in addition to the Harris and Rowland parties. In 1751 Thomas Bowen of Builth declared independence from both groups, gaining the support of a number of societies in Breconshire and Radnorshire.[26] The brothers James and John Relly broke away from the Pembrokeshire Methodists in 1750 to establish their own religious sect. In addition, the Moravians in Pembrokeshire provided serious competition to the Methodists, particularly in the more Anglicized areas in the south of the county, and managed to recruit some of their more prominent members, including John Sparks and George Gambold.[27] There can be no doubt that the Methodist movement suffered as a result of the division. The internal quarrelling distracted from active recruitment, and the reputation of the movement was damaged by the allegations against Harris. William Williams Pantcelyn acknowledged in his poetry and prose that these were troublesome times. In *Ateb Philo-Evangelius*, published in 1763, he described the dark days that had preceded the renewed revival in 1762:

> Ymhen rhai blynyddau daeth rhwygiad i ganol y gyn'lleidfa; daeth Satan i mewn at feibion Duw ... Cymylau tywyll a dudew, swn griddfan, galar a gwae oedd ymhob pulpit; yr utgyrn arian oedd yn rhoi sain anhynod, heb neb yn paratoi i ryfel ...

> [After some years division came to the centre of the congregation; Satan came in among the sons of God ... Black and dark clouds, the noise of groaning, grief and woe were heard in every pulpit, the silver trumpets made unremarkable sound, without anyone preparing for war ...][28]

Williams acknowledged in his elegy for Harris in 1773 that the consequences of Harris's retreat to Trefeca had been unfortunate for the movement. It was generally accepted that Rowland lacked Harris's abilities to lead and organize the Association, and meetings were said to be increasingly aimless without Harris to direct them.[29] On a visit to Trefeca in January 1756, according to Harris's diary, Williams admitted that: 'Stupidity and slumber is come over their People and Preachers, and that they have lost ye spirit of ye Reformation and are going worse and want me to send some body among them, and they never thrived since ye Breach.'[30] His former colleagues were highly critical of Harris's decision to dedicate his time and energy to his religious community at Trefeca. Harris was outraged when Daniel Rowland accused him of doing nothing during the years of separation.[31] In his elegy for Harris, William Williams described him as skulking in a cave during the 1750s, tending a flock of one hundred and ignoring the thousands further afield who had need of his care.[32] Methodism undoubtedly suffered greatly as a result of the withdrawal of Harris's organizational skills and, indeed, of his ability to connect with the rank-and-file membership in the societies.

Despite all these difficulties, however, Methodism survived. It has to be acknowledged that one of the main reasons for this survival, ironically, was Howel Harris, despite the fact that he was probably the chief cause of the division in the first place.

By the time he withdrew to Trefeca it was clear that Rowland's party was the official continuation of the Welsh Methodist movement. They had the blessing of George Whitefield and had control of the movement's major assets: the society houses and any funds collected in aid of the movement. Harris himself in a sense acknowledged their legitimacy when he complied with their request to submit an account of money he had collected and to transfer it to them by the end of 1750.[33] In reality, of course, Harris had little option but to retreat and leave the field to Rowland, but the fact that he did so at least prevented further unseemly competition and faction.

More importantly, one could argue that Harris's organizational skills were an important factor in the survival of the Methodist movement. Harris had expended a considerable amount of time and energy in planning the organization of the movement, well before the first meeting of the Methodist Association in 1742. The Association was an assembly of Methodist clergy and exhorters which decided on the rules and order of the movement in a series of meetings between 1742 and 1743. The driving force behind these decisions was Howel Harris as the major organizer and administrator. What emerged from these discussions was a multi-tiered structure. Each society had a steward and was under the care of a private exhorter. Each private exhorter was in turn supervized by a local superintendent. Each superintendent reported to the General Association and also to a monthly society which met in each county. Harris, as general superintendent of the societies, had supervision of this whole edifice, yet he could be removed and the structure could still stand, since it had a firm foundation at its base in the form of the societies and those appointed to oversee them. Even without Harris and his followers, Rowland's party was numerous enough to maintain the General Association and the movement at large. There were still exhorters and superintendents in many areas to minister to individual societies and alleviate whatever misgivings they might have about the division. Many people undoubtedly missed Harris's presence, since as general superintendent he had visited the societies more frequently than any of the other leaders, but the movement could continue without him. The structure which was so much his creation proved strong enough to stand in the absence of its architect.

The efforts of local exhorters were also essential in offering reassurance to bemused members and in helping to ensure continuity. This was especially true in the south-west, where allegiance to Daniel Rowland was at its strongest, as, for instance, in south Cardiganshire. The local superintendent was William Richard of Llanddewibrefi, a man from Daniel Rowland's own locality and one of his most stalwart supporters. William Richard was one of the earnest, literate farmers who formed the backbone of the movement. Under his supervision, Methodist activities in south Cardiganshire continued unabated during the 1750s. There is perhaps more information about this area than most others during this period, because of the diary written by John Thomas of Tremain, a schoolmaster in Griffith Jones's circulating schools in the region. He kept a spiritual diary in which he recorded faithfully all the Methodist meetings he attended.[34] This diary reveals that south Cardiganshire was particularly well served, sandwiched as it was between Daniel Rowland in Llangeitho and Howel Davies in Llys-y-frân in Pembrokeshire. Both Daniel Rowland and Howel Davies visited the chapel of ease at Llechryd regularly to conduct communion services. Despite the fact that this chapel had largely fallen into disuse, it remained consecrated by the Anglican Church, which meant that it, like other chapels of ease, provided a solution to the problem that faced many Methodists regarding taking communion from parish clergy whom they deemed to be unfit for their calling or who were openly hostile to their Methodist parishioners. There were, therefore, ample opportunities in the area to receive communion from the hands of the Methodist clergy and to hear them preach. In the course of one week in November 1758, for instance, John Thomas attended Sunday morning service at Tremain church and went to hear William Richard at Cwm-howni in the neighbouring parish of Blaenporth in the afternoon. On Tuesday evening he again attended a meeting conducted by William Richard, this time in Tŵr-gwyn, and on Saturday he was present when Howel Davies held a service in Llechryd chapel. In the previous month he had also attended services conducted at Llechryd by Daniel Rowland and by

William Williams.[35] Meetings two or three evenings a week, in addition to Sundays, appear to have been the norm for this devout Methodist, and there was scarcely a month when he did not have the opportunity to hear either Daniel Rowland, William Williams, Howel Davies or Peter Williams. One of the places he frequently attended was Twr-gwyn chapel in Troed-yr-aur parish, built in 1752, possibly on the site of a previous Anglican chapel of ease.[36] A further seventeen chapels were built by the Rowland Methodists between 1751 and 1762, largely in west Wales, further evidence of their continued efforts to maintain and expand the movement.[37]

The other essential factor in the survival of the Methodist cause was the emergence of William Williams, Pantycelyn, as one of the main leaders. Derec Llwyd Morgan suggests that if Methodism had died out at the time of the division in its ranks, history would have had little to say about Williams.[38] He had only just begun to publish the first of his hymns prior to 1750, and his role in the movement was chiefly that of assistant to Daniel Rowland. With Harris's departure, he rose to greater prominence and also to a large extent inherited Harris's mantle as pastor to the societies. His first prose works, *Llythyr Martha Philopur* and *Ateb Philo-Evangelius*, which both appeared in 1763, were largely based on his experience of visiting societies during this period. These works did much to define and describe the nature of the revival, drawing on the experiences of the rank-and-file membership whom Williams had spent hours counselling.

The result of all this ongoing activity was the 1762 revival associated with Llangeitho. It is often attributed to the publication of a volume of Williams's hymns, *Caniadau y Rhai sydd ar y Môr o Wydr*, but was also the product of Daniel Rowland's ministry at Llangeitho.[39] Llangeitho had become a focus for Methodist pilgrims from far and wide, who travelled to hear Rowland preach and to receive communion at his hands.[40] Rowland's congregation constructed the chapel of Capel Gwynfil, a stone's throw from the parish church, for their pastor's use, and faithfully attended there when Rowland, for reasons which remain unclear, was expelled from his benefices at Llangeitho and Nancwnlle in 1763. David Lloyd, the Arian minister of Llwynrhydowen in Cardiganshire, described the renewed outburst of energy centring on Llangeitho in a letter to his brother Posthumous in April 1764:

> The Methodists after having kept quiet for several years have of late been very active. Their Number increases, and their wild Pranks are beyond Description. The worship of the day being over, they have kept together in ye Place whole Nights, singing, capering, bawling, fainting, thumping and a variety of other Excercises. The whole Country for many miles around have crowded to see such strange Sights.[41]

From 1762 onwards the Methodist movement continued to grow steadily, having transcended the testing period of the 1750s. In 1763 Harris was finally reconciled with his colleagues, although he never regained his former prominence in the movement. This reconciliation was actually made possible in the first place by the death of Madam Sidney Griffith in 1752. The building work for the community at Trefeca began on 14 April 1752 and on 31 May Madam Griffith died in London, as the grief-stricken Harris recalled on the first anniversary of her death:

> Ye memorable Day on which ye dearest and most favoured spirit I ever saw went to Glory and I sustained ye greatest Loss indeed, suffering then in my spirit with her as appears by Journals tho' absent from her and knowing nothing of her Conflicts &c and wrestling and prevailing for her and uniting to her – and afterward raisd above ye Devil and Conquering him having dreamt then I had seen ye Dragon dead and held in a River up with this Inscription in its Mouth – Honi Soit qui mal y pense.[42]

This was a devastating blow for Harris, shattering his vision of the Trefeca community presided over by himself as Father and Sidney Griffith as Mother. Poor Anne Harris, his long-suffering wife, by this stage was considered by Harris to be barely fit to be mother to her own daughter, Elizabeth, let alone to an extended religious family. Indeed, in his first will, in October 1751, Harris decreed that the upbringing and 'entire government in every respect whatsoever' of his daughter was to be left to Thomas William, who was to be advised in this matter by

Sidney Griffith.[43] Harris grieved for his prophetess for the rest of his life, but, callous as it may sound, her death was ultimately his way back into the Methodist fold. Who knows what further indiscretion Harris might have committed or what further scandal might have circulated if he and Sidney Griffith had become joint 'parents' of the Trefeca community?

The first tentative approaches towards reconciliation with the Methodists were made as early as 1754, when Daniel Rowland and William Williams visited Trefeca, which suggests that the accusations of heresy against Harris were not, after all, the major cause of the division. It also demonstrates that the two sides were not divided by as unbridgeable a chasm as has often been depicted. There was quite regular contact, if not with Harris himself, then with his supporters, Thomas William and, later, Evan Moses. As early as April 1751 when Daniel Rowland visited Glamorgan and encountered some of Harris's supporters, he argued that he wanted union between both sides and regretted that 'the Devil had thrown a black ball in the air between people and that they were kicking it instead of looking to the Lord'.[44] The comparison with football is an interesting one, considering how vicious and prolonged games of football could be in the eighteenth century. The fact that the two sides were on speaking terms by 1754 does not, however, alter the intensely personal and painful nature of the dispute between them. There is no disguising the real grief expressed in Harris's letter to Rowland, written in August 1750 when the scars of the separation were still painfully fresh: 'come fight no longer – nothing stabs so sore as to find Daniel – my dear Brother Daniel – among them that cry Crucify him crucify him – come lay aside thy Prejudice lest other measure to you ye same measure you measure your Brother'.[45] Even so, reconciliation might actually have occurred much sooner were it not for Harris's poor health in the mid 1750s and his subsequent involvement with the Breconshire militia, which entailed long periods of service in England. There was also some opposition from some of the exhorters, who did not relish the prospect of Harris returning to dominate the movement once more, given his reputation for authoritarianism. Despite these setbacks, Harris was formally invited back to the Methodist fold by a letter from Daniel Rowland, William Williams, Peter Williams,

William Richard, David Williams and John Harry, written in May 1762 when news circulated that Harris was about to surrender his commission with the militia and return to Wales.[46] It was not until the end of 1762 that he was able to resign his commission, but by February 1763 he was negotiating his return with Rowland. He met Rowland, along with William and Peter Williams, on 15 February, and an association of the reconciled movement was held in Trefeca on 18 May 1763.[47]

By this time, Methodism had already been reinvigorated by the 1762 revival, but, even so, there was still a sense that Harris was needed in order to shake up the Association. It must have been tempting to Harris also to return to a movement going through experiences similar to those to which he had grown accustomed in his early years as an evangelist. Going out once more at the age of fifty to preach to large, enthusiastic crowds throughout Wales must have been a moving experience for Harris, even though his activities were but a pale shadow of his previous work. Both sides were therefore motivated to reunite. The result was a period of steady growth from 1763 onwards, with the movement succeeding in gaining ground in the new industrial communities and, as Iolo Morganwg complained, in the previously hostile north. It survived its most testing time in the 1750s and was reinvigorated by fresh revival. As a result, the 1750s as a period has been relatively ignored within the history of Welsh Methodism. Yet the period of division was significant, and Methodism in the 1760s was not quite the same as in the 1740s. A new generation had emerged, literally, since young Nathaniel Rowland, Daniel Rowland's son, was present at the Trefeca association in 1763. What this period demonstrates is that the 'Great Awakening' in Wales was not one continuous period of revival, as it is sometimes perceived, leading almost inevitably to the triumphant Nonconformity of the nineteenth century. There were individual revivals within the general revival period, indeed the story of Methodism is punctuated by recurring revivals at various points in its history, but there were also times when progress was halted and the future of the movement looked very uncertain indeed. Thomas Burgess, of course, remained in his infancy at the time of these developments and was blithely unaware of the dramas that were unfolding in his future diocese. However, these events did have a major significance for the nature of the task that faced him as Bishop of St David's and, indeed, for the nature of religion and society in Wales during the early nineteenth century.

Notes

1 National Library of Wales, Calvinistic Methodist Archive, Diary of Howel Harris, 241, 18 May 1763.
2 Gomer M. Roberts, 'Ymwahanu oddi wrth Eglwys Loegr', in Gomer M. Roberts (ed.), *Hanes Methodistiaeth Galfinaidd Cymru, Cyfrol II: Cynnydd y Corff* (Caernarfon, 1978), pp. 316–19.
3 For instance, NLW, Calvinistic Methodist Archive, Diary of Howel Harris, 145, 21 June 1750.
4 Ibid., 144, 23 April 1750.
5 Ibid., 145, 24 June 1750.
6 Ibid., 146a, 7 December 1750.
7 For example, ibid., 145, 22 June 1750; 146, 5 October 1750.
8 NLW, Calvinistic Methodist Archive, Trevecka Letters, 2017, 12 November 1751 (in Welsh).
9 Ibid., 1997, 2 July 1751 (in Welsh).
10 Ibid., 2035, 17 November 1752 (in Welsh).
11 John Hughes, *Methodistiaeth Cymru*, 2 vols (Wrexham, 1851–4).
12 John Morgan Jones and William Morgan, *Y Tadau Methodistaidd*, 2 vs (Swansea, 1895–7).
13 John Roberts, *Methodistiaeth Galfinaidd Cymru* (London, 1931), pp. 18–19.
14 See B. S. Schlenther and E. M. White, *Calendar of the Trevecka Letters* (Aberystwyth, 2003), pp. vii-x.
15 NLW, Calvinistic Methodist Archive, Trevecka Letters, 2029, 16 May 1752.
16 NLW, Calvinistic Methodist Archive, Diary of Howel Harris, 145, 17 July 1750.
17 Gomer M. Roberts, 'Calvinistic Methodism in Glamorgan, 1737–1773', in Glanmor Williams (ed.), *Glamorgan County History. Volume IV: Early Modern Glamorgan* (Cardiff, 1974), pp. 519–24.
18 For example, NLW, Calvinistic Methodist Archive, Trevecka Letters, 1943, 23 June 1750; 1948, 1 August 1750; 1977, 24 March 1751; 1989, 18 May 1751. These letters are all in Welsh.

[19] NLW, Calvinistic Methodist Archive, Diary of Howel Harris, 146a, 7 December 1750.

[20] NLW, Calvinistic Methodist Archive, Trevecka Letters, 1968, 7 January 1751 (in Welsh).

[21] Ibid., 2002, 24 September 1751 (in Welsh).

[22] Ibid., 1984, 20 April 1751 (in Welsh).

[23] Geraint H. Jenkins, *The Foundations of Modern Wales: Wales 1642–1780* (Oxford, 1987), p. 197.

[24] NLW, Calvinistic Methodist Archive, Trevecka Letters, 2006, 2007, 2008, 2009, 2011.

[25] For the history of the Family, see Alun Wyn Owen, 'A study of Howell Harris and the Trevecka "Family" (1752–60) based upon the Trevecka letters and diaries and other Methodist archives at the NLW', unpublished MA thesis, University of Wales, 1927; and also Alun Wyn Owen, 'Yr Ymraniad', in Gomer M. Roberts (ed.), *Hanes Methodistiaeth Galfinaidd Cymru, Cyfrol I: Y Deffroad Mawr* (Caernarfon, 1973), pp. 314–55.

[26] Richard Bennett, *Methodistiaeth Trefaldwyn Uchaf* (Bala, 1929), p. 187.

[27] Gomer M. Roberts, 'The Moravians and John Relly and his people', *Journal Historical Society of the Presbyterian Church of Wales*, 38 (1953), pp. 2–7; Roberts (ed.), *Cynnydd y Corff*, p. 16.

[28] *Gweithiau William Williams Pantycelyn*, II, ed. G. H. Hughes (Cardiff, 1967), p. 24.

[29] Roberts (ed.), *Cynnydd y Corff*, p. 15.

[30] NLW, Calvinistic Methodist Archive, Diary of Howel Harris, 25 January 1756.

[31] Ibid., 19 February 1755.

[32] N. Cynhafal Jones (ed.), *Gweithiau William Pant-y-celyn, Cyfrol I* (Holywell, 1887), p. 494.

[33] NLW, Calvinistic Methodist Archive, Trevecka Letters, 1952, 14 August 1750; 3196, 9 January 1751.

[34] NLW MS 20515–6; R. Geraint Gruffydd, 'John Thomas, Tre-main: Pererin Methodistaidd', *Journal Historical Society of the Presbyterian Church of Wales*, 9 (1985–6), pp. 61–6.

[35] NLW MS 20515.

[36] NLW, Morgan Richardson MS 749; Eryn M. White, *Praidd Bach y Bugail Mawr* (Llandysul, 1995), p. 104.

[37] Gomer M. Roberts, 'Pobl Rowland yn ystod yr Ymraniad 1750–1763', in Roberts (ed.), *Y Deffroad Mawr*, pp. 3838.

[38] Derec Llwyd Morgan, *The Great Awakening in Wales*, trans. Dyfnallt Morgan (London, 1988), p. 85.

[39] R. Geraint Gruffydd, 'Diwygiad 1762 a William Williams o Bantycelyn', *Journal Historical Society of the Presbyterian Church of Wales*, 55 (1970); Llwyd Morgan, *The Great Awakening*, p. 101; Eifion Evans, *Daniel Rowland* (Edinburgh, 1985), p. 309.

[40] Ibid., pp. 294–5.

[41] G. Eyre Evans (ed.), *Lloyd Letters (1754–91)* (Aberystwyth, 1908), p. 52.

[42] NLW, Calvinistic Methodist Archive, Diary of Howel Harris, 77a, 31 May 1753 Old Style, 11 June 1753 New Style.

[43] NLW, Calvinistic Methodist Archive, Trevecka Letters, 2014, 30 October 1751; 2016, 30 October 1751, for a copy of the will.

[44] Ibid., 1984, 20 April 1751 (in Welsh).

[45] Ibid., 1952, 14 August 1750.

[46] Ibid., 2472, 19 May 1762.

[47] NLW, Calvinistic Methodist Archive, Diary of Howel Harris, 240, 15 February 1763; 241, 18 May 1763.

5

Wind, Rain and the Holy Spirit: Welsh Evangelicalism in a Pan-Celtic Context 1750–1850

NIGEL YATES

The purpose of this essay is to address a theme that has grown out of my recent series of separate, but inevitably interrelated, studies of the religious life of Wales, Ireland and the Isle of Man in the late eighteenth and early nineteenth centuries. These were all areas with much in common: a surviving native language which competed with English, high levels of rural poverty, and the prevalence of wet and windy weather. In all three areas churches had to be repaired frequently after damage by storms, and the reputation of the bad weather was enough to deter some of those Englishmen offered bishoprics in those inhospitable lands from accepting them. When the younger Thomas Wilson visited his ageing father, Bishop Wilson of Sodor and Man, in 1750, he noted in his diary several days of fierce winds and driving rain, even at the height of summer.[1] In 1757 Bishop Wilson's successor, Mark Hildesley, was prevented from carrying out his planned visitation of Lonan church by 'the severity of the weather'.[2] Many of those rural deans, responding to Archbishop Beresford of Armagh's visitation queries in 1839, noted the damage that had been caused to their churches and parsonage houses by the 'big wind' in January of that year.[3] It is not the purpose of this essay to endeavour to establish a correlation between evangelicalism and bad weather, but merely to point out that there was something in the religious spirituality of the western parts of the British Isles which responded with a generally high degree of enthusiasm to evangelicalism, and to suggest that the individual character of what has been termed the 'Great Awakening' in Wales needs to be set in a broader Celtic context than has been the case in the past.

Most scholars writing about the evangelical revival in Wales accept that this phenomenon, which has had such important consequences for the subsequent religious history of Wales, was part of the much wider movement, usually termed pietism in Europe, which had an impact on all the Protestant churches of Europe and North America at different dates between the late seventeenth and early nineteenth centuries. They acknowledge the relationship between the early evangelicals in Wales and their exact contemporaries who were instrumental in establishing evangelical movements in England and Scotland, though they stress that the way in which the movement developed in Wales was highly individualistic and different from developments elsewhere.[4] Again, it is not the argument of this essay to deny that there was an individuality to the Welsh evangelical revival which differentiates it from similar movements in other parts of the British Isles, though I would suggest that this individuality may have been exaggerated and that more should be done to investigate the similarities, as well as the differences, between the Welsh revival and those in Cornwall, Ireland, the Isle of Man and Scotland, especially the western Highlands and Islands of Scotland. It is these similarities and differences which I intend to explore during this essay, but I should like to begin by addressing some of the myths that have grown up about the reasons for the success of the Welsh evangelical revival.

During the second half of the nineteenth century there was a consensus among Welsh religious historians, whether Anglicans or nonconformists, that the Established Church during the late eighteenth and early nineteenth centuries, the Church of England in Wales, was moribund, and that it was this state of affairs which had stimulated the evangelical revival in Wales and had led to the most significant religious event of this period, the decision in 1811 by the Calvinistic Methodist Associations to ordain their own ministers and, eventually, to create a new denomination outside the Established Church. The impact of this was seen in the religious census of 1851, when, across Wales as a whole, only one-fifth of those who attended religious services on the census Sunday did so in an Anglican church. The vast majority of the remaining four-fifths attended services in a place of worship belonging to one of the four main Nonconformist groupings in Wales: the Baptists, the Independents, the Calvinistic Methodists or the Wesleyan Methodists. The Calvinistic Methodists were in 1851 the group that attracted the largest congregations in Wales, one-quarter of those attending religious services on the census Sunday.[5] It was statistics such as these that led to the eventually successful campaign to disestablish the Church of England in Wales, resulting in the setting up of an independent Church in Wales in 1920. It is hardly surprising, therefore, that Nonconformist historians, keen to support the disestablishment campaign, should have been so willing to discredit the Established Church and to attribute the success of Nonconformity to its failings. Anglican historians had different reasons for doing so. They were involved in the movements, both evangelical and Tractarian, that were transforming the nature of Anglicanism in the second half of the nineteenth century, and they had a vested interest in discrediting their predecessors as a means of justifying the new directions in which they wished to lead a reformed church. In Wales, one of those new directions was to demonstrate the Welsh credentials of an Established Church now committed to identifying itself with the spiritual aspirations of the people. It suited its own agenda to accept the Nonconformist criticism of an unreformed church and to argue that, as the Church of England in Wales was now a thoroughly Welsh institution, it could justify its position as an Established Church.

Recent research into the state of the Established Church in Wales before the appointment of Joshua Hughes, the first Welsh-speaking Welsh bishop in almost two hundred years and a graduate of St David's College, Lampeter, to St Asaph in 1870, is beginning to show that its poor reputation is far from justified. Indeed, there is evidence to suggest that the movement for reform, led by the bishops of what became from 1 January 1801 the United Church of England and Ireland, which began in the last quarter of the eighteenth century, was more advanced the further west one went. Certainly, Wales had, in bishops like Thomas Burgess, Samuel Horsley, Henry William Majendie and Richard Watson, leading episcopal reformers who had made their respective marks on all the Welsh dioceses by 1820.[6] Many of the allegations made against the Established Church are rapidly being disproved. For example, the widely held view that English-speaking bishops did nothing to promote the use of the Welsh language and, in some cases, sought to discourage its use, has been effectively undermined by the work of Eryn White, who has shown that in early nineteenth century Wales the vast majority of parishes still held most, if not all, of their services in Welsh.[7] The threat to the Welsh language came, not from Anglican bishops and clergy, but from demographic change, increased mobility and the successful promotion of the scenic charms of Wales in the guidebooks that began appearing from the first quarter of the nineteenth century.[8] The evidence for this will be found in the visitation returns. For example, in the Carmarthenshire parish of Llanfynydd it was reported in 1828 that the services, which had been wholly in Welsh in 1813, were now 'in both languages, to accommodate an English family residing in the Parish'. At Pembrey in 1813 the single Sunday service was in English once a month, but in Welsh on the remaining Sundays. By 1828 more services were in English, as Pembrey 'is becoming a very fashionable bathing place'.[9]

If the causes of the evangelical revival in Wales are not to be found in what was thought, erroneously, to be the state of the Established Church in Wales at the time, then the case for looking more broadly at the nature of this revival in other parts of Celtic Britain and Ireland appears to be greatly strengthened, and it may help to provide some alternative interpretations of events in Wales. Whilst there were clear common roots between the evangelical movements in the Established Churches of England, Scotland and Wales, and in Ireland within both the established Anglican and non-established Presbyterian churches, these were to some extent distorted by somewhat different chronologies. An important common root was the influence of the Moravians, who provided one of the main links between British evangelicalism and mainland European pietism. Links between the Moravians and England began in 1728 and developed through the 1730s. In 1738 John

Wesley visited the German Moravian congregation at Herrn-hut but he had fallen out with them by the 1740s. They maintained somewhat better relations with George Whitefield and they had considerable influence on Howel Harris, who was accused by his enemies of having become a Moravian.[10] One of those linked with both Wesley and Whitefield, John Cennick, did join the Moravians in 1745 and subsequently worked in Ireland, establishing congregations at Dublin and Gracehill (Co. Antrim) in 1746; Moravian congregations were also established at Ballinderry (Co. Antrim) and Kilwarlin (Co. Down) in 1754–5.[11] The Moravians also received support from Bishop Thomas Wilson of Sodor and Man who, despite his orthodox High Churchmanship, was impressed by their missionary activities in the American colonies, the West Indies, the Baltic lands and Greenland.[12] How far Wilson himself promoted Moravian ideas of personal piety is far from clear, but it is not without significance that when Wesleyan Method-ist activity in the Isle of Man began in the 1770s, it received strong support from Henry Corlett (Vicar of German 1761–1801) and Daniel Gelling (Vicar of Malew 1761–77 and Rector of Ballaugh 1777–1801), both of whom had been trained by Wilson and spent time in his household in the 1740s and 1750s.[13]

The time-lag that was experienced in the Isle of Man between first acquaintance with evangelical ideas and the success of evangelical missions was replicated in Ireland and Scotland, but not in Cornwall and Wales. In Cornwall there was regular Wesleyan preaching from the 1740s, which attracted large congregations. When the Methodists eventually seceded from the Established Church they left it in a similar minority position to the one that it held in Wales: in the 1851 religious census the various groups of Methodists – Wesleyans, Primitives and Bible Christians – significantly outnumbered Anglicans in twelve out of the fourteen registration districts, the only exceptions being St Germans and the Scilly Isles.[14] In Wales the progress of evangelical missions was slightly more complicated. The early success of Calvinistic Methodism was largely confined to the western half of the diocese of St David's, particularly the area that fell within the influence of Daniel Rowland of Llangeitho, where substantial numbers of converts had been made by 1760. It was the success of this mission, and the unorthodox methods by which it had been achieved, which almost certainly persuaded Bishop Squire of St David's to withdraw Rowland's licence as curate of Llangeitho in 1763.[15] It was not until the 1770s that Calvinistic Methodism began to have similar successes in the northern and south-eastern parts of Wales. It was also in the last quarter of the eighteenth century that comparable evangelical movements began to make an impact on the Established Churches of Ireland, the Isle of Man and Scotland.

In discussing what was taking place throughout the Established Churches of Celtic Britain and Ireland from the 1730s I have used the term evangelical. It is, however, important to note that this term does not, in this context, denote a particular doctrinal stance but, rather, an attitude to church order and personal piety. Eighteenth-century evangelicalism was deeply split between those who would have defined themselves as Calvinists and those that were Arminian. The great distinction that has been drawn by the historians of religion in Wales has been between the Arminianism of the Wesleyan Methodists in England and the Calvinism of most Methodists in Wales. In truth, however, whilst Wales may have been out of step with England, including Cornwall and the Isle of Man in this respect, it had very much in common with both Ireland and Scotland, in both of which the evangelical revival was strongly linked with Calvinism. The evangelical revival in Wales, therefore, should be seen as part of what might be termed a pan-Celtic Calvinistic evangelicalism, which provided the dominant element within the evangelicalism of Ireland, Scotland and Wales. Where Wales differed from Ireland and Scotland was that in Wales the majority of the Calvinists chose to withdraw from the Established Church, whereas in Ireland and Scotland they were able to work so successfully within the structures of existing churches as not to be forced by opposition to them to set up separate ecclesiastical organizations. What were the differences that made this happen?

It was certainly not a different attitude on the part of the bishops in Ireland and Wales. Whilst there were certainly bishops in Wales, such as Horsley at both St David's and St Asaph, and Randolph at Bangor,[16] who were extremely hostile to Calvinistic Methodism in the years leading up to the eventual schism of 1811, there were others, like Burgess of St David's and Watson of Llandaff, who believed that a measure of benevolent tolerance could result in Calvinistic Methodism being kept within the Established Church. The Irish bishops before the 1820s were, with the sole exception of Archbishop Trench of Tuam, uniformly hostile to evangelicalism.[17] In the 1820s Archbishop Magee of Dublin also began to take a more tolerant line, but it was only after 1840, with the appointments of Robert Daly to Cashel and Waterford and James O'Brien to Ossory, that the evangelicals could count on the unconditional support of bishops drawn from their own ranks. The leadership of the main Presbyterian churches in Ireland and Scotland was likewise in the hands of those usually termed moderates, who had little sympathy for evangelicals. It was, however, a leadership that had made little headway in the western Highlands and Islands of Scotland, which were still bastions of either Roman Catholic or episcopalian allegiances in the early eighteenth century, and where it was difficult to attract non-Gaelic-speaking ministers from lowland Scotland to serve vast parishes with few roads or habitations of any size. Faced with these problems, the Established Church of Scotland was forced to rely heavily on evangelical missionaries to establish effective ministries in these areas, with the result that most ministerial charges were in evangelical hands by the end of the eighteenth century.[18] It was from this strong base, and the development of evangelical ministries in other parts of Scotland, that evangelicals were able by the 1830s to wrest control of the General Assembly of the Church of Scotland from the moderates. It was the failure of this majority to secure parliamentary legislation to abolish private patronage and achieve satisfactory arrangements for the creation of new parishes and the building of new churches, not the frustration of a minority unable to influence the leadership of the Church (as had been the case in Wales), that led to the disruption of 1843.[19] The strength of evangelicalism in the western Highlands and Islands was revealed all too clearly in the religious census of 1851: in the counties of Argyll, Inverness, and Ross and Cromarty only 19.3 per cent of the churchgoing population still worshipped in the Church of Scotland, compared with 63.6 per cent who were worshipping in the Free Church of Scotland created by the disruption.[20] It was a discrepancy even greater than that between the Established Church and the Calvinistic Methodists in Wales, though similar levels of support for the Calvinistic Methodists could be found in some of the registration districts in the dioceses of Bangor and St David's.[21]

Whereas in Scotland much of the evangelical revival developed within the structure of the Presbyterian churches and owed little to Methodism, in Ireland Methodism was as critical a factor in the evangelical revival as it was in Cornwall, the Isle of Man and Wales, but it had significantly different consequences. Most importantly, it did not lead to significant secessions from either the Established Church of Ireland or the non-established Presbyterian churches; rather, it acted as a catalyst to bring about an evangelical movement inside the churches that led to evangelicals becoming the dominant groups within them. Methodism itself did not benefit. Secession from the Church of Ireland was long delayed. In the surveys of church attendance in Ireland in 1834 Methodists, whether Wesleyan or Primitive, are generally described as being 'in connexion with the Established Church',[22] though a degree of separation had occurred in 1816. From a peak of 44,314 members in 1844, what was by then an independent church, though still willing to cooperate with Anglicans and Presbyterians, quickly collapsed to 31,527 members by 1850 and 26,790 by 1855. This was partly, but by no means wholly, attributable to the deaths and emigration caused by the Irish famine of the 1840s.[23] It was as a result of Methodist influences from the 1750s that a separate strand of evangelicalism, which did not regard itself as Methodist, had established itself within both the Established and Presbyterian churches by the end of the eighteenth century. Initially, within Presbyterianism this took the form of increased support for reformed Presbyterian congregations, but increasingly a number of congregations within the main Presbyterian body, the Synod of Ulster, acquired evangelical ministers. As a result of serious divisions in the Synod over the doctrinal orthodoxy of some staff within the Belfast Academical Institution in the 1820s, the evangelicals, under the charismatic leadership of Henry Cooke, managed to gain control over the Synod and proceeded to force their moderate opponents to withdraw. In 1840 the Synod of Ulster united with the even more evangelical Secessionist Synod to form what subsequently became known as the Presbyterian Church in Ireland.[24] The growth of evangelicalism within the Church of Ireland was a somewhat slower process, which did not result in evangelicals gaining effective control until the legislation to disestablish the Church was approved by parliament in 1869.[25]

In Ireland and Scotland there were factors that, on the whole, encouraged evangelicals to work as far as they could within the existing Protestant, mostly established, churches. In Ireland all Protestants were a minority numerically, if not in terms of status, in a country which had remained predominantly Roman Catholic, and they could see that further divisions among Protestants, especially at a time of increasing political agitation by the Roman Catholic majority, were likely to be counter-productive. In Scotland the orthodox Calvinism of the Established Church created at least a doctrinal, if not an emotional, bond between evangelicals and non-evangelicals. In Wales there was both doctrinal and emotional division between Calvinistic Methodism and the prevailing Arminianism, as well as distrust of evangelical enthusiasm, within the Established Church. Nevertheless, it has to be emphasized that the schism that was formalized in 1811 was far from inevitable. For the best part of a century the Calvinistic Methodists operated, admittedly with some difficulty, within the Established Church, and, even after the decision to ordain their own ministers, good relations between Anglicans and Calvinistic Methodists were maintained in many places for several years thereafter. On the other hand, many Anglican clergy had been bitter opponents of the Calvinistic Methodists for a generation or more before the formal secession took place, and the pressures for separation were more difficult to withstand, as there were fewer mitigating factors to support the arguments of those who wished to remain within the Established Church.[26] The arguments against separation were not confined to Wales. In the Isle of Man, for example, Methodists continued to worship both in their own chapels and in their parish churches until well into the nineteenth century. This practice is recorded in the surviving diary of an anonymous Wesleyan local preacher covering the years 1826–8 and it is attested to by the fact that in the 1851 religious census only nine out of thirty-nine Anglican places of worship had services on Sunday evenings, whereas only seventeen out of fifty-nine Wesleyan, and four out of twenty-seven Primitive, Methodist places of worship had services on Sunday mornings.[27]

I have tried so far in this essay to demonstrate that we must not overemphasize the individuality of the evangelical revival in Wales, by illustrating the ways in which evangelical movements throughout the western parts of Britain and Ireland shared many characteristics. Indeed, it is difficult to find a feature of the Welsh revival which was not replicated in at least one of these Celtic areas, and several appear to have been replicated in more than one. In some respects, most notably in the separation of a large number of evangelicals from the Established Church, Wales shares common characteristics with the Isle of Man and Cornwall, and, indeed, with the rest of England as well. In other respects, the similarities between Ireland, Scotland and Wales put their evangelical movements in a different category from those in Cornwall and the Isle of Man. The pattern is complicated, but the broad trends can be clearly detected. Throughout the western parts of Britain and Ireland, however, evangelicals formed either a majority or at least a substantial minority within the Protestant churches to a degree that they did not in most parts of England, though there were areas of evangelical strength there as well. I want to conclude by endeavouring to answer the question: why should this be so? We can, I think, exempt the wet and windy weather, though perhaps it might have been a factor, just as the long winter nights are in northern Europe, in producing emotions that respond well to the ethos of evangelicalism. I would, however, like to suggest two possible reasons for the ready reception of evangelical initiatives in the western parts of Britain and Ireland.

The first relates to historical religious traditions. Robert Currie's somewhat fanciful suggestions about the survival of pre-Christian religion have been modified, in respect of

Cornwall, by Bruce Coleman to notions of the survival of 'a popular rather than an officially determined religious culture'.[28] The survival of what might be termed folk religion was equally strong in other Celtic regions. In both Wales and the Isle of Man Anglican bishops complained of the survival of 'reliques of popish superstition', such as prayers for the departed at the graveside, the ringing of bells before corpses, prayer stations during funeral processions, the cults associated with holy wells, and strong beliefs in charms and fairy doctors, which survived until well into the nineteenth century.[29] In Brittany Roman Catholic bishops and clergy had to struggle with superstitious practices such as baptisms immediately after birth, the refusal to receive back women into society until they had attended a special mass to give thanks for their safe delivery, and the removal by hysterectomy of foetuses from women who had died during childbirth so that the foetus could be baptized.[30] Breton *pardons*, the festivals and processions in honour of local saints, were, too often, excuses for drunkenness and sexual licence. Although these have survived, in Ireland their counterparts, the 'patterns', and the even more dissolute behaviour associated with funeral wakes, were effectively suppressed by a reforming Roman Catholic episcopate during the first half of the nineteenth century.[31] It does not seem unreasonable to argue that the sort of popular religious culture that existed in the Celtic parts of Britain and Europe, though it was by no means wholly confined to these areas, may be a factor in explaining the popularity of the more extravagant manifestations of religion. For Roman Catholics these might include cults, festivals and pilgrimages. For Protestants the comparable manifestations of religious exuberance were those associated with evangelicalism: the singing of hymns, the personal testimonies, the love-feasts and preachers who cried in the pulpit. Certainly, all these were on offer from the Welsh evangelicals. A contemporary account by Howel Harris of the celebration of Holy Communion by Daniel Rowland at Llangeitho illustrates this clearly:

> I was last Sunday at the Ordinance with Brother Rowland where I saw, felt and heard such things as I cant send on Paper

any Idea of . . . such crying out and Heart Breaking Groans, silent Weeping and Holy Joy, and shouts of Rejoicing I never saw . . . Tis very common when he preaches for Scores to fall down by the Power of the Word, pierced and wounded or overcom'd by the Love of God and Sights of Beauty and Excellency of Jesus, and lie on the Ground.[32]

It was, of course, precisely such manifestations of uncontrolled emotionalism that created the backlash against the Calvinistic Methodists from the more orthodox Anglican bishops and clergy who, on this point at least, were not on the same wavelength as their laity.

Whilst I certainly would not discount the temperamental attraction of evangelicalism, one also needs to consider whether it might not also have had a political attraction in Wales and the other Celtic regions. Britain and Ireland differed from many parts of mainland Europe in not developing significant anti-clericalist movements in the late eighteenth and early nineteenth centuries. It seems to me that they may have compensated for this by finding ways of religious expression that could, at the very least, be regarded as anti-establishment, and that there was a correlation between the strength of such attitudes and an absence of political power. In the late eighteenth and early nineteenth centuries political power was concentrated in the hands of a fairly small and close-knit oligarchy. Its main power base was in London, with smaller concentrations, for the governments of Ireland and Scotland respectively, in Dublin and Edinburgh. From 1801 all parliamentary business was, with the final suppression of the Irish parliament, conducted in London. Wales had no political centre; it did not even have any really important towns. Whilst the leaders of the evangelical movements throughout Britain and Ireland protested, quite genuinely, their loyalty to existing, mostly established, churches, and deeply regretted in most cases the separations that eventually took place, there does seem to be at least a prima facie case that they were appealing to feelings of political alienation. That the strength of British evangelicalism was to be found in those parts of Britain and Ireland furthest from London, and in an Irish and Scottish context furthest from Dublin or Edinburgh, is therefore not surprising. Evangelicalism was what might be described, initially at least, as a non-establishment strand within the religious establishment. The fact that when evangelicals set up their own chapels within that establishment they were obliged by law to register them as Dissenting meeting-houses only served to emphasize this point. Whilst more work needs to be done, through studies of the contemporary literature, to discover to what extent those at the time recognized the connection between the attractions of the new evangelical movements and feelings of political alienation, there does seem to be a reasonable hypothesis here. In the case of Wales a good illustration of the connection is to be found in an essay that won a prize at an eisteddfod of the London Cambrian Institution in May 1831. It argued that 'ecclesiastical misgovernment' had been 'the sole cause of ... Dissent in Wales' and that 'the unpopularity of Episcopal clergy [was] ascribable to two causes ... Their want of sympathy with the feelings and tastes of the people [and] their neglect of the language of the people – Both these causes themselves the effects of an English Hierarchy'.[33]

This attempt to link political alienation with issues of nationalism, language and indigenous culture in the case of Wales has, however, to be treated with caution, and it is certainly difficult to see these as a main cause for the growth of evangelicalism in either Ireland or Scotland. Irish evangelicals, somewhat late in the day and after generations of Protestant attempts to marginalize the native language, recognized that there might be some value in taking a more positive view, and in 1818 set up the Irish Society for the Education of the Natives through the Medium of their own Language, largely as a means of converting Roman Catholics to Protestantism.[34] It was dismissed by Roman Catholics at the time as a paternalistic and opportunistic move, and indeed it was the case that by the early years of the nineteenth century Irish nationalism was increasingly being seen as something that was synonymous with Irish Roman Catholicism. In Scotland the link between evangelicalism and Gaelic culture was stimulated by similar considerations to those in Ireland, namely a recognition that if the people of the western Highlands and Islands were to be converted from their Roman Catholic or episcopalian allegiances to the Calvinism of the Church of Scotland, it had to use the language the people spoke. The difficulty of attracting university-educated ministers who would have to learn Gaelic resulted in much of this missionary work being undertaken by catechists, some of whom had had little education and were obliged 'to depend on their memory, rather than their ability to read' to instruct the people in Gaelic from the Bible and the catechism. At a later stage, when basic levels of education were rising in these Gaelic-speaking areas, some evangelical schoolmasters discouraged the use of Gaelic, to the extent that one recent commentator has observed that 'Highland evangelicalism, as a whole, has been a deracialising influence. It has fostered a British rather than a local and Celtic patriotism.'[35] It is certainly the case that in Wales the use of Welsh was strongly encouraged by the evangelicals within the Established Church, and this support for the language was seen as one of the great strengths of Calvinistic Methodism once it had ceased to be part of the Established Church. What I would want to take issue with is the view that the evangelicals differed from other members of the Established Church in their support for the Welsh language, or that support for the language and indigenous culture of Wales was to be found largely outside the Established Church after the Calvinistic Methodist schism of 1811. Generations of Welsh historians have dug up notorious examples of monoglot Englishmen serving parishes with a predominantly Welsh-speaking population, such as Dr Bowles of Trefdraeth (Anglesey),[36] but the fact that the same examples are trotted out again and again suggest that they were few and far between. Non-anecdotal evidence, in sources such as visitation returns, suggests that most English-speaking bishops were fully alive to the need to provide worship, preaching and catechizing in, to quote the Thirty-Nine Articles (Article 24), 'such tongue as the people understandeth', and that this provision was being almost universally met in the late eighteenth and early nineteenth centuries. Support for the language among non-evangelical Anglican clergy was, however, much more positive than that and can be seen, for example, in the production of Welsh translations of the major works of Anglican instruction and spiritual direction, as well as in the involvement of the clergy in the early movement for the revival of eisteddfodau and the work of the various Welsh societies for the study of antiquities.[37]

I wrote at the beginning of this essay that I do not, in any way, seek to diminish the importance of the evangelical revival in Wales in the eighteenth century or the long-lasting effects it has had on the subsequent development of the Protestant churches in Wales. Neither would I wish to deny that there were certain features of this revival in Wales which were individualistic, perhaps even idiosyncratic. It is, however, my contention that Welsh evangelicalism, and its particular manifestation in Calvinistic Methodism, cannot be properly understood except in the broader context of the evangelical and pietist movements that swept across all the Protestant churches of Europe and North America in this period, or, perhaps more importantly, in the particular context of evangelical movements within the western parts of Britain and Ireland. Just as these areas were, and still are, susceptible to wet and windy weather, so they were also, in the late eighteenth and early nineteenth centuries, receptive to evangelical preaching and piety. It is impossible in a single essay to do more than offer, as I hope I have done, a few suggestions of why this was the case, and to illustrate some aspects in which there were differences between the five main Celtic regions of the British Isles – Cornwall, Ireland, the Isle of Man, the western Highlands and Islands of Scotland, and Wales – in the way in which evangelicalism was received and the impact it had on their different religious establishments. It is, however, a topic that deserves, and would benefit from, further study.

Notes

1   *The Diaries of Thomas Wilson D.D., 1731–7 and 1750*, ed. C. L. S. Linnell (London, 1964), pp. 242–7.
2   Manx National Heritage Library, MS 791C.
3   Public Record Office of Northern Ireland, DIO/4/29/1/14.
4   D. L. Morgan, *The Great Awakening in Wales* (London, 1988),

pp. 10–15. For the international impact of the pietist and evangelical revivals see W. R. Ward, *The Protestant Evangelical Awakening* (Cambridge, 1992).

5   The actual breakdown was Calvinistic Methodists 25%, Independents 23%, Church of England 21%, Baptists 18%, Wesleyan Methodists 13%; see J. Davies, *A History of Wales* (London, 1993), p. 427.

6   See D. T. W. Price, *Bishop Burgess and Lampeter College* (Cardiff, 1987), pp. 24–57; F. C. Mather, *High Church Prophet: Bishop Samuel Horsley (1733–1806) and the Caroline Tradition in the Late Georgian Church* (Oxford, 1992), pp. 163–77, 191–9; P. G. Yates, 'Neglect or reform? The diocese of Bangor under Bishop Henry William Majendie 1809–17', unpublished M.Th. thesis (University of Wales, Lampeter, 2003); T. J. Brain, 'Some aspects of the life and works of Richard Watson, Bishop of Llandaff, 1737–1816', unpublished Ph.D. thesis (University of Wales, Aberystwyth, 1982), pp. 159–92

7   E. M. White, 'The Established Church, dissent and the Welsh language, c.1660–1811', in G. H. Jenkins (ed.), *The Welsh Language before the Industrial Revolution* (Cardiff, 1997), pp. 270–80.

8   E.g. T. J. L. Pritchard, *The New Aberystwyth Guide* (Aberystwyth, 1824), pp. 39–54, 118–29.

9   National Library of Wales, SD/QA/68 and 70.

10   C. Podmore, *The Moravian Church in England, 1728–1760* (Oxford, 1998), pp. 5–96; G. Tudur, *Howell Harris: From Conversion to Separation* (Cardiff, 2000), pp. 167–73.

11   D. L. Cooney, *The Methodists in Ireland: A Short History* (Dublin, 2001), pp. 29; S. Walker, *Historic Ulster Churches* (Belfast, 2000), pp. 37, 79–81.

12   Podmore, *Moravian Church*, pp. 194–5, 212–15.

13   J. D. Gelling, *A History of the Manx Church 1698–1911* (Douglas, 1998), pp. 13, 16, 42–3, 48.

14   N. I. Orme (ed.), *Unity and Variety: A History of the Church in Devon and Cornwall* (Exeter, 1991), pp. 97, 141.

15   Morgan, *The Great Awakening*, pp. 65–71.

16   S. Horsley, *The Charge ... to the Clergy of his Diocese Delivered ... in the year 1790* (London, 1792), and *A Charge to the Clergy ... of St Asaph* (London, 1806); J. Randolph, *A Charge Delivered to the Clergy of the Diocese* (Bangor, 1808), esp. pp. 12–29.

17   See, for example, the attacks on evangelicals in R. Laurence, *A*

Charge Delivered at the Triennial Visitation of the Province of Munster (Dublin, 1826), pp. 20–1.

[18] See C. G. Brown, *Religion and Society in Scotland since 1707* (Edinburgh, 1997), pp. 85–8; J. MacInnes, *The Evangelical Movement in the Highlands of Scotland 1688–1800* (Aberdeen, 1951); D. Ansdell, *The People of the Great Faith: The Highland Church 1690–1900* (Stornaway, 1998), pp. 10–11, 22–3, 47–50, 114–16.

[19] See S. J. Brown, *Thomas Chalmers and the Godly Commonwealth in Scotland* (Oxford, 1982), pp. 242–71, 296–335.

[20] *British Parliamentary Papers: Population 11* (Shannon, 1970), pp. 515, 522, 526.

[21] For the raw figures see *The Religious Census of 1851: A Calendar of the Returns Relating to Wales*, ed. I. G. Jones and D. Williams, 2 vols (Cardiff, 1976–81), I, pp. 681–7, and II, pp. 425–8.

[22] *First Report of the Commissioners of Public Instruction, Ireland*, House of Commons, Parliamentary Papers 1835, vol. XXXIII.

[23] See Cooney, *Methodists in Ireland*, pp. 58–73.

[24] See R. G. Holmes, *Henry Cooke* (Belfast, 1981), and *The Presbyterian Church in Ireland: A Popular History* (Blackrock, 2000), pp. 87–97.

[25] See A. R. Acheson, *'A True and Lively Faith': Evangelical Revival in the Church of Ireland* (Belfast, 1992).

[26] See my forthcoming discussion of these issues in 'Calvinistic Methodism: growth and separation', in *The Welsh Church from Reformation to Disestablishment 1603–1920* (University of Wales Press, forthcoming).

[27] Manx National Heritage Library, MS 994C; *British Parliamentary Papers: Population 11*, pp. 604–5.

[28] Orme, *Unity and Variety*, p 135.

[29] A. W. Moore, *Diocesan Histories: Sodor and Man* (London, 1893), pp. 97–8, 174; D. Craine, *Manannan's Isle* (Douglas, 1955), p. 28; W. Gibson (ed.), *Religion and Society in England and Wales, 1689–1800* (Leicester, 1998), pp. 141–2; F. Jones, *The Holy Wells of Wales* (Cardiff, 1954), pp. 63–87.

[30] J. Delumeau (ed.), *Histoire des Diocèses de France: Rennes* (Paris, 1979), pp. 200–4.

[31] S. J. Connolly, *Priests and People in Pre-Famine Ireland* (Dublin, 1982), pp. 135–74.

[32] Quoted in T. A. Campbell, *The Religion of the Heart: A Study*

of European Religious Life in the Seventeenth and Eighteenth Century (Columbia, 1991), p. 105.

33 A. J. Johnes, *An Essay on the Causes which have produced Dissent from the Established Church in the Principality of Wales*, 3rd edn (London, 1835), p. 7.

34 I. M. Whelan, 'Evangelical religion and the polarization of Protestant–Catholic relations in Ireland', unpublished Ph.D. thesis (University of Wisconsin-Madison, 1994), pp. 283–5.

35 MacInnes, *Evangelical Movement in the Highlands*, pp. 209, 247.

36 See W. Hughes, *Diocesan Histories: Bangor* (London, 1911), pp. 111–12.

37 See A. H. Dodd, *A History of Caernarvonshire* (Denbigh, 1968), pp. 348–9; R. L. Brown, 'The effects of Queen Anne's Bounty and the Ecclesiastical Commission on some Montgomeryshire parishes', *Montgomeryshire Collections*, 86 (1988), 105–7; H. T. Edwards, *The Eisteddfod* (Cardiff, 1990), pp. 14–20; R. T. Jenkins and H. M. Ramage, *A History of the Honourable Society of Cymmrodorion and of the Gwyneddigion and Cymreigyddion Societies* (London, 1951, pp. 138–41, 145, 155–9, 169; D. Miles, *The Royal National Eisteddfod of Wales* (Swansea, 1978), pp. 46–56; E. Humphreys, *The Taliesin Tradition* (Bridgend, 2000), pp. 128–33; T. Parry, *The Story of the Eisteddfod* (Liverpool, 1963), pp. 34–6.

6

Catholicism Renewed: Controversy and Reconstruction in the English Catholic Community, 1790–1850

DOM AIDAN BELLINGER

Thomas Burgess was no friend to Roman Catholicism. He remained an implacable opponent of Catholic Emancipation until his last breath, considering Romanism a monstrous growth and any movement in the direction of freedom for Catholics to be a foolhardy error, the end of toleration, not its completion. Emancipation was, for him, a constitutional impossibility, 'Adherence to the principles of the REFORMA-TION and REVOLUTION being necessary qualification for any free-born Englishman'.[1] Indeed, the Bishop thundered, Rome's sanction of idolatry and superstition undid the providential work of the Reformation, which had saved England from popery and returned it to its 'ancient independence and Protestant character' after a few brief centuries of papal dominance.[2] The primitive British church, Burgess had proved to his own satisfaction, owed its origin to St Paul rather than St Peter.[3] Emancipation was an affront to reason, Enlightenment and the true principles of the Church of England:

> How then may he hope most effectively to shew the injustice and unconstitutional nature of the Roman Catholic claims? By keeping constantly in view the false foundations of Popery, and the *Apostolical origin*, and *ancient Protestant character* of our own church; the statutes of Praemunire; the exclusive principles of the REFORMATION and REVOLUTION; and the inviolable covenants of the two UNIONS.[4]

His historical interpretation of the development of England and its church, which he commented on at length in a number of works,[5] was clearly in sympathy with those who wished to exclude all those who did not belong to the Established Church from any active role in the state. In this he shared Lord Eldon's view that that the church was 'essentially and inseparably connected with part of the state . . . the Constitution required that the Church of England should be supported and the best way of affording that support to her was to admit only her own members to office of trust and emolument'.[6] Burgess would not consider any accommodation or compromise with Catholicism.

This essay will look at the threat posed by Catholicism to the Established Church in the early nineteenth century and at the Catholic response to the continued and strengthened Protestant attack which accompanied the gradual amelioration of Catholic restrictions. It takes a considerable intellectual shift from the milieu of Burgess to see the events of this period through Catholic eyes, and the observations of the Italian Rosminian Luigi Gentili (1801–48) may help to illustrate the contrasted mindset. This, on his arrival in 1835, is how Gentili saw Burgess's ordered and steadfast church-state:

> The people had only an apparent religion. The sky is always dark, people look sad, the countryside had nothing to cheer you or to raise your spirits; all is melancholy, a heavy atmosphere hangs over a monotonous countryside, the poverty is frightening. People shout at you that they are free, but they are slaves to a nobility that wallows in opulence. This idea of independence which in fact they have not got, acts like a drug and hides from them their temporal and spiritual ruin.[7]

For Gentili, emancipation was not the issue; he was one of a new generation of 'missionaries' to England who were concerned with revitalizing the struggling Catholic community and bringing the Gospel to the unchurched; to him, church establishment was an irrelevance.

The Roman Catholic Church at the time of Catholic Emancipation (1829) was not in a good state. The papacy, harried by the French Revolution and Napoleon, and challenged in its temporal authority from every direction, had never seemed more fragile. The English Catholics, growing numerically,[8] were, in all other ways under acute pressure; their continental safe-houses of education and formation had been closed during the French Revolution, and there was a chronic shortage of priests[9] which deprived many of the sacraments. The structure of vicariates apostolic, virtually autonomous religious orders and local chapels depending on either gentry patronage or lay subscribing committees was unstable, and bore little relation to the model of the integrated diocesan structures of the Tridentine Church. Yet, by the end of the 1830s the community was presenting itself with a new confidence and self-awareness, encouraged by both a sense of a part in the recovering continental church and the unexpected vitalization of the Oxford Movement.

Peter Nockles, notably in his work on Catholic apologetic against the Church of England from 1778, has shown how a new assertiveness among Catholic controversialists was evidenced by the priest John Milner's *End of Religious Controversy* (1818)[10] and by the publications of the layman William Eusebius Andrews (1773–1837), including (from 1813) his influential and significantly titled *Orthodox Journal*.[11] Individual initiative was critical in the change of tone from irenic submissiveness to stubborn pugnacity, and much of this leadership was clerical.

Peter Augustine Baines (1787–1843), a Lancastrian educated at Lamspringe, the baroque English monastery near Hildesheim in Germany (closed in 1803), and at Ampleforth, where he became a monk, was perhaps the most pertinacious of the new breed. He made his mark as a preacher, teacher and evangelist in Bath, where he was a priest at the Catholic chapel, one of the most important in the south of England and the jewel in the Benedictines' rather meagre crown.[12] His theological and devotional approach was strongly based on the 'forgiveness of sins', and his sermons had an evangelical fervour. His long clash with his own Order and the financial ruin brought by his venture at Prior Park have overshadowed his real achievement and his role as a herald of a new age. Prior Park failed, but it was a magnificent idea. Prior Park was to be the episcopal heart of the Western District, of which he became

Vicar Apostolic. It was to be cathedral, bishop's palace, university and school, housed in a great mansion made even more splendid with grandiose classical additions. 'I saw in Prior Park', Cardinal Wiseman reflected, 'the beginnings of a new era for Catholic affairs, in education, in literature, in public position, in many things which are now realities and which then were hopes.'[13]

Baines had formidable energy and missionary zeal. He combined a fierce clericalism and episcopalism with a growing distrust of monasticism, which seemed to him both romantic and ill-suited to the nineteenth century. He displayed a strong emotionalism and, occasionally, a lack of discernment and discretion. Like many prophets, his immediate impact was great and his long-term bequest limited. Wiseman, in the end, judged him harshly:

> He had a power of fascinating all who approached in spite of a positive tone and manner which scarcely admitted of a difference from him in opinion. He had sometimes original views upon a certain class of subject; but on every topic he had a command of language and a clear manner of expressing his sentiments which commanded attention, and generally won assent. Hence his acquaintances were always willing listeners, and soon became warm admirers, then warm partisans. Unfortunately this proved to him a fatal gift. When he undertook great and even magnificent works, he would stand alone: assent to his plan was the condition of being near him; anyone that did not agree, or that ventured to suggest deliberation, or provoke discussion, was soon at a distance; he isolated himself with his own genius, he had no counsellor but himself; and he who had at one time surrounded himself with men of learning, of prudence and of devotedness to him, found himself at last alone, and fretted a noble heart to a solitary death.[14]

Baines, the battling bishop, was handicapped by poverty and by the nature of the English Catholic community. Luigi Gentili, in his letters to Rome, written mainly at the end of the 1840s, suggested a new strategy – the preached mission. Missions varied in detail but included numerous sermons and frequent opportunities for confession. The missions were highly charged emotionally and generally culminated in a great closing ceremony and the unveiling of a mission cross: 'The multitudes who flocked to the confessionals at the mission were a true witness to the effectiveness of the preaching of the missioners.'[15] Gentili identified the lack of unity among the clergy as 'the greatest wound of holy church in this island':

> Except for the new orders who get on well with the secular clergy, there is hostility between order and order and secular and secular, District and District, bishop and bishop, and little obedience from priests to their bishop. These latter criticise one another. They meet once a year, and there never seems to be any result, for there is no one at their head. They are all equal and no one dares propose a reform, each does what he thinks best . . . The bishops never make a canonical visitation of their dioceses, not dare to do it; but from the experience I have had in giving missions, I can assert without hesitation that they do not know a third of what is wrong in their Districts . . . One of them, Mgr Briggs, who has been present at all the missions that we have given in his District, and saw the abuses with his own eyes . . . wanted me last year to attend the Bishops' Meeting in London, to give an account of things as we saw them in practice during our missions, so that they might know what was going on.[16]

Gentili preached in town and country with equal passion, but his audiences were sometimes reduced by the pew rents which restricted entrants to the more fashionable London Catholic places of worship.

The appeal of Nicholas Wiseman was less popular than Gentili's, but he established himself as an outstanding spokesman for Catholicism long before his appointment as first Archbishop of Westminster in 1850. Learned, energetic and cosmopolitan, a native of Seville with Irish parentage, a wunderkind at the Venerable English College, Rome, Wiseman entered the controversial list in the 1830s. In November 1835, while looking after the chapel of the Sardinian Embassy in Lincoln's Inn Fields, Wiseman delivered a course of lectures in English (the Sardinian chapel also had Italian sermons) on the Catholic Church, intended especially for Protestants. It was a unique occasion and one who was present, with the hyperbole which often surrounded Wiseman's activity, said the lectures marked 'the beginning of a serious revival of Catholicism in England'.[17] The lectures, given in Advent 1836 on Sunday afternoons, were repeated the following Lent at Moorfields chapel, and published in two volumes the same year. Wiseman's lectures were intended to be expository rather than controversial, but he was prepared to cover all subjects, including such hardy perennials of anti-Catholicism as indulgences and transubstantiation. Wiseman's lectures were part of a Europe-wide revival of Catholicism, although the greatest Catholic scholar of the time, Johannes Döllinger (1799–1890), was concerned that his contemporary English scholars of the time had not learned German and were unable to benefit from the historical work in that country. Döllinger, Professor of Church History at Munich from 1826, had formidable linguistic and learned accomplishments, and proposed a new social and religious order based on Catholic principles. He was a sustained critic of liberalism, Protestantism and rationalism, and saw the Reformation as an unhappy rupture in the continuity of Christian Europe. English Catholics, he suggested, were suffering from 'a sort of literary apathy and inactivity' and 'your numerous adversaries take too much advantage of your silence'. Dollinger asked: 'Are there no persons of literary pursuits among your Catholic clergy who are capable and inclined to study our theological literature of the last years?'[18]

The most impressive of the English Catholic writers of the period was John Lingard (1771–1851), whose *Anglo Saxon Church*, published in 1806, came, with impeccable academic credentials, to quite different conclusions on the identity of early English Christianity from those reached by Burgess and Henry Soames, whose Bampton lectures of 1830 suggested that historical separateness of the English Churches from Rome.[19] Lingard's programme in returning to the original sources was explicit: 'My object is truth, and in the pursuit of truth.'[20] Lingard's education at Douai, the university in northern France attended by generations of English Catholic seminarians, had provided him with a good historical background. The English College in the town made a particular contribution to critical historical scholarship in the person of Alban Butler (1709–73), whose scientific use of sources was at the core of his hagiographical writings most associated with his *Lives of the Saints*. Douai took a full part in the French tradition of historical scholarship, most associated with the Maurists, and took part too, no doubt, in the Cisalpine and Gallican spirit which Milner, another alumnus of Douai, considered had infected Lingard. Lingard, for Milner, was too open to lay participation in the administration of the Church, too democratic, too much a man of the age. Yet, as a writer respected by his opponents Lingard's pen was even mightier than Milner's. Using primary material from English and continental libraries and archives, many for the first time, he not only demolished old myths, like the Burgess theories on the Pauline origin of the English Church, but also constructed an alternative anti-Whig interpretation of history which still has its adherents and apologists; Lingard, in his quiet scholarly way, was perhaps the greatest Catholic champion of his generation, and those who crossed swords with him rarely came away unbloodied.[21]

The fight was on, and it was a fight with increasingly high stakes as the cities flooded with immigrants, many of them Irish, and Catholics and Protestants vied for their souls. In London the Catholic community experienced a great rise in numbers. In round figures the Catholic population in metropolitan London expanded from some 50,000 in 1815 to about 250,000 in the late 1830s.[22] New chapels began to be built, adding to those of the ambassadors and the French exiled clergy, which already provided some spiritual care. The most important of the new chapels was St Mary's Moorfields, opened in 1820, near what is now Finsbury Circus (the church was demolished in 1889), a magnificent and capacious building with a dramatic interior.[23] In time this church, a metropolitan cathedral in all but name, became the pro-cathedral of the restored Westminster diocese, and, although not in the same architectural league as similar churches in Baltimore or Dublin, its splendid sanctuary set it apart from the other London chapels.[24] It showed the way in which the framework of an effective parochial and diocesan structure was being established long before the official restoration of the hierarchy in 1850. Nevertheless, shortage of money and of priests made effective pastoral ministry to the poor very difficult. Pew rents and designated areas for the rich within the new chapels kept the poor at bay. This was also the case at Lincoln's Inn chapel, the long-established chapel of the Sardinian Ambassador, but Moorfields was 'quite as bad, if not worse, for there it is impossible to fulfil our obligations unless we pay *at least* twopence, and so on till we mount to a shilling'.[25]

A new pastoral strategy was needed, and this had to wait until the dynamic leadership of Wiseman and Manning later in the century, but the shortage of clergy, aggravated by the forced closure of the continental colleges, was being addressed by the foundation and endowment of seminaries. The great college of St Patrick at Maynooth near Dublin and the controversial grant which endowed it[26] provided a model for the English Catholics, and the newly established colleges of St Edmund at Old Hall Green, near Ware in Hertfordshire,[27] and St Cuthbert's at Ushaw in County Durham[28], successors to the closed college at Douai in France, were both fully operational by 1815. Old Hall (1793) and Ushaw (1808) both had spacious, if somewhat spartan, buildings (their Gothic glory came later), and their Englishness was obvious from the first.[29] The Catholics now trained in England were most keen to lose any trace of an alien status. These two colleges, which provided lay education as much as clerical training (as at Douai) were, in scale and aspiration, on a level with the best of contemporary 'dissenting academies' and were comparable, too, to the somewhat moribund colleges of Oxford and Cambridge.

The religious orders, too, were beginning to establish permanent homes in England, despite the hostility of public opinion and the perceived force of law against their existence. The Jesuit College at Stonyhurst was in existence in the 1790s,[30] and the Benedictines had monasteries and schools at Downside in Somerset[31] and Ampleforth in Yorkshire before 1815.[32] The religious orders continued their work in missions in town and country and, after a half-century of stagnation, were beginning their greatest period of expansion and influence. Religious orders of women, some refugees from the French Revolution, were beginning to develop and to work among the poor, although their major impact was to come in the second half of the century.

The laity, dominant in the recusant period, continued to influence the working of the Church and the old recusant families maintained their patronage and financial aid. Charity dinners and other public functions, predominantly in the 1830s, reflected the growth of a Catholic middle class and the development of social standing in the community. An indication of a growing lay self-confidence was reflected in the numerous journals which proliferated. The first issue of the *Dublin Review* appeared in May 1836; its title was an obvious challenge to the *Edinburgh Review*, placing the Catholic associations of Dublin against the Protestantism and Enlightenment credentials of Edinburgh. Wiseman was the *Dublin Review*'s first editor but it remained under lay management. The *Orthodox Journal*, mentioned already, like a tabloid version of Lingard's history, trumpeted the causes of Catholicism's inherent Englishness and the negative influence of the Reformation. Many of the numerous Catholic journals of the early nineteenth century had short lives, on account of financial difficulties, and few ever attained a sale of more than 1,000 (in a period when the *Methodist Magazine*, in 1821, had a circulation of about 25,000 copies a month), but they did show the depth and vigour of Catholic polemic, comparable in its intensity, if not in its volume, to its Protestant counterparts.

Nothing in England came near to the thrice-weekly newspaper *The Pilot*, which fired the Irish Catholics in their search for emancipation. Ireland was far ahead of England, not only in the number of its Catholics, but in its lay and clerical organization. In Ireland the emancipation question had galvanized Catholic opinion and led, in 1823, to the establishment of Daniel O'Connell's 'Catholic Association', which, crucially, won the support of both the poor and the clergy; the latter saw it as a crusade against the propagators of the 'New Reformation' movement. This 'New Reformation' was intended to complete the unfinished business of the first Reformation and took its lead from the 1822 Charge of the Protestant Archbishop of Dublin, who described Catholics as possessing 'a church without what we can properly call a religion' and as being blindly enslaved to a supposed infallible ecclesiastic authority.[33] Mass meetings and intense local campaigns were the techniques used by both the Catholic Association and the various New Reformation societies. Their example was soon followed in England. The Reformation Society's English operations were originally subsidiary to the Irish venture, but the work soon flourished.[34]

The Catholics soon found a particular champion in Thomas Michael McDonnell (1792–1869), ordained in 1817, stationed in Birmingham from 1824, a vocal supporter of O'Connell and a natural ally of Midland radical dissent,[35] who based the Catholic response to the Reformation Society onslaught on the bedrock of religious liberty.[36] Numerous meetings were held across the country and some of them left a permanent record, not only in local newspapers, but in the form of publications. One such was the Downside discussion of 1834, held at the chapel of the Benedictine monastery which had been opened in 1823; its façade was adorned with the papal keys.[37] This followed a meeting of the Reformation Society at the Old Down Inn on the road from Bristol to Shepton Mallet, near Downside, on 10 January 1834. McDonnell played a leading part, as did the Franciscan Francis Edgeworth (1799–1850) of Bristol, who had conducted a similar defence in his home city in 1828. The third Catholic was Joseph Brown (1796–1880), who taught theology at Downside and was to go on to be a pioneering and missionary-minded bishop in Wales. The Protestants were Edward Tottenham, minister of Kensington chapel in Bath, an Irishman who had been secretary of the Dublin Reformation Society, and John Lyons, minister of All Saint's, Liverpool. The Downside event, which took place over six days, was the first such meeting on Catholic property and was conducted on a 'civilized' basis. The discussion took two subjects under consideration: 'The Rule of Faith' and 'The Sacrifice of the Mass'. At the end of the first sessions it was made clear how well proceedings had gone:

> In Conclusion, permit me to say that this has been the most orderly meeting I ever witnessed, and is worthy the imitation of every meeting in this great land, and from one extremity of the British Empire to the other, I trust it will be duly appreciated.[38]

The open-handed approach of the meeting was perhaps not typical of the genre, but it indicated the way in which the

Catholics were increasing in confidence as the implications of emancipation became clearer. There was an increasing involvement in public life. One of Joseph Brown's pupils, Bernard Ullathorne (1806–89), before the 1830s were out, was playing a significant role in the important Molesworth Commission on the end of transportation.[39] Mission was becoming the inspiration of the English Catholics, rather than the survival mentality which had sustained them since the Reformation.

Burgess's certainties made less sense in the reforming political world of the 1830s when the *ancien régime* was being deconstructed. The fight for the souls of men and women as populations grew and moved was becoming more urgent and insistent than a constitutional status quo, which was appearing increasingly unsustainable. Evangelicalism had made good use of a number of strategies – public meetings, church- and school-building and controversial and devotional writing – which were also used by the emerging Roman Catholics. Indeed, evangelicalism, especially in the Reformation societies, had learnt much from the activities of the Catholic Association in Ireland. Moreover, much of the language of debate between Catholics and Protestants shared a vocabulary where words like 'orthodox', 'historical' and 'apostolic' took on a sectarian guise.

The similarities in strategy and vocabulary do not conceal the fact that the 1830s saw the emergence of clear, separate identities in the Protestant and Catholic communities. The Holy See might be showing more favour to Great Britain and to the English Catholics, but principally on account of the possible advantage of British protection of Roman interests.[40] There was no meeting of minds. The Catholics of the post-French Revolution world turned their back on the irenic overtures of the century of the Enlightenment and faced the new world of the nineteenth century, which in England reached its apogee in the restoration of the Catholic hierarchy in England and Wales in 1850. This ultramontanism was combined with an English enthusiasm for a lost Catholic world, especially appealing to converts who feared Catholicism's forgiveness, given form in the churches of Pugin and in the writings of Lingard. What was emerging in the English Catholic world of the 1820s and 1830s was an alternative church and a counter-culture. If Burgess had realized the threat posed by the Catholic Church to the Establishment his disquiet might have been greater and his prolixity might have scaled even greater heights.

Notes

1 T. Burgess, *The Protestant's Catechism on the Origin of Popery and the Grounds of the Roman Catholic Claims*, 2nd edn (London, 1818), p. 21.
2 Ibid., p. iii.
3 Ibid., p. 9.
4 Ibid., pp. v–vi.
5 See, for example, T. Burgess, *Tracts on the Origin and Independence of the Ancient British Church*, 2nd edn (London, 1815), and *Remarks on the Western Travels of St Paul* (London, 1820).
6 H. Twiss, *Lord Chancellor Eldon*, III (London, 1844), p. 39.
7 C. Leetham, *Luigi Gentili* (London, 1965), p. 62.
8 See J. Bossy, *The English Catholic Community 1570–1850* (London, 1975), especially pp. 303–22.
9 Just over 300 (309) ordinations for the English Mission in the last quarter of the eighteenth century, as compared to 735 in the same quarter of the seventeenth century. See D. A. Bellenger, *English and Welsh Priests 1558–1800* (Bath, 1984), p. 246.
10 P. B. Nockles, '"The difficulties of Protestantism": Bishop Milner, John Fletcher and Catholic Apologetic against the Church of England in the era from the First Relief Act to Emancipation, 1778–1830', *Recusant History*, 24 (1998), 193–236.
11 B. Carter, 'Catholic charitable endeavour in London 1810–1840. Part II', *Recusant History*, 25, 648–9. P. B. Nockles considers the definition of 'Orthodoxy' within the Established Church in 'Church parties in the pre-Tractarian Church of England 1750–1833: the "Orthodox", some problems of definition and identity', in J. Walsh, C. Haydon and S. Taylor (eds), *The Church of England c.1689–c.1833: from Toleration to Tractarianism* (Cambridge, 1993), pp. 356–8.
12 See J. A. Williams, *Bath and Rome: The Living Link* (Bath, 1963), and J. S. Roche, *History of Prior Park College* (London, 1931).

[13] B. Ward, *The Sequel to Catholic Emancipation I* (London 1915), p. 70.

[14] N. Wiseman, *Recollections of the Last Four Popes* (London, 1858), p. 325.

[15] E. Larkin, 'The Parish Mission movement, 1850–1880', in B. Bradshaw and D. Keogh (eds), *Christianity in Ireland* (Dublin, 2002), p. 201.

[16] Leetham, *Gentili*, p. 288.

[17] B. Fothergill, *Nicholas Wiseman* (London, 1963), p. 74.

[18] R. J. Schiefen, *Nicholas Wiseman and the Transformation of English Catholicism* (Shepherdstown, 1984), p. 65.

[19] P. Phillips, 'John Lingard and the Anglo Saxon Church', *Recusant History*, 23 (1996), 179.

[20] Ibid., 178.

[21] See E. Jones, *The English Nation: The Great Myth* (Stroud, 1998), esp. pp. 168–217.

[22] See B. Carter, 'Catholic charitable endeavour in London 1818–1840. Part I', *Recusant History*, 25, 489.

[23] *The Laity's Directory*, 1820.

[24] R. O'Donnell, 'The interior of St Mary Moorfields', *The Gregorian Group Journal*, 7 (1997), pp. 71–4.

[25] Carter, 'Charitable endeavour II', 665.

[26] See P. J. Corish, *Maynooth College 1795–1995* (Dublin, 1995), and J. Newman, *Maynooth and Gregorian Ireland* (Galway, 1979).

[27] See B. Ward, *History of St Edmund's College* (London, 1893).

[28] See D. Milburn, *A History of Ushaw College* (Durham, 1964).

[29] See Ward, *St Edmund's College*, p. 148, and Milburn, *Ushaw College*, facing p. 113, for contemporary illustrations.

[30] See T. E. Muir, *Stonyhurst College 1593–1993* (Stonyhurst, 1992). Established at Saint Omer in 1593, the college resettled at Stonyhurst in Lancashire in 1794.

[31] See N. H. Birt, *Downside* (London, 1902).

[32] See A. Cramer, *Ampleforth* (York, 2001), and A. Marett-Crosby, *A School of the Lord's Service* (London, 2002).

[33] D. Kerr, 'The Catholic Church in the age of O'Connell', in Bradshaw and Keogh, *Christianity in Ireland*, pp. 172–3. See also D. Bowen, *The Protestant Crusade in Ireland* (Dublin, 1978).

[34] See J. Wolffe, *The Protestant Crusade in Great Britain 1829–1860* (Oxford, 1991).

[35] See J. Champ, 'Priesthood and politics in the nineteenth century: the turbulent career of Thomas McDonnell', *Recusant History*, 18 (1987), 289–303.

36 Wolffe, *Protestant Crusade*, p. 46.
37 See D. A. Bellenger (ed.), *Downside: A Pictorial History* (Bath, 1998), p. 30.
38 *The Authenticated Report of the Discussion ... Downside* (London, 1836). The Downside Abbey Archives contain some excerpts of letters between Brown and Tottenham on proofs of his book (e.g. DAA, Birt, Papers, J 83, 84, 93) and also a manuscript of an anti-transubstantiation sermon given by a Mr Shanks at Midsomer Norton Methodist Church in January 1834 (ibid., I 155).
39 For Ullathorne see D. A. Bellenger, '"The normal state of the Church": William Bernard Ullathorne, first Bishop of Birmingham', *Recusant History*, 25 (2000), 25–34. The Benedictine mission to Australia which was to lead to the establishment of a Roman Catholic hierarchy there began in the 1830s.
40 Some tentative diplomatic moves were made between the Holy See and Britain during the Napoleonic period, and in 1820 Pope Pius VII presented the new Moorfields chapel with a gold chalice (a gift he had received himself from Mexico), saying 'there is nothing too good for me to give to the English Catholics'. On 1 May of that year a Latin letter from 'the King of England' arrived in Rome, the first such since 1688. (See N. Wiseman, *Recollections*, pp. 142–3.)

7

Drawing up the Battle Lines: Elementary Schooling in the Diocese of Bangor in the Second Decade of the Nineteenth Century

PAULA YATES

There has recently been a renewed interest and a renewed debate over the pros and cons of faith schools, and not all those who show an interest in this issue realize that they are taking part in an argument which has exercized the minds of Christians, on and off, over at least a century and a half. The debate peaked a century ago, when the Education Act of 1902 sparked off an unprecedented response from Christians of all denominations.

This Act was designed to set up a national system of education. It abolished the non-denominational Board Schools, which had been set up by the Forster Act of 1870 on the insistence of the influential Nonconformist lobby within the Liberal Party. At the same time it offered funding to denominational schools, both Anglican and Roman Catholic. It may not be surprising that members of the Free Churches objected, but the sheer force of the campaign it aroused is perhaps more hard to account for.

All over the country Free Churchmen refused to pay that portion of their rates which went towards education. Meetings were held at which, amidst considerable religious fervour, men queued up to take solemn oaths to go to prison, rather than pay it. Here in Wales, with its powerful Nonconformist lobby, some were spared this necessity by the fact that county councils with Nonconformist majorities refused to levy the tax and had government grants withheld.[1] The repeal of the Act was a key issue at the general election of 1906, which saw the final flowering of the alliance between Nonconformity and the Liberal Party. The Free Church Council publicly announced its support for the Liberals; Free Church ministers campaigned on behalf of Liberal candidates; and the Baptist leader, Dr John Clifford, toured the country, sharing platforms with Lloyd George. On election day students training for the Free Church ministry had their exams postponed so that they could help encourage voters to the polls. It was the last and greatest set-piece battle in the war over education which had been fought between Nonconformity and the Established Church throughout the second half of the nineteenth century.

So why were Nonconformists so agitated about the Act? Why was it that William Nicoll, editor of the *British Weekly*, could describe the Act as dealing 'the deadliest blow to the very existence and future of Nonconformity'? Nonconformity is usually seen to have been at its peak at the turn of the century – about to suffer a rapid decline, of course, but nevertheless at its peak. Was it really so essential that its young people be protected from Anglican education that the end of Board Schools could mean the end of Nonconformity? How had the churches got themselves into the position where feelings could run so high on this issue? Well, of course there were a number of factors, and a complete answer would need an examination of the full course of the war, but to see the first skirmishings, to see the two sides drawing back and looking at one another for the first time across the hostile divide, we need to travel back another hundred years, to the time of Bishop Burgess himself, though not, in this essay, to his own diocese.

In north Wales in the second decade of the nineteenth century Burgess's fellow bishop, Henry William Majendie of Bangor, was setting about an energetic programme of reform.[2] An earnest, conscientious bishop, he was struggling, not always successfully, to ensure that the church buildings were in good order, the services more frequent, the clergy in residence in their parishes, and the people's spiritual needs met. His task was made more difficult by the fact that the Established Church was much troubled by the great number of dissenters from its ranks and the popularity of the services of various Dissenting churches, most notably the Calvinistic Methodists.

To those who have worked on this period in many parts of England, the extent of this problem in Bangor may come as something of a surprise. There were almost no clergy in the diocese who were not more or less concerned about this issue. Of the 124 clergy who returned forms nearly 30 per cent reported that many or all of their parishioners regularly attended Dissenting worship, whereas only about 10 per cent reported few or none. As elsewhere, of course, the situation was complicated by the fact that the dividing lines were still extremely blurred, with even the most faithful Anglican communicants going to hear Dissenting preachers from time to time and even the most committed members of the Dissenting societies continuing to attend church occasionally, especially for communion.

Officially the Calvinistic Methodists remained within the Church of England until 1811, when they broke away by taking the step of ordaining their own ministers, but this event, at least as evidenced in these returns, seems to have made very little difference on the ground. There seems no doubt in the minds of any of the clergy that Methodists were just another set of Dissenters, and this was almost equally true in the 1801 returns, so the situation was not new. In each of the three years in this decade for which visitation returns survive a small percentage of the clergy felt that Dissent was on the increase (and a similar percentage felt that it was declining), but most seem to have seen it as a long-standing problem which had changed little over twenty years or more. The decision to ordain ministers is mentioned only four times, in each case in the 1814 return and generally as a matter of report or as a reason for a small decline in communicant figures. Only one man seems to be seriously surprised or affronted by the development. David Jones at Gyffylliog claims that the Calvinistic Methodists 'have lately presumptuously invaded the sacred office, by appointing their spurious Priests to administer the Holy Sacraments; and ever since have carried on a kind of Spiritual Conspiracy against the Established Church with redoubled Zeal and Vigour'. The use of this vehemence of language is interesting. Jones may have had strong views but he was not alone; similar and, indeed, more colourful invective against Dissent comes from others of his colleagues. Attitudes amongst the clergy to Dissenters varied considerably, from ignorance and complacency, through sneering disdain, to frustration and fury. For some of the poorer clergy in remote parishes, surrounded by uncooperative Dissenters, things could be very difficult. Edward Hughes, the curate of Llanfihangel-y-Pennant wrote in 1814 that 'The neighbourhood seems to be the very Focus of Fanaticism. It is an uncomfortable situation. Having not the Means of doing Acts of Hospitality and of extensive Charity with the View to conciliate the affections of the People, I find Preaching availeth but little.' Under the relatively smooth surface of these returns there runs a definite current of defensiveness, anxiety and discomfort.

Part of the reason for this was undoubtedly politically based. The French and American revolutions were still quite a recent memory. Even in a diocese as remote as Bangor the establishment was anxious about an uprising of the masses and, for many, political and religious dissent went hand in hand. In the 1817 return, in the aftermath of the end of the Napoleonic Wars, the curate of Aberffraw described an increasing enthusiasm for Dissent in the previous year, which he linked to '2nd Decr 1816, and the other days fixed for the general downfall of all Order and Law', but said that when this attempt failed the people began to come back to the church 'and it is better filled since the failure of the Revolutionists'.

In his 1817 Charge Majendie noted

> with what abhorrence must we not recently have seen the most blasphemous and seditious tracts industriously circulated, gratis, among the lower orders, and from the poison of which not even the seclusion of this Principality, and the peculiarity of its language has entirely protected us . . .

and referred to two occasions when

> our consecrated Churches have . . . been most audaciously violated by preoccupation of a number of persons not in communion with us [on Sundays at service time] . . . I speak of

large congregations – in full possession of the Churches – to the exclusion of their own Rector, or licensed Minister . . .[3]

It is clear that some at least of the clergy were feeling threatened, not only about the loss of congregations, but also about the potential loss of authority, position and dignity.

Various possible solutions to the problem of Dissent were put forward by the clergy, but for Majendie, as for many others, the key to solving it was education. In his 1814 Charge, struck by accounts of congregations going from chapel to chapel as well as to church, he concluded that this could be made possible only by serious ignorance and that more catechetical instruction was required. He warned that Dissenting schools 'have greatly multiplied, while their zeal . . . is become more fervent and the teaching of their Disciples . . . without any motive of Pecuniary recompense. On the other hand the Schools of the Established Church . . . especially in some of the larger towns, are evidently in languishing . . . condition.'[4] In his 1817 Charge, in an inverted foreshadowing of Edward Nicoll's dire warning of 1902, he described the flourishing nature of Dissenting schools in the diocese and predicted that this would inevitably lead to 'the fall of the Constitution of this Country, both in Church and State, and probably at no distant period'.[5]

So why were the schools of the Established Church in such a languishing condition? Certainly, something seems to have been causing problems for the smaller charity schools. The chief bequest for schools in the diocese was that by Dean Jones of Bangor, who had died in 1727. Owain Jones says that the bequest established a chain of twelve schools in Caernarfonshire specifically to educate children in the Welsh language.[6] By Majendie's time only three seem to have remained in Caernarfonshire, though a further three were reported in Anglesey and two more in Merioneth.

The circulating schools, of which there had been sixty-seven in the diocese in 1760, had collapsed after the death of Madam Bevan, their chief funder, in 1779. Her will, which left all her fortune to the schools, was contested by her family and mouldered away in Chancery until 1808. By 1811 only one such school in the diocese was specifically linked to the Bevan charity, and though two or three others are mentioned in the returns they all seemed to have stopped functioning properly, except for one, which served a group of parishes at the western end of the Llŷn peninsula.

There are hints in the returns that there may have been a problem getting teachers. In several cases it is reported that schools have ceased to function for want of a teacher. This may have been partly caused by a problem with revenues for their provision. At Llanengan, for example, there was a bequest of £6 to instruct youth in the catechism, but as the interest amounted to only 6s. a year 'no Teacher will teach it'. At Llanllechid it was stated that the endowment did not pay enough so the master was given 'a small payment . . . now and then' and 'few shillings Overplay Money after paying for White Bread which is distributed to the poor according to Legacy'.

Another problem for schools was to do with church buildings. In many cases the church had traditionally been where the school was held, and no other suitable building existed, but children are not noted for the care with which they treat their surroundings. The problem had already been identified before Majendie's first visitation. At Llanllyfni, in 1811, it was reported that about fifty children were being taught in a voluntary school in the church 'rather unhappily to the injury of the Church and Churchyard which has been noted by the Rural Dean as well & unfortunately no place occurs for the purpose so as to be at all under the influence of church discipline'. The rector of Llandwrog told Majendie, 'Houses for Parochial Schools are much wanted. In consequence of the want of such Houses, youths are now instructed in the Churches, which they greatly injure, or they are brought up in Conventicles in Principles, I fear, very detrimental to the establish'd Religion of the Land.' However, it was undoubtedly exacerbated by the Bishop's reforming zeal. Not long after his arrival in the diocese in 1809 Majendie set about a determined campaign of church repair, which lasted until 1817. In doing so he probably had not considered that his clergy, having endured all the fund-raising rigours of such a campaign, would become even more unwilling to subject their spanking new churches to the activities of a bevy of schoolchildren.

Even before the advent of the National Society attempts were being made to solve this problem. A small number of new schoolrooms were reported and several new schools were being founded, both day schools and Sunday schools, but many found it hard to become established. Peter Bailey Williams, for example, had founded a Sunday school in his parish of Llanrûg in 1793, but this had disappeared by 1811. In 1814 he was trying to establish a permanent school, but in 1817 he reported that he had not yet managed to acquire a building for it, and it was not clear whether or not it was actually functioning. At Llandyfrydog in 1814 the curate explained that: 'I endeavoured last year with the assistance of my Clerk and the Churchwardens to establish a Sunday school in the Church; but it was discontinued in consequence of its being so indifferently attended.'

In 1811, fifteen clergy reported new or recent day or Sunday schools in their parishes, and in 1814 there were thirty-two more, though not all of the previous ones had survived. Frustratingly, the 1817 returns, in which the first National schools are reported, are nothing like so complete. Anglesey, in particular, is hardly represented at all, so we must just take Majendie's word for it when, in his 1817 Charge, he rejoices that, 'we have made some progress in founding schools of a higher class, with the encouragement and in union with the National Society, not only in some of the principal towns of the Diocese, but even in sequestered villages'. This is, he says, particularly true in Anglesey.[7]

The question of control over schooling, which was mentioned by several of the clergy, was a new problem, but it was becoming an important one. In the 1801 returns there is a clear understanding that where a school exists it will be instructing the children in the church catechism. By 1811 this is beginning to be in doubt. The clergy can no longer assume that this will be the case and, for the first time, they are having to wonder how they can be sure a school is sound if it is not held in the church or, preferably, taught by the minister.

This problem is clearly brought out in the case of Sunday schools. Some worked very well, but there is something of a pattern of Sunday schools being at risk of falling into the hands of Methodists. Who, after all, are the members of a congregation most likely to volunteer to help teach a Sunday school? They are those who are energetic, zealous, enthusiastic and, all too often, Methodistically inclined. Richard Lloyd at Llanallgo, for example, reported in 1811 that there were no schools 'excepting a Sunday school now kept by the Methodists at their own Chapel which had been kept in the Parish church: but as soon as their Chapel was ready they frequented the Church no longer'. More detail is given by William Ellis at Rhiw. In 1811 his predecessor had reported simply 'a small Sunday school under my inspection, taught by a few of the Parishioners'. By 1814 either the situation or the attitude of the minister, or indeed both, had changed. Ellis writes:

> At the time of my collation to this Parish the Calvinistic Methodists kept a Sunday school in this church, as soon as they found me to be ready to enter church for reading divine service the school would be dismissed and both teachers and scholars would turn their back on the divine service and would in all directions immediately depart, which indeed was very painful to me and had reason to think they were not of God. After bearing with them for some months and finding the Ch. Catechism was entirely neglected by them, no not even the Lord's Prayer, Creed, nor the Ten Commandments were taught by them to the Children, then I represented to them that they would be no more suffered to teach in the church for the future unless the Ch. Catechism and divine service would be attended to, which they refused to comply with but went on to teach, and sang hymns and prayed after school time was over, extempore; to which business I put a stop to & attempted to establish a Sunday school myself but was not able to do it for a long time as they always continued to keep school or to have a preaching at the same time.

There is an awareness that schools were recruiting grounds for both Anglicanism and dissent. At Llandwrog in 1814 it was reported that the Calvinists were:

> very zealous in bringing up the children in their own persuasion by teaching them to learn by heart detach'd Parts of Scripture which they suppose make for their own doctrine –

These Chapters the children learn to repeat very perfectly to the great astonishment of an ignorant but crowded assemblies.

However, it may be that the correlation between school attendance and denominational adherence was not always entirely simple. Richard Jones of Llanynys had founded a very successful evening school in church because his Sunday school could not compete with that of the Methodists, and this was attended by many of those who also went to the Methodist school on Sundays. He gives us this explanation of the situation in his parish and more widely:

> this Sunday School has been given up, on account of the Methodists having opened up a Sunday school ... where the parents of the children have sent them in preference of the Church Sunday School, because the teachers are more numerous, and the children and grown up people, men and women, are brought forward sooner than in the Church Sunday Schools, as the Church Teachers require payment for their trouble, whereas the Methodists do it all gratis, and there are plenty of Instructors, who offer their services; so that there is a Teacher for every half dozen children and they continue their schools for a whole half a day on Sundays ... but I do not consider the grown up people instructed in these schools as having deserted the Church. They frequent them only as a means of Instruction.

The picture, then, that emerges from these documents is one of a worthy Church, generally well-run but perhaps a little tired, not yet fully realizing the changes which are on the way but beginning to be forced to rethink ancient certainties; under threat, both in terms of adherents and, much more widely, in terms of authority and political status. On the other side we see an energetic underclass, aware of its ability to threaten and disturb, enjoying the excitement of flourishing congregations and fiery preachers. And between them lie the schools, beginning to be identified on both sides as the most appropriate field on which to fight the battle for the hearts and minds of the people.

Notes

1 John Davies, *A History of Wales* (Penguin edn, 1994), p. 481.
2 This essay is largely based on the virtually complete set of diocesan visitation returns for 1811 and 1814, and the less complete but still extensive returns for 1817, the first three visitations of Majendie's episcopate. They are NLW, B/QA/19–20 (1811), 22–3 (1814) and 24–5 (1817). Unless otherwise stated all quotations and information about the diocese come from these volumes.
3 H. W. Majendie, *A Charge to the Clergy of . . . Bangor . . . 1817* (Bangor, 1817), pp. 7, 26.
4 W. H. Majendie, *A Charge to the Clergy of . . . Bangor . . .* (Chester, 1814), p. 24.
5 Majendie, *Charge 1817*, p. 29.
6 O. W. Jones, 'The Welsh Church in the eighteenth century', in David Walker (ed.), *A History of the Church in Wales* (Penarth, 1976), p. 106.
7 Majendie, *Charge 1817*, p. 28.

8

Two 'Western Seminaries': Bishops Burgess and Chase and the Founding of Saint David's College, Lampeter and Kenyon College, Ohio

PETER MILES

In 1997 and 1999 the University of Wales, Lampeter (originally Saint David's College) and Kenyon College, Ohio, celebrated the 175th anniversaries of their respective foundations – each without reference to the other.[1] However, an attention to the interaction of their founders, Thomas Burgess (Bishop of St David's) and Philander Chase (Bishop of Ohio), suggests that these two institutions can consider themselves long-lost cousins.

The stories of these foundations are well known on their respective sides of the Atlantic but it remains to draw them into a single narrative. To effect that conjunction is to enrich the history of each college and estimates of the personalities of their founders, to throw further light on the cultures of evangelicalism and philanthropy in early nineteenth-century Britain and on the Trollopian day-to-day party politics of both the Church of England and the Episcopal Church in America.

The conjunction is principally achieved by reading Thomas Scandrett Harford's biography of Thomas Burgess against the *Reminiscences* of Philander Chase, and also in the light of more recent scholarship, as represented by G. F. A. Best's study of 'Church parties and charities' and William Price's *History of Saint David's University College*. Chase's *Reminiscences* (published first in serial form in 1841–4 and then in two volumes in 1847–8) provides a particularly detailed focus on the life-changing episode of the Bishop of Ohio's visit to Britain in 1823–4.

Philander Chase

Then it was that the forty-eight-year-old Chase found himself far from his family and, for the first time in his life, celebrating Christmas in London. As so often for the nineteenth-century traveller entering the greatest city in the world (indeed, *in the cosmos*, as the rural writer Richard Jefferies was to put it), the 'backwoods bishop'[2] found the experience overwhelming – and one made even more of a trial for him by anticipation of his reception: 'LONDON – a world within itself – and not a soul within its vast bosom with whom he had the least acquaintance; and what was more, none had ever heard of him but through a hostile medium.'[3] Two days before Christmas he wrote plaintively to his wife of his feelings of isolation and of his doubts concerning the outcome of this very special expedition:

> I am quite lonely, scarcely seeing any one but Mr. Pratt.[4] He called on me to-day, and manifests the same kind zeal in my behalf as ever. He told me he had a desire to get something inserted in the periodical papers; but such is the prejudice against me, and the fear of awakening the wrath of mine opposers, that I fear nothing of this sort can be done as yet. What a peculiar situation I am in! The duty I owe to the peace of our Church at home compels me to silence, though that silence seems to be my ruin. My cause is known in its merits but to few; those few all approve of my measures and desire to help me, but find insurmountable difficulties at every step. Will not a kind Providence help me, by opening some door of mercy and peace? I pray he may. I have tried to submit to my lot of separation from you and our lovely children as well as I can, but I fear I do it in a very imperfect manner. What would I give to see you and all in these lonely moments! (*Reminiscences*, I, p. 260)

While Chase's isolation was personal and domestic, in respect of 'mine opposers' (whom he is largely conscientious in not naming) it was also a matter of church politics. Uplifted by the religious experience of the season (and by Christmas dinner with Pratt and his family), he confided to his diary on Christmas night not just his troubles, but his hopes and his determination: 'Jesus, though he had not where to lay his head, by *waiting* his Father's time and pleasure, was raised to glory, and power, and might, and majesty, and dominion' (*Reminiscences*, I, p. 261). The particular allusion was not fortuitous. What preoccupied Chase was the particular place where *he* dreamed of 'laying his head': this was his proposed frontier college, back in Ohio, where he might promote the training of clergy and teachers to work in the American West. On Boxing Day he found, as he had anticipated, that the prospects of support in Britain for his project were by no means good. As his *Reminiscences* note, Chase was visited that day by the Reverend Mr Wilks,[5] who began by speaking of one of Chase's 'opposers' who had also been visiting London. This was John Henry Hobart, Bishop of New York:[6]

[Mr Wilks] observed that there was great care taken on the part of that gentleman that the intimacy which was forming between them should have a corresponding aversion to me and my object in coming to England. He said that the said gentleman left an impression on his mind that, if not a schismatic, I was a disturber of the public peace and harmony of the Church; that my object was selfish, and opposed to the great body of the Church in America; that the institution of a seminary in Ohio would be against the public law of the Convention, and be that which they would condemn; and that the General Theological Seminary had the exclusive right to say 'when and where all branch schools should be fixed,' and that, not having obtained their consent, I was opposed in my own country, and ought to be opposed in this. These were the impressions made on his mind by the conversation of my opponent, and to his knowledge the same were the impressions made on the minds of the Bishops here in England, particularly on that of the Bishop of St. David's, now in London, as I think he (Mr. Wilks) said he had from that Bishop's own mouth. 'But,' said Mr. W., 'after reflection, and the putting together a few facts, and the holding of a little conversation with others, the tide of opinion begins to turn, not only in my own mind, but in that of others.' (*Reminiscences*, I, pp. 262–3)

Chase had journeyed to Britain specifically in search of support and donations for his planned college. Ohio was the first diocese fully west of the Allegheny Mountains, and for Chase the task of founding such an institution was an automatic responsibility of his position; it was also one that gave expression to the practical evangelizing side of his outlook. However, the problems he faced were as much matters of Episcopal Church politics and metropolitan hegemony as they were of money. New York was the home of the General Theological Seminary (GTS) of the Episcopal Church (although itself founded only as recently as 1817), and Chase's idea constituted a concern to the interests vested in that fact and to the conservative-minded, who saw no need of a further seminary and certainly saw no need for one outside New York. Best makes clear that Chase was but one figure in a larger pattern of quasi-republican–federalist conflict between New York and various dioceses contemplating their own seminaries. However, the tensions between Bishops Hobart and Chase (which already had a history) were accentuated by Hobart's being both founder and principal of the GTS. Moreover, Hobart was competitively engaged in seeking funds for a permanent home for the GTS (only realized in 1827). Recognized in England as a strong High Churchman, Hobart also maintained as a matter of ecclesiastical polity the necessary primacy of the GTS.[7] Widely credited with revitalizing the Episcopal Church in post-revolutionary America, Hobart could entertain the possibility of branches of the New York seminary but not the idea of such a semi-independent body as Chase planned for Ohio. Something of this spirit is understandably still apparent in *The General Theological Seminary's* current website account of its own history:

> Although it is frequently dropped in informal reference, the tiny article 'the' in the Seminary's name is an important reminder of the institution's national origin. For the Seminary was intended from the very beginning to be a Church-wide resource for the national Episcopal Church which created it. In 1814, with American victory in the War of 1812 having brought final freedom from European entanglements, the Diocese of South Carolina, with a burst of national vision, made a proposal for the foundation of a theological institution that would belong to the whole national Episcopal Church. It was hoped the Church's general seminary would strengthen the bonds of affection among the separate dioceses because of their joint responsibility for the maintenance of one institution

of learning, and because of the intimate association that would be experienced by students from all parts of the country who came to the national school to study for the priesthood.[8]

This loyal, Hobartian characterization of the historical conception of the Seminary implicitly highlights the distance that lay between Chase and Hobart, and clarifies the significance of Hobart's frequent, apparently harsh description of Chase and his plans as 'schismatic'. (In return, though normally practising a politic restraint, Chase was not beyond reaching for the term 'papacy' to characterize what he saw as Hobart's and New York's high monopolizing tendencies.) Best records how Hobart stymied Chase's chances of support in America; ironically enough, Hobart left the Ohio bishop little option but to journey to Britain. Yet this was precisely the voyage that Hobart was making in pursuit of funds for the GTS. Hobart again warned Chase off: he declared he would have to take a different ship from Chase, and that if asked in Britain about the Ohio project he would make very clear his antagonism, just as he had done in America.[9] There was no paranoia in Chase's characterization of Hobart as a 'hostile medium'; indeed, as Best shows in some detail, Hobart's High Church friends in Britain were scorching the earth before Chase arrived and pre-emptively souring his reception.

The Bishop of St David's who, as Wilks reported, had been persuaded by Hobart against Chase's plans, was Thomas Burgess. Ironically, just the previous year, Burgess had seen eighteen years of work, planning and soliciting of donations culminate in the founding of his own 'western seminary', in the form of Saint David's College, Lampeter, in Cardiganshire.[10] Burgess had been convinced of the need for an institution that would both locally and economically meet the educational needs of a proverbially under-trained Welsh clergy by preparing them for ordination. The dilapidated state of the diocese of St David's before Burgess took charge in 1803 (both in terms of buildings and clergy) was frankly recognized in an Address presented to Burgess in Carmarthen on the occasion of his departure for the diocese of Salisbury. As the Address had it, in those days 'many of the clergy were incompetently educated, and disgraced their profession by ebriety and other degrading vices'. Bishop Jenkinson, Burgess's successor at St David's, specifically pointed to the fact that those ordinands who had previously attended only grammar schools for their training 'had often been obliged to live at inns or public houses', and had consequently been exposed to scenes and temptations quite counter to the purposes of their education. As late as 1826, the year before Saint David's College first admitted students, Jenkinson commented on his having had to exclude candidates for ordination on the grounds of their not having attended a grammar school for seven years – and in one case for sheer 'insufficiency' of education:

> I have since learned that the latter candidate, within three weeks after his rejection, enlisted as a common soldier!! Another whom I refused to admit for want of a title, has, I am told, subsequently married a woman who keeps an alehouse at Llandilo. All this shows that it is impossible to be too cautious in admitting young men to holy orders in this diocese.[11]

Clearly, if Ohio had its problems, south and west Wales had had their own. In time – and this was to be crucial for Chase – the parallel between the respective needs of the two western provinces, Wales and Ohio, proved an irony anything but lost on Burgess.[12]

Chase had come to Britain armed only with a letter of introduction to Lord Gambier ('the very dregs of religious fanaticism and faction', according to the strongly partisan High Churchman H. H. Norris).[13] After some consideration (for even he had not proved immune to the advance counter-propaganda), Gambier wrote to Chase on 29 December 1823 effectively throwing his hat into the ring: the American bishop could now make public use of the peer's name and Gambier would busy himself writing letters, making introductions and smoothing Chase's way among potential supporters (*Reminiscences*, I, pp. 270–1). Yet there remained the obstacle of the hierarchy of the Church of England, and of Thomas Burgess in particular. As it happened, Chase had a practical as well as a political reason for wanting to see the Bishop of St David's on his side. After Pennsylvania, Ohio was proving the second most attractive destination in the United States to Welsh settlers. By 1900 Ohio would be able to number some 36,000 inhabitants of Welsh stock; many of them brought the Welsh language with them.[14] Even in the 1820s Chase needed to accommodate his 'Welsh colony' (as Wilks termed it) and so on 3 January 1824 he decided to take the bull by the horns:

> I wrote a letter to the Rev. Mr. Wilks, with a view of his showing it to the Bishop of St. David's, Dr. Burgess, with whom Mr. W. said he was intimate. For Mr. W. had previously told me that this good Bishop, in his hearing, had been addressed in words very disadvantageous to the cause of Ohio, and now that his own mind had been disabused on that subject, I hoped he would take pleasure in correcting that of the Welch Bishop. Another motive of writing the letter was that of obtaining a Welch preacher, for the benefit of the people of that language who had emigrated from Wales to Ohio, and who, if attended to in time, might be retained in the fold of our primitive Church. (*Reminiscences*, I, p. 275)

At this point Chase was on the verge of departing for more evangelically minded Manchester to meet potential supporters, but, thanks to his friend Wilks, events in London now moved very swiftly. As Wilks explained to Chase:

> As the Bishop of St. David's attends the chapel in which I minister, I contrived so as to walk home with him after divine service. In doing so I mentioned the subject of your affairs. He told me that your name was familiar to him; that he had heard from several quarters what you were about, and *lately* had formed a very favourable opinion of you; – that the opposition latterly was not viewed in a favourable light, even by the members of the Bartlet Buildings Society; – that he (the Bishop of St. D.) had heard the secretary speak unfavourably of the opposition. This frank declaration on the part of the Bishop of St. David's gave me an opportunity to show him the letter which I had received from you. He read it with much interest, and said he would endeavour to find the man you wish. 'I will write,' said he, 'to my *rural dean*, who is acquainted with the country people, and if such a man as the Bishop of Ohio wants is to be found, he shall be forthcoming.

Pray may I keep this letter of Bishop C.'s, and send it to Wales?' (*Reminiscences*, I, pp. 276–7)

Burgess, known for 'withholding institution from all who were not competently skilled in the language of their parishioners', was certainly the man to approach in this respect (*Life of Thomas Burgess*, pp. 361–2). This spirit would be preserved in the curriculum of Saint David's College: William Price notes that when the Reverend Rice Rees of Llandovery was appointed as the third member of staff at the college, at the age of 22, his was the first Chair of Welsh in any college.[15] (For his part, Burgess doubtless saw such linguistic competence as essential in contesting the inroads being made into Wales by Unitarianism.)

Following Wilks's conversation with him, Burgess was quite ready to call on Chase in person, but with Chase committed to his journey to Manchester, Wilks urged the American bishop to waste no time and to join a party calling on Burgess that very evening. At 11 p.m. on Monday 5 January 1824 an excited Bishop Chase was back in his lodgings and recalling for his diary his first impressions of Burgess and the for him momentous events that had taken place:

> We found a venerable, but very intelligent gentleman, with a small, snug wig, black, old-fashioned, long-waisted coat, and Bishop's silk cassock. He received us without the least unnecessary ceremony, seated us, and ordered coffee, which being before him, he, doing just as our ladies do in America, poured it out and handed the cup across to us as we sat around the fire. The primitive simplicity and godly sincerity of this very learned gentleman immediately took possession of my heart's best affections, and in a few minutes put me at my ease, and induced, in answer to his judicious and pertinent questions, a very free conversation.

Luckily for Chase, Burgess 'never allowed names of contumely to prejudice his mind, a priori, against any individual' (*Life of Thomas Burgess*, pp. 340–1). In short, Burgess had indeed changed his view of the Ohio project. And he had done so for the very good reason that what Chase was trying to do in the

American West was precisely what Burgess had been doing in west Wales. As Chase reported Burgess's observation that evening:

> If you are a schismatic I am such, for I am establishing a school for the education of ministers in Wales, although Oxford is comparatively so near. If this is required in this country, where the distances are so little compared with America, how much more forcibly can you urge the necessity of a school for the education of young men for the ministry in Ohio! (*Reminiscences*, I, p. 278)

The parallels between the locations of Saint David's College (with its three acres of the Castle Field) and Kenyon College (to be set in thousands of acres of virgin forest) can be overstated – even though it was once said of Rowland Williams, an early and distinguished Vice-Principal of Saint David's College, that 'he went to Lampeter in the same spirit in which Bishop Heber went to India'.[16] However, the symmetry of relationships between centres and margins in their respective countries was in principle by no means dissimilar, and in relative terms the sites of the two colleges had much in common; John Scandrett Harford observed of the Lampeter site: 'The situation is healthy, and the view which it commands beautiful, extending over the vale of Lampeter and the windings of the Tivy, and surrounded by a fine range of lofty hills' (*Life of Thomas Burgess*, p. 311). Henry Caswall, a student from England at Kenyon in 1828 (and a relative of Burgess's[17]) wrote home that, in the case of Bishop Chase's foundation:

> The College now stands upon a beautiful hill a few hundred yards north of Owl Creek and 6 miles east of Mount Vernon. From the top of the college is an extensive view of many miles, but nothing is seen except the almost interminable forests of the country, which extend for hundreds of miles every side. The trees are most majestic.

Admittedly, he also added: 'The wild animals are numerous; there are three kinds of bears, 2 of which are very fierce; there are likewise many wolves. The rattlesnakes are innumerable.'[18] Such differences of fauna, however, failed to mask the essential similarity of the two bishops' projects. No wonder Chase recorded of Burgess that he was now 'delighted with this excellent Bishop' (*Reminiscences*, I, p. 279). To his joy, Chase now began to make more converts to the Ohio project. Objections in the press, notably in the *British Critic* (in May and June 1823), were subsequently reversed, and a meeting of the London Clergy resulted in both a statement of the case for the seminary (a copy of which was sent to Burgess) and the setting up of a subscription fund, to be administered under Lords Gambier, Kenyon and Henry Hoare as trustees. Chase gained a particularly enthusiastic supporter in the form of George Wharton Marriott, shortly to be collated Chancellor of the diocese of St David's and as early as 1813 a man to whom Burgess had referred as 'my oldest and best friend' (Life of Thomas Burgess, p. 300). This was fortunate, because gaining the particular support of Burgess appears to have been crucial in extending support for Chase beyond a strictly evangelical base. In April 1824, hearing from Marriott that Burgess was about to arrive in London from Durham, Chase duly hurried to see the Bishop of St David's that very evening:

> We found him sitting in his modest chair, neatly but plainly dressed, with his books and papers before him. He received me in a friendly manner, and entered warmly into my cause: said he was happy to learn that the opposition, for which he had never seen any reason, had been withdrawn: that he had subscribed five pounds some time ago to Mr. Wheaton, and now would contribute ten guineas to Ohio: that he would thank me to send him a dozen of the Appeals, and he would see that they were communicated to the Bishops: that *he had no doubt of my success*. This opinion, as the event proved it to be, might be set down as *prophetical*. (*Reminiscences*, I, p. 329)

Chase was delighted but slightly bewildered by the prophetical Burgess's new confidence on his behalf. The inner machinery of British power, influence and society still remained something of a mystery to him, and even now he could reflect grimly that 'all London was prepossessed against him' and that 'the prelates of the Church of England and all their friends, excepting as above [that is, Burgess], were of this opinion, and viewed the writer as a factious schismatic' (*Reminiscences*, I, p. 329). One consideration that helped sway British opinion in Chase's favour was the story that began to be disseminated of how, back in America, Bishop Chase had freed a slave of his. In 1824 the slavery debate was in full flow in Britain, and Chase's reputation in this context endeared him to many (such as the abolitionist John Scandrett Harford) and must certainly have reinforced Thomas Burgess's revised sentiments about him; many years previously Burgess had published a pamphlet in which he had made his own thoughts about slavery, with particular reference to the West Indies and America, abundantly clear. Burgess was now clearly taking the diplomatic initiative among the Church of England hierarchy, unsurprisingly beginning with Shute Barrington, the ninety-year-old Bishop of Durham and Father of the Bench of Bishops, the prelate whom Burgess had served as chaplain during his own appointment to the Diocese of Durham – and friend of the philanthropist Hannah More (whom Chase would later visit in person).[19] In 1821 Barrington referred in correspondence with Burgess to 'the cordial friendship which has subsisted between us [Barrington and Burgess] for thirty-five years' (Life of Thomas Burgess, p. 317). In consequence, as Chase recorded, the Bishop of Ohio and the Bishop of Durham duly met at Burgess's Upper Montagu Street residence:

> I showed him the map of the western states, and pointed out the waters of the Mississippi. 'And your plan is to found a seminary for the supply of this vast country with Christian ministers, according to our primitive Church?' 'The same, my Lord,' said I. 'It is good,' said he; 'I like you and your plan, and I hope to hear more of both.' (*Reminiscences*, I, p. 343)

This was a conversion, for Barrington had already been approached by Hobart's British supporters, but Burgess had doubtless known that there were particular reasons why Barrington could be swayed towards Chase's plan. In another context, John Scandrett Harford observed:

> The existence of a branch of the Church in England in our remaining North American Colonies is very much to be ascribed to the influence and exertion of Bishop Barrington. In

1786 his lordship drew up a very valuable and able paper, entitled 'Thoughts on the Establishment of the Church of England in Nova Scotia'.

Following the American Revolution, Barrington had argued the case for an Anglican seminary to be set up in Canada, an institution that was duly inaugurated in 1788 and granted a charter in 1802 (Harford, p. 394). While Chase's British opponents tended to cast the institution in Nova Scotia as having first claim on any support from the Church of England, Barrington himself, poring over maps of Mississippi, may have discerned an echo of his own earlier ambitions. He took the more adventurous line. One by one, Chase found access to members of the Church of England hierarchy opened for him: for one reason or another, the Bishop of London withdrew his opposition; meetings followed between Chase and the Archbishops of York and Canterbury: both agreed to subscribe to the Ohio cause. While Chase thanked God for these apparently miraculous changes of heart, he also had the practicality to thank Burgess. Contact between Burgess and Chase continued through Chase's stay in Britain. On 12 May 1824, for example, Chase recorded:

> Dined to-day with the venerable Bishop of Durham; present, the Bishop of St. David's, and the two Mr. Duncans, of New College, Oxford. The conversation was at once learned, pious and cheerful; at times like the majestic flow of a deep river, strong and peaceful;at others, more swift, exhibiting the transient rainbow sprays of wit and humor. (*Reminiscences*, I, p. 365)

Chase's stay in Britain was greatly darkened by news of the death of his ailing son, also named Philander, but as far as his plans for Ohio were concerned, his anxious Christmas of 1823 must now have seemed far in the past. New subscribers included Lady Rosse, who gave a hundred pounds; Hannah More, a generous contributor to Saint David's College, would become a substantial subscriber. In the West Country Chase received an invitation to dine at Blaise Castle from John Scandrett Harford. Perhaps needless to say, Thomas Burgess was also among Harford's guests:

There were present at Blaise Castle on the occasion referred to, 1st July, the following persons – Lord and Lady William Somerset, the Bishop of St. David's, Sir Thomas and Lady Acland, Rev. Mr. Trevelyon, Rev. Mr. Gray, Mr. Gray, Sir Edmund C. Hartopp, Mr. Grove, Mr. and Mrs. Harford, the Bishop of Ohio, the Dean of Bristol, and Mr. Harford Battersby. To describe an afternoon and evening spent in such company in England, would be to write a book. The good Bishop of St. David's seemed, when on the subject of the Ohio claims, to open his heart and pour forth his good wishes without measure. The conclusion of one of his sentences to the writer was a blessing most fervent. 'May God bless you in this work!' said he: 'may God bless you in all you think, in all you say, and in all you do!' (*Reminiscences*, I, p. 404)

Harford claimed that this meeting of Burgess and Chase was entirely fortuitous, but at the same time he highlighted how others began to understand and relish the parallelism, under such different circumstances, of the two bishops' projects:

In June 1824, [Bishop Burgess] paid a visit to the author at his residence in Gloucestershire, and by a happy but fortuitous coincidence, the American Bishop of Ohio, Dr Chase, together with Sir Thomas and Lady Acland, and part of their family, were at the same time assembled under his roof. Many neighbouring friends joined the party on the day of their arrival; and few of them will easily forget the lively interest which all felt in witnessing the meeting, in a place so remote from the metropolis, of two Bishops presiding over sections of the Church of Christ in such opposite hemispheres, both men of primitive and devout feelings, both also, at that very time, engaged in furthering the erection of a college for clerical education; the one for a diocese, comprehending nearly the whole of South Wales, the other for the vast and semi-cultivated province of Ohio, in North America. They were themselves no less gratified by this unexpected meeting. (*Life of Thomas Burgess*, p. 355)

A little later the 'urbane and tolerant' Harford would be present at a meeting at the chapter-house of Bristol Cathedral where a sum of two hundred pounds was donated to Chase's cause.[20] On 8 July 1824, Burgess wrote to Harford from the Bishop's Palace at Abergwili:

I had allotted yesterday for an excursion to Lampeter, but was prevented by the rainy weather. Today there is an amendment in the wind and the barometer, therefore I hope soon to get a sight of St. David's College. [. . .] Pray be so good as to add Mrs Burgess's name to Mrs Harford's list of guinea donations towards a printing press for Bishop Chase, which, if you will pay for me, I will repay you when we meet.' (*Life of Thomas Burgess*, p. 358)

Such was Chase's success, in no small part thanks to Burgess and his circle of lay friends, that on American Independence Day 1824 Chase could announce to his wife that he now planned to return to Ohio, though not without musing on the ironies of his having received so much support for his plans from 'foreigners', when he had encountered so much coldness at home. The British Fund had risen to £5,000 by the time of Chase's return to the United States, a sum equivalent to the initial government grant to Saint David's College. (By this point Bishop Hobart had attempted to muscle in on Chase's financial success and had even come to terms over the status of Chase's college.) As Chase was to express it in an address to the 1825 Convention at Zanesville, Ohio, 'though on the bosom of the tempest which surrounds us, British benevolence has painted the rainbow of hope' (*Reminiscences*, I, p. 449).

As the date for Chase's departure neared, there were many affectionate farewells to be taken, particularly in respect of Lords Kenyon and Gambier, whose names would be enshrined in the title of the new college and in the name of the settlement in which it was located. Kenyon also knew of the Lampeter project, as Marriott reported to Burgess: 'Lord Kenyon writes me as follows: – I am very glad [Bishop Burgess] is so well pleased with the appearance of his College and trust that, by the goodness of God, he will be spared many years to witness and to contribute to its prosperity' (*Life of Thomas Burgess*, pp. 454–5).

On 12 July 1824 a letter was being written to Chase from John Scandrett Harford, donor of the Castle Field in Lampeter, where Bishop Burgess's own seminary of the west, Saint David's College, that parallel 'spiritual oasis in the desert', was still being built and awaiting its first students. But Harford was talking about progress with the Ohio subscriptions:

> Our subscription amounts at present to about two hundred and forty pounds. Mrs. Harford has more than collected the twenty guineas. Mrs. Burgess, the Lady of the Bishop of St. David's, has sent her a message to add her name to the list. We are taking means to promote the subscription in Bristol, by means of a printed circular, with a list of subscribers, and a short but forcible appeal annexed to it. [. . .] I presume you have already written to Lady William Somerset. Her direction is Frenchay, near Bristol. I desired several newspapers, containing our Bristol list of subscriptions, to be forwarded to you by Saturday's post. (*Reminiscences*, I, p. 413)

At Christmas 1824, Chase made sure to take time to write to Thomas Burgess:

> My VERY DEAR LORD BISHOP OF ST. DAVID'S.
>
> I never reflect on my visit to Old England but with gratitude to God and good-will towards men. What I heard there instructed me; what I suffered there, I trust, has made me better. God was gracious unto me, and gave me favor in the sight of those whom, by every book, precept and line in my education I had been taught to admire and love, the sound and pious of the Church of England. Among the most excellent of such, I must ever, with great veneration, rank your Lordship; and if this is not said in so courtly a manner as might be, I entreat that its sincerity may plead its apology and make amends for its roughness.
>
> I remember every instance of your Lordship's goodness to me with great delight. It was in your Lordship's eyes I first read that there was favor amongst the British prelates for Ohio; it was your Lordship who introduced me to the father of the English bench of Bishops; and it was your Lordship who so solemnly and in such plenary terms blessed me, in the name of the Lord, at Blaise Castle. God hath indeed blessed me, according to that prayer, ever since your mild eye beamed on me. [. . .] Several places offering very liberally to contribute in lands and buildings, provided the contemplated seminary can be placed in their vicinity, the convention have appointed a

committee to receive all proposals of that nature, and report at the next June convention, when the question as to where the seminary will be established will be finally determined.

In the mean time the act of incorporation is to be obtained of the civil legislature, and I am to do what I can to get together a few students with whom to commence with some promise. One teacher is already with me, and a few, say from eight to ten, scholars, will constitute our incipient school. Another teacher will be with me in June, and we humbly hope to succeed; but it must be a work of great labor, and time, and patience. (*Reminiscences*, I, pp. 428–9)

Two days later, across the high mountains and on the other side of the Atlantic, on Christmas night 1824, Marriott penned a letter to Chase that indicates, even more pointedly, how the connections that Thomas Burgess had fostered in founding Saint David's College had in turn rallied to support Kenyon College. To such as the Burgesses, the Harfords, Sir Thomas Acland and Hannah More one may also add the name of the Bowdler family, donors of the Tract Collection to Saint David's College and now exercising a similar generosity towards Ohio:

You will also, I trust, soon receive a parcel of books for the future seminary, which the eldest son of the late excellent Mr. John Bowdler, the donor of the chapel sacrament plate, has made up for this purpose. The parcel will contain a memoir of his father, and some engravings of English worthies, whose example may be useful to excite your disciples of a Protestant Episcopal seminary to imitation. I intend to solicit one of the venerable Bishop of Durham: you have already got one of the Bishop of St. David's. Their two names stand first on the pocket sacrament plate, and their veneration for you justifies the compliment which will thus be paid to them. (*Reminiscences*, I, pp. 435–6)

The image of Bishop Burgess, it was evidently hoped, would look down on future students from the walls of Kenyon College, as he has done from the walls of what is now University of Wales, Lampeter. John Bowdler, indeed, had left Chase a 'large set of communion plate [. . .] viz., a flagon. Two chalices, two patens, and collection plate' (*Reminiscences*, I,

p. 421). And back in England even Lord Kenyon could report the continuance of Burgess's support and interest:

> The dear good Bishop of St. David's (Dr. Burgess) I have seen several times lately. He is, thank God, quite well, and busy as ever in endeavoring to fulfil his every duty. He showed me your kind letter to him, which he highly prizes, and talked of you with true affection and regard. I wish we could send you some clergymen to relieve you in your duties, which must be overpowering. God grant you may have a supply. (*Reminiscences*, I, pp. 440–1)

A little later Marriott reported to Chase the news of Burgess's movement to the diocese of Salisbury:

> Bishop Burgess' translation to Salisbury, on the death of Dr. Fisher, has led to such public testimonies of the reverence and affection felt for him by his Welsh clergy as are hardly to be paralleled in any period of the history of the Church. I enclose you the Carmarthen address, which you will delight to peruse, and read to others. I fear that I must request it may not be published. I trust that the well-deserved laurels which adorn his brow may operate usefully on all other Bishops, and especially his successors in St. David's.

Marriott added a postscript that suggested that the transatlantic traffic in spiritual strength between Wales and Ohio was by no means one-way:

> PS I have just opened a letter from a South Wales clergyman, to whom I sent a copy of yours to Lord K[enyon]. He says, 'I have transcribed the whole of it, with the view of showing it to my friends in the diocese of St. David's, and becoming perhaps the humble instrument in promoting in some small degree the pious designs of the apostolical American Bishop, in our poor principality. May his truly Christian exertions be crowned with every success, is my sincere wish and humble prayer!' (*Reminiscences*, I, p. 454)

Information and letters from Ohio in fact readily circulated in Burgess's circle. While Saint David's College found half of its initial intake of students stemmed from local farming families,

Burgess must have been delighted by this account, through Marriott, of student recruitment in Bishop Chase's diocese:

> I write chiefly to tell you the substance of a most interesting recent communication from Bishop Chase [. . .] He has been a visitation of more than 800 miles, on one horse, this autumn, and was solicited, in the course of it, to visit a tribe of Oneida and Mohawk Indians, who were said to be well disposed to the Church. He went with the aid of a guide, who introduced him to the Chiefs. From them he learnt that they had long been in possession of our Liturgy published in London in 1787, in their language, and that the Elders of the tribe used it in morning and evening services every Sunday. They also administered Baptism, and lamented this as a great irregularity, from which they much desired to be relieved by an authorised Ministry. The Bishop preached to them through an interpreter, and chose five of their most intelligent young men for gratuitous education at his College, hoping finally to ordain them. What a delightful instance of his persevering zeal, of the value of his Diocesan Seminary in the extension of the true Church, and of our Liturgy! With its aid these poor Indians were able to form themselves into something like a Christian Body, and are quite ripe for the benefits of a regular Church. (*Life of Thomas Burgess*, pp. 458–9)[21]

The traffic from Burgess's erstwhile diocese of St David's included one particularly tangible contribution, in the form of the Reverend John Herbert. Chase's felt need for a Welsh tutor had been a major consideration in his first approaching Thomas Burgess at all. By meeting the Bishop of St David's Chase had gained so much more, but the presence of John Herbert in Ohio may well yet be shown to constitute evidence of a very practical response on Burgess's part. Sadly for Herbert, however, his appointment to Kenyon College was his last. When Bishop Chase addressed the Episcopal Convention in September 1830 he referred to four new graves in the College Cemetery (although he hastened to add that the climate of Ohio had played no part in those deaths). One grave was that of the wife of the Professor of Greek and Latin; two were of students:

> The fourth and last grave, which you see in the college burying-ground, is that which covers the body of the Rev.

John Herbert, late of the Diocese of St. David's, in Wales, where he was ordained to the Christian ministry by the Rev. Dr. Burgess, now Lord Bishop of Sarum. He came to us in great simplicity and godly Sincerity, with full intention of doing good to the Christian cause. He was appointed tutor in our college, and, so far as his feeble health would allow, discharged his duty well. As a Christian, he lived exemplarily; and although his death was unexpected, even by himself, yet we have great consolation in believing him now among the faithful in Paradise. (*Reminiscences*, II, p. 58)

In the course of time, Chase was himself translated from Ohio to the diocese of Illinois. By all accounts, those around him felt that he might have raised himself a little too much by way of 'power, and might, and majesty, and dominion' in his authoritarian control of the management of Kenyon, and in due course he resigned his position. A different diocese now faced him, but with essentially the same problems of supplying clergymen and teachers for the needs of the expanding west. His answer – of course – was to found another college. In this enterprise (Jubilee College) he was to meet with less success than in the case of Kenyon, and the new college was eventually to fail; but his tactics echoed his previous labours. To Britain he must go, and in 1835 he revisited familiar scenes, although now changed by intervening deaths and altered circumstance in the lives of many on whom he might otherwise have hoped to call. Among those missing faces were such as had fostered the two seminaries of the west at Lampeter and Gambier – and most missed was Burgess:

He looked around for his friends and warm supporters. But alas! many of them could no more be seen. George W. Marriott, Esq., of queen's square, who so kindly had sought him out in No. 10 Featherstone buildings, had died and was sleeping by the church of good Mr. Bowdler, with this Christian inscription on his tomb: '*Blessed* are the dead that die in the Lord'. That heavenly-minded prelate, Bishop Burgess, once of St. David's, and then of Sarum, who so sweetly smiled on the writer when the whole nation was frowning by reason of false reports, was now no more to be seen. Not meeting with this most learned and best of men, and warmest friend, was a heavy blow to one who needed a pillar to rest on now more than ever in his life; for there was something in the character of this most estimable prelate that united innocence with discernment, and fearlessness with most perfect suavity. Surely the writer found it so when the Bishop of St. David's, Dr. Burgess, was the only prelate who stepped forward to speak in favor of the writer amid the obloquy which was heaped upon him from New York. He did this to the Bishop of Durham, saying that 'if Bishop Chase were condemned for endeavoring to found a theological seminary in Ohio, he himself must be equally censured for founding one in Wales.'

Burgess in fact lived until 1837, but by 1835 he was extremely ill and had effectively 'passed away' into 'a state of inability and suffering that forbade all useful intercourse'.

The interwoven narrative of the founding of Saint David's and Kenyon colleges testifies to the energies of two singular men who each recognized the singularity of the other, and who came together with conviction, understanding, warmth and great practical strength. If such as Kenyon, Gambier and Wilberforce gave Chase access to the resources of evangelical Christianity, Burgess facilitated Chase's approval and support by the less party-bound members of the Church of England hierarchy (while Norris and Hobart doubtless fumed). The narrative also provides a remarkable insight into Burgess's mountain-moving network of supportive relationships, including such mediators as Marriott, and of course John and Louisa Harford and their Bristol set, which he made freely available to Philander Chase. This is the more interesting for the fact that in 1823–4 Burgess's own project was still short of funds to complete building; Saint David's College would teeter through its early days from one financial crisis to the next. Had Burgess protected his circle of philanthropic contacts, Lampeter might have gained by Kenyon's loss, but Burgess was no dog in the manger: 'I well remember, on a particular occasion, that on my strongly commending any of [Burgess's] many generous acts, his reply was, "As to money, I regard it as no more than dirt, when an important object calls for support"' (*Life of Thomas Burgess*, p. 327). The narrative also testifies to that nineteenth-century ardour for education that was prepared to move beyond the metropolitan. Marriott put it this way in a letter to Chase in 1826, shortly before 'the blessed institution' of Saint David's College admitted its own first students:

> You must have heard that the Church is profiting, as in so many parts it has lately done, by the spirit of *education* which characterizes our age. At Edinburgh, an Episcopal college is in the course of being established, and Bishop Jolly has already devoted his extensive theological library to its use, forever after his death, as good Bishop Burgess has his, to St. David's college. By-the-bye, that blessed institution (the greatest boon, I believe, that any English or Welsh Bishop ever gave to his diocese, and which led the venerable founder to say, 'Bishop Chase is just as much a schismatic as myself') has just commenced its operations, and takes in, at one time, (in the very heart of a diocese of almost unexampled extent, and peculiarly destitute previously of the means of clerical education,) seventy-five students, at the expense of fifty pounds per annum, for each. I trust that you have long ago received, what I know you will highly value, both for its own and for the Right Reverend donor's sake, the engraving for the college, which the Bishop sent you through my hands. I saw the original last summer, and the engraving might have done *much more*, without an iota of flattery. (*Reminiscences*, I, pp. 501–2)

That particular gift to which Marriott referred generates a final footnote to the narrative. Tom Stamp notes that Bishop Chase himself participated in the architectural design of Kenyon College, and that:

> We know from his writings that Chase had fallen in love with Gothic architecture, which was closely associated with Christianity, during his time in England, when he visited the colleges of Oxford University and numerous cathedrals [. . .] Chase chose the style, as he would later at his Jubilee College in Illinois, to emphasize ties with England and the English church.[22]

The aesthetic environment in which Bishop Chase found himself when he became caught up in the Burgess–Harford circle was one that, through Blaise Castle and Saint David's College, Lampeter, promoted the Gothic.

Saint David's College, Lampeter

Kenyon College, Ohio

Historians of Kenyon College have long been amused by the tale that when Kenyon started to rise, there were anxieties in the locality that the British had returned and were building a fort. At least to the untrained eye, the original plan for Kenyon seems particularly haunted by the image of Saint David's College. Steeples apart (a particular enthusiasm of Chase's) – and the matter of an odd storey – there is much in the planned Gothic design of Old Kenyon that echoes the Gothic quadrangle of what is now the St David's Building at Lampeter. Both were to have particular problems with the construction of their wings, and Old Kenyon, when built, was, in the event, to be much changed from its original design. (It was also destroyed by fire in 1949 and subsequently rebuilt.) Nevertheless, it is hard to avoid the inference that Chase's aspirations for the aesthetic appearance of his college were significantly influenced by his conversations with Harford and with the Bishop of St David's – not to mention that 'engraving for [Saint David's College]' from 'good Bishop Burgess' that pursued Philander Chase back across the Atlantic to Ohio.

Notes

1   Though founded earlier, the University of Wales, Lampeter only celebrated the 175th anniversary of its first admission of students in 2002–3. Kenyon, admitting students in its year of foundation, was ahead of Lampeter in this respect, thanks to its greater hardiness in temporarily embracing a log farmhouse as Bishop's Palace, hall of residence and lecture room.

2   G. F. A. Best, 'Church parties and charities: three American visitors to England, 1823–4', *English Historical Review*, 78 (1963), 243–62, (244). I am grateful to Peter Nockles and Nigel Yates for drawing my attention to Best's study.

3   Philander Chase, *Reminiscences: An Autobiography*, 2 vols, 2nd edn (Boston, 1848), II, p. 225. Further references to this work are given in the body of the text. Kenyon houses a project under the editorship of Andrew Richmond to give online access to Chase's writings. The collection includes 'over two thousand manuscript letters, nearly one hundred manuscript sermons, two journals, two editions of [the Reminiscences], as well as over one hundred other publications (including pamphlets, circulars,

and addresses) which Chase authored over the course of his life'. *http://www2.kenyon.edu/khistory/chase/project/*.

4   Josiah Pratt, Rector of St Mary Woolnoth and Secretary of the Church Missionary Society. See Best, 'Church parties and charities', 234.

5   C. S. Wilks, 'editor since 1817 of the *Christian Observer*, "the most popular and useful religious publication in the world"': Best, 'Church parties and charities', 254.

6   See Frederick S. Arnold, 'Bishop John Henry Hobart', *American Church Monthly*, 41 (1937), 23–30.

7   'His chosen position was "Evangelical truth with Apostolical Order"': Arnold, 'Bishop John Henry Hobart', 30.

8   'Our Heritage of Service.' *http://www.gts.edu/catalogue/heritage.pdf*.

9   Best, 'Church parties and charities', 249.

10 An early published reference to Burgess's project occurs in the appendix to his biography ('Thomas Lord Bishop of St David's, and Prebendary of Durham') in *Public Characters of 1809–10* (London, 1809), pp. 1–27, 586: 'This worthy prelate [. . .] has actually laid the foundation of a Provincial College, to qualify young clergymen of the establishment, for the Welch church. To attain this object, his lordship has appropriated a tenth of his revenues, during life, and all his beneficed clergy have added their contributions, to a meritorious institution which has, for its objects:
    1. The purchasing, printing, and distributing of moral and religious tracts;
    2. Clerical education and exhibitions;
    3. Building and establishing a clerical seminary; and
    4. The relief of superannuated curates.'

11 John Scandrett Harford, *The Life of Thomas Burgess D.D.* (London, 1840), p. 385. Further references to this work are given in the body of the text.

12 Chase also 'wanted to remove his students from the influences of cities and villages where there were "persons who find it in their interest or malicious pleasure to seduce young men from their studies into vice and dissipation". He found his ideal location, "a retreat of virtue from the Vices of the World," on top of beautiful Gambier Hill.' Thomas B. Greenslade, 'The history of the College', *http://www.kenyon.edu/publications/studenthandbook/history. pdf*.

13 Best, 'Church parties and charities', 250.

14 'Why do Welsh names seem to be so common within the African American community?'
http://www.data-wales.co.uk/plantations.htm.
15 William Price, *A History of Saint David's University College Lampeter: Volume One: To 1898* (Cardiff, 1977), pp. 36–8.
16 Price, *Saint David's University College I*, p. 47
17 I am grateful to Peter Nockles for this information.
18 'Exhibit Hall: Slide 25', *http://www2.kenyon.edu/khistory/ch ase/exhibit/earlyknoxcounty/slide25.htm.*
19 Anne Stott, *Hannah More: The First Victorian* (Oxford, 2003), *passim.*
20 Stott, *Hannah More*, p. 313.
21 Chase's account of these events occurs in *Reminiscences*, I, p. 457–60.
22 Tom Stamp. 'The Kenyon campus at 175: how it grew', *http://www1.kenyon.edu/crc/pa/175th/howitgrew/03.phtml.*

9

State Churches and Diversified Confessionalization in Scandinavia[1]

ANDERS JARLERT

Background

In the Nordic countries, the Reformation led to a transformation of the papal Catholic Church into national Lutheran churches. They played an important part in the forming of a national identity and culture. Their developments were not identical. The Danish Reformation was much more 'German' in its character than the Swedish one, which kept more medieval customs and a higher esteem for episcopacy, including the preservation of the historical apostolic succession. While the main point was national independence of Rome, Norway lost its former ecclesiastical independence, and became totally dependent on the Danish sovereign.

From the point of ordinary people in the provinces, being a Lutheran, in all the Scandinavian countries, became a practical and cultural matter more than a doctrinal one, since no alternative faith was possible, and taking part in Lutheran church life was a common duty. Doctrinal errors were interpreted not only as false belief, but also as a threat to national or local Christian unity. While Denmark had an important period of state pietism (1730–60), and a limited religious liberty had been opened to Jews as early as 1682, the severity of the Swedish religious statutes was further intensified in the 1730s. The new, restricted tolerance towards Catholics and Jews in Sweden, from the 1780s onwards, was practised in only a few cities, and since ninety per cent of the population in 1810 still lived in rural areas, most people had never encountered any 'foreign' believer. During the nineteenth century, this setting was challenged and changed.

Part IV of the 1996 report of the joint meeting of British and Scandinavian church historians, held at the University of York in 1995, dealing with the 'long' nineteenth century, was titled 'Religion and National Identity', and an extensive 1998 volume with articles from all the five Nordic countries was dedicated to 'Church and Nationalism in the Nordic North'. In the study of the state churches of Scandinavia, *nationalism* has been the dominating concept for a long time, but during the last years other aspects as well, such as secularization and confessionalization, have been emphasized in the international debate.

A second confessional age

The nineteenth century has often been called an 'age of secularization'. An important reason for this is the lack of historiographic understanding of the meaning and significance of religion that has permeated a large part of twentieth-century academic research. In later years, its critics have spoken of a 'blindness of religion'. Theorists of modernization have taken their self-evident starting-point in a continuing increase of secularization since the early modern period. From the point of ecclesiastical history, it is especially important to observe the complexity of the situation, with strong religious forces of defence provoked by secularization, emphasized by the German historian Hartmut Lehmann as 'rechristianization'.[2] These forces did not only emanate from traditions, but also brought forth a new traditionalization of church life,[3] and created profiled anti-cultures.[4] The German theologian Friedrich Wilhelm Graf has – in a somewhat incendiary wording – stated that the secularization concept mirrors a dogmatism in modernization theory of high resistance to empirism.[5] Other designations for the nineteenth century have been the 'Age of Liberalism' or the 'Bourgeois Age'. But still it is obvious that the 'long' nineteenth century showed an unusual mobilization of the Christian religion as a driving force in different areas of society, as well as on different social levels.

In its original concept, the first confessional age refers to the period of confirmation of the confessional split of the Reformation, in Germany up to 1648. In Scandinavia, it lasted longer, especially in Sweden, where the Church Code of 1686, or even the Sacramental Code of 1735, may be regarded as its peak.

With his idea of the 'long' nineteenth century as a second confessional age, the German historian Olaf Blaschke has suggested a new interpretation of German church, society and culture. Significant elements of this process are a new uniformity of church life, an increasing clericalization, and the professionalization of the clergy.[6] Such elements are easily recognized in the Scandinavian churches as well. A clericalization is obvious even in revivalistic, anti-clerical circles, in the establishment of employed, full-time lay preachers. And in Sweden, academical studies in theology were not made compulsory for ordination until 1831.

Though the rechristianization of the nineteenth century started in a harmonizing way, under the influence of Romanticism and across confessional borders, it was soon characterized by sharp confessional antagonism. Blaschke speaks about the super-confessional euphoria in the years around 1800.[7] But, as in the first confessional period, relations between the different positions were soon to be made clear through their conflicts. Blaschke describes confessionalization as a 'wave', rolling over society, carrying with it 'the demon of confessionalism'.[8] His point is that *confession* is much more than a short chapter in history books, and that a certain 'blindness of confession' has prevented us from understanding the importance of confessional culture. He explicitly states that his concept does not have to expand to a new paradigm – it serves as an explanation, and is only one decisive motive or force among others.[9]

Confessionalization makes belonging to a specific confession an important part of the everyday culture of ordinary man.[10] Though *confessionalization* is a much broader, cultural concept than confessionalism, it is simultaneously a more specific concept than *rechristianization*.[11] This implies, of course, nothing like a dominance of confessionalism, but a rather complicated struggle between secularizing and confessionalizing forces, as described by Hugh McLeod in his *Secularisation in Western Europe, 1848–1914*. Confessionalism is only one important feature of the second confessionalization, a part that should not be overemphasized, as has sometimes been the case with Blaschke himself, and certainly very often, and in an exaggerated way, with his critics.[12] Confessionalization does not at all times imply a confessional conflict, but always implies a cultural division. Still, the term confessionalization remains slightly ambiguous – just like secularization, rechristianization and other actual designations.[13] To abstain from their use would, however, be still worse.

Hugh McLeod has successfully introduced the idea that pluralism, and not only secularization, was the result of the victory of tolerance, and he finds the balance between religious and secular forces to be characteristic of western Europe up to the 1960s.[14] McLeod is especially observant of how things were before secularization. With examples from Germany, he states that:

> the idea that *everyone* should be attending church regularly seems only to have become widely accepted in the early nineteenth century – partly under the influence of the evangelical movements of the time, and partly because of fears that the irreligious were potential rioters or radicals.[15]

It may be questioned if a common attending of church services ever succeeded in the whole of Scandinavia. It certainly did not in the far north, with its long and difficult journeys to churches, but neither did it in the south of Sweden, where services were not held in every parish every Sunday during the darker part of the year, but sometimes only every third Sunday.[16] The Swedish historian Göran Malmstedt has stated that individual, intellectual listening, motivated by the Lutheran confession, did not gain its popular breakthrough until the Schartau revival in the second and third decades of the nineteenth century.[17] This implies that the confessional ideal to a great extent was realized only during the second confessional age. In his dissertation, *Change and Identity*, Erik Sidenvall analyses what I would call a diversified confessionalization – after the first nationalistic reactions to John Henry Newman's conversion, the Roman Catholic Church was gradually accepted as yet another English confession.[18]

Because of his emphasis on the nineteenth century as a *second* confessional age, Blaschke has been criticized for identifying the church struggles of the nineteenth century with those of the sixteenth or seventeenth century. His answer has been that, in speaking of the First and Second Enlightenment or the First and Second World Wars, the intended meaning is not that history repeats itself.[19] In the German Lutheran sources of Scandinavian theology, no longer *Rechtgläubigkeit*, but *das Sonderbekenntnis der Konfessionen* was emphasized. 'Confessionalism' succeeded 'orthodoxy'.[20] As Nicholas Hope has shown, Lutheran ecclesiology was emphasized in the mixed confessional situation in Livonia.[21] In Scandinavia, the second confessional age is certainly not a repeat of the confessionalization of the seventeenth century.

Other critics have turned against Blaschke's wide concept of confession, especially his use of 'Protestantism' as a whole, which, from a Scandinavian view, certainly seems to be a rather German Catholic perspective, since the gap between Lutheran and Calvinist theology had been emphasized in Scandinavian Christian teaching since the sixteenth century.[22] This point was stressed further in the nineteenth century, when not only Reformed principles of organization, but Reformed theology as well, formed a distinct Free Church culture from the middle of the century.

Church historian Martin Friedrich has asserted that the confessionalization of state and society in the nineteenth century was only a 'broken' one.[23] However, this is a matter of qualification, and I cannot see that Blaschke's concept has any 'total' claim. With my own idea of a *diversified* or *manifold confessionalization*, it is obvious that the second confessional age – in contrast to the first one – had precisely a 'broken' character.

On the other hand, I cannot see why a more narrow definition of *confession* would change the whole concept. Friedrich emphasizes that the idea of mediation is contrary to confessionalization,[24] and indeed it is, from a strict theological angle. But the idea of mediation can, of course, in itself construct a confessional position, just as, for example, plain biblicism with explicit repudiation of any creed can form a rather profiled confessional platform. Martin Friedrich has suggested that the nineteenth century could be described as the era of *Kirchwerdung* ('churchification') – obviously a more limited concept – and the response from Blaschke has been that whether this remains a partial process in the confessionalization, or whether it is the decisive category, is open to question.[25] When applying Blaschke's concept to Scandinavia, I will try to make it clear that confession in this broad, cultural sense is *wider* than the Church, it can be applied on more levels, and it opens our understanding for the importance of confessional identities and mentalities formed also by religious societies or even formally unorganized religious movements – identities that carried a cultural importance to its so-called 'neighbours' or 'grandchildren' as well.

I will explore Blaschke's ideas, applying them to the various developments in Scandinavia, trying to combine them with Hugh McLeod's ideas of pluralism and a balance between religious and secular influence as characteristic of the western European development, with special attention to nationalism and conversion.

This connects also to the continuing movement in the sociology of religion from the old secularization paradigm to an emphasis on religious change, an altered view that in Sweden has been emphasized especially by the sociologist of religion Göran Gustafsson.[26] In modern religion, José Casanova has observed a 'deprivatization', defined as 'the process whereby religion abandons its assigned place in the private sphere and enters the undifferentiated public sphere of civil society to take part in the ongoing process of contestation, discursive legitimation and redrawing of boundaries'.[27] This view is relevant to the historical study of the nineteenth century as well, since it questions the previously reigning concept of privatization as secularization. According to Casanova, the development of the 1980s showed 'the revitalization and the assumption of public roles by precisely those religious traditions which both theories of secularization and cyclical theories of religious revival had assumed were becoming ever more marginal and irrelevant in the modern world'.[28]

Among Scandinavian historians, Hanne Sanders from Denmark has connected to John C. Sommerville, who has described secularization as 'the change of a religious culture into religious belief' or to 'a distinct part of culture'.[29] The label 'secularization' for this change is questioned by the diversification concept. Sommerville's observation works, rather, as a description of 'confessionalization' that directs our attention towards the development of several parallel religious or secular cultures, often overlapping one another.

However, we have to consider that the religious pluralism of the nineteenth century was something quite different from the religious pluralism of the twenty-first century. We have to study nineteenth-century pluralization on its own conditions, not just as a more or less anachronistic explanation to twenty-first-century pluralism.

Diversified or manifold confessionalization

As developed by Hugh McLeod, the secularization problem must be studied in several areas. McLeod has stressed six of them: individual belief; formal religious practices; the place of religion in public institutions; its part in public debate; its significance as an aspect of identity; and its relationship with popular culture. In his study of England, France and Germany, he has found the clearest evidence of secularization in the first two areas, concerning individual activity, whereas the results in the public areas were more mixed, and in the fifth and sixth areas, of identity and popular culture, the evidence for secularization was much less.[30] There are also wide national and geographical variations. McLeod states that if one of the possible ways of 'telling the story' of religion in modern western Europe is to be given pride of place, it should be not secularization, but pluralism.[31]

Increased religious pluralism may – as the Swedish theological migration researcher Eva M. Hamberg has emphasized – lead to different effects in different phases of a historical development.[32] Pluralism does not necessarily lead to secularization. I find the construction of a gap between pluralization and confessionalization rather unnecessary and perhaps even somewhat superficial.

It might seem as if Olaf Blaschke would place *pluralism* – in its German sense of dissolution or disintegration – only in the post-confessional era.[33] Others have found that pluralism was to become the initial position in a more and more liberal society, and have emphasized 'pluriformity' as significant to the disparate tendencies in the paradigm shift from *l'ancien régime* to a modern society.[34] While *pluralism* in McLeod's concept is used as a characterization of a whole period (including both confessionalization and secularization), I will use *diversified* (or *manifold*) in a more limited way as a description of one variation of confessionalization.

As an introduction to the sixth volume of the new history of the Swedish Church, dealing with the years 1810–65, I have contributed a chapter called 'The century of Luther reading'. In 1817, the very first Swedish Luther centenary was celebrated. Before then, only the centenaries of the political/religious 'liberation' of King Gustavus I and of *Confessio Augustana* had been celebrated.[35] During the nineteenth century the writings of Martin Luther were translated, published and read to a hitherto unprecedented extent in Sweden, often used in a polemical way between combatants in matters like lay preaching, baptism of children or anti-clericalism. Actually, several of Luther's criticisms of the Catholic priests in Germany of his time were not translated until the nineteenth century, when this was done with allusion to the present Lutheran clergy of the Church of Sweden.[36] Some anti-Jewish sermons from the sixteenth century, also of German origin, were simultaneously translated for the first time, without any explicit reflection on the fact that the homiletic situation had changed, with the existence of a Jewish population in Sweden. All this nineteenth-century use of Martin Luther did create, in some circles, varying forms of a new Lutheran confessionalism, but in much wider circles it contributed to a new confessional culture, where not only the Lutheran catechism and hymns, or Lutheran theology, but the actual, pugnacious way of arguing in a confessional language, expressed 300 years earlier by Martin Luther, suddenly acquired contemporary relevance and importance in a quite different context. Luther could be used against the new Prayer Book of 1811 and the new catechism of the same year, and against the new hymn-book of 1819. Instead of the old uniformity, parishes were allowed to keep the old hymn-book of 1695, and some did, even up to the very last years of the nineteenth century. Still, a strong uniformity, with new confessional motivations, was kept in the liturgy. Proposals for freedom to use the liturgy of 1693 for baptisms or common confession were repeatedly rejected, with strong, popular protests in the north of Sweden in consequence. Thus, the diversified confessionalization of nineteenth-century Sweden can be understood only in the framework of old ecclesiastical uniformity with new confessional motivations.

I find *diversified confessionalization* to be one of optional possibilities, just like *dualistic confessionalization* (the German model in Blaschke's original concept) or *monistic confessionalization* (which, of course, has nothing to do with theological or philosophical dualism or monism). However, as we already have seen, these three dimensions of confessionalization do not exclude each other. The example of Norway may clearly show this.

In Norway, diversified confessionalization was a matter mostly inside the state church, organized in various Lutheran missionary and Home Mission societies. Sociologian Pål Repstad even states that in Norway, within the framework of the state church, 'religious pluralisation has been the main pattern in the last two centuries'.[37] And yet we must be reminded that Jews were not allowed to settle in Norway until 1851 and Jesuits not until 1956, and that full religious freedom was not established there until 1969. Here, the mostly conservative missionary societies, in their own pietist way, for a long period strengthened the confessional Lutheran character of the country. This became clear, not least in the first half of the twentieth century, in their continuing tensions with the liberal or modernist Lutheran theologians; hence the two theological faculties in Oslo, the State faculty and the Norwegian Lutheran School of Theology, both underlined the importance of the Lutheran confession, though interpreting it in different ways. These inner Lutheran tensions reveal that while Norway on the level of practical tasks and the organization of laymen's work was very diversified, theology was for a long time rather dualistic, and all this within the monistic confessional framework of the Lutheran state church.

In Denmark, the tension between the two distinct confessional cultures of Grundtvigianism and Home Mission started in opposed theological views, different ways of preaching and so on, but gradually built up two distinct cultures with different schools, different insurance companies, different shops and so on, as a remarkable parallel to the different confessional cultures in Germany. The significance of these different cultures was sometimes taken from matters of Christian teaching, such as the special Home Mission's dairies being closed on Sundays, while some, such as different colours of working trousers sold in different shops, attached to different Christian traditions, were only secondary consequences of the shop-owners' confessional identity.[38] In its Scandinavian adaptation, the most important point of Blaschke's concept is its deep understanding of the new confessional culture of the nineteenth century.

In Sweden, a discussion on the Lutheran Articles of religion versus the Bible was inaugurated by the young theologian Peter Wieselgren in 1827. In a pamphlet on the question of which was the religion of Sweden, he distinguished two different forms of religion, the biblical one and the symbolical – that is, the confessionalist – one. Since the continuing debate was part of the discussions on Church Statutes and Church Law, much of it was later concentrated on the extent of the Lutheran Articles of religion – whether to stick to the directions of the Church Law of 1686, with the Formula of Concord of 1577 as an authorized explanation of the earlier Lutheran Articles of religion, or to harmonize the Swedish confessional position with the Danish and Norwegian one, where only the *Confessio Augustana* and Luther's Small Catechism were prescribed. Not until 1893 was the later position defeated. This led to an unparallelled popular circulation of the Lutheran Articles of religion, in a new edition of 1895. In some parishes in the diocese of Gothenburg, more than 500 copies were distributed. It is not known if more than some parts of the book, such as Luther's cathechisms and the *Confessio Augustana*, were also read by laymen to any greater extent, but the effort certainly is to be labelled as a very ambitious form of popular confessionalization.

Confessionalization may be observed in many areas, as when the Swedish bishops tried to replace the old quarterly communion, collectively organized by villages in annual semesters, by a continuous system with a communion service every third to ninth week.[39] These strivings can be explained, not as pietist fervour, hardly as expressions of a conscious individualization, but as confessionalization: to make Holy Communion an ecclesiastical practice, not primarily a social custom, and to let it become a recurrent moment in church life even in small parishes. Another significant feature in confessionalization is what in English church history of the 1840s is known as the growth of party. In his much-debated book on awakenings and church parties in Denmark, Professor P. G. Lindhardt emphasized the appearance of the awakening movements from the 1860s and onwards as church parties as a consequence of social development, with its political parties and class antagonisms.[40] The extensive building of new churches may also be interpreted as part of the confessionalization process, and the development of foreign missions can easily be described as a confessionalization, where pluralization or Christian competition was magnified, in an often strange way.

Up till 1860, Swedish citizens were not permitted to resign from the Church of Sweden in order to transfer to any so-called foreign religious denominations, and until 1859 a child of parents belonging to the Church of Sweden could be baptized only by its parish priest. Church members were not allowed to go to Holy Communion anywhere but in their parish church – except in cases of emergency. The common duty of an annual communion was not abolished until 1863. Until that year, communion was necessary for entering into matrimony, for admission to official positions, for burgher rights and academic exams, as well as for witnessing in court. The change meant, of course, a secularization of society on a formal level, but at the same time a confessionalization of communion attendance as such. This is a process distinct from the parallel process of privatization. It may have had secularizing effects on large groups of individuals, but it must not be labelled *only* as secularization.

A parallel change appeared in the reading of public announcements from the pulpit, a custom that had been institutionalized during the first confessional age, in the seventeenth century, and was gradually limited in 1849, 1875, 1894 and 1917, to be finally abolished only in 1942 and 1947. This decline may be labelled as a secularizing phenomenon – the Church was not so important in society any more, though it was mostly the clergy who criticized the pulpit announcements, especially during the seventeenth century, and again from 1818. The change in 1849 meant that the reading was moved to the end of the service.[41] Thus, the religious character of the service was strengthened, which is a clear sign of confessionalization.

The religious bourgeois culture of the later part of the nineteenth century may be judged as secularization or as confessionalization – or, rather, as a combination of both. The German historian Thomas Nipperdey has emphasized that listening to Bach's *St Matthew Passion* or Wagner's *Parsifal* is two steps of distance away from the traditional Christian celebration of Good Friday.[42] On the other hand, while the bourgeoisie in Stockholm during the largest part of the nineteenth century had listened to Haydn's *Creation* every Good Friday, in the 1890s this was replaced by works like Bach's *St Matthew Passion* and the *Seven Words* by Schütz, music that did not try to escape from the ecclesiastical address of the day, but interpreted it.[43] This was clearly a cultural manifestation of confessionalization, which renewed the values of ecclesiastical convention, though at the same time it confirmed the establishment of a cultural alternative to traditional worship.

When included in the Russian Empire in 1809, Finland was transformed into an autonomous nation within this Empire. The attitude of the Russians varied between great liberty and brutal enforcement, and shifted with the different emperors and their differing political attitudes. Owing to the Russian supremacy, the country had two state churches, the Lutheran majority church and the very small Orthodox minority church. This meant on the national level a clear dualistic confessionalization, though in 1892, when a separate Finnish Orthodox Church province with its own archbishop was established, still only about 60,000 persons, or less than two per cent of the population, belonged to the Orthodox Church.[44] In the Lutheran

Church, the awakening movements, while opposing each other, strengthened the common confessional framework.

The Finnish Dissenter movements of the 1850s differed from the dominating Lutheran culture. Like the corresponding movements in Sweden, they regarded the Church as founded from below, on the religious character and individual activity of its members.[45] This meant the construction of a different confessional position, but since the quantitative support for the Anglo-American Dissenter movements, in contrast to Sweden, remained very limited,[46] the confessional culture in Finland was kept in its traditional framework: dualistic at a national level, and diversified within the Lutheran Church at a popular level. Thus, the consequences of the first law of Protestant Dissent, in 1889, were rather insignificant.[47]

Up to the later part of the nineteenth century, Scandinavia saw no religious competition comparable with that in England or Germany. The distinguishing label 'Church of Sweden' did not appear in Swedish law until 1860, in the first law of Dissent.[48] That indicated a new situation of competition and the start of a new form of confessionalization, the diversified one.

Diversified confessionalization and state churches

The state churches in the Scandinavian countries may from the outside seem to have been very much like each other. With the exception of the Orthodox Church of Finland, they were all Lutheran, and despite their various differences in defining the Lutheran confession, and their varying views on historical episcopacy, their theological foundations have been rather similar. However, the development of church–state relations in the nineteenth century went in quite different directions, and to explain and understand this development, the concept of diversified confessionalization may have an illuminating function.

To get a realistic picture of the actual church–state relations, we must observe not only how these relations were organized on a national level, but also how they were revealed on a local level. This is clear already from the popular phrase, that we may talk about the Church of Sweden, the Congregations of Denmark and the Christians of Norway.

In the Church of Sweden, the bishops and dioceses had had a strong, independent position since the end of the Reformation struggles. But it was an independence intertwined in state politics. Up to 1865 the Clergy constituted a separate estate in parliament, and several church leaders played important political roles over the centuries. At the local level, the independent peasantry voted in the parish meeting, under the presidency of their vicar, in matters both secular and ecclesiastical.

The debate on church–state relations was closely linked to the discussions on the organization of the church on other levels. Especially important are the different suggestions of more lay influence in the parishes, suggestions motivated primarily by the Christian responsibilities of the laity, and a refining and concentration of local church work to the Christian commission of the church, something that is significant to the second confessional age.

Church–state relations changed seriously in Sweden with the new legislation of the 1850s and 1860s. The parishes were 'secularized' in 1862, which means that new local councils were established for common purposes, while separate church councils at the local level were to deal with ecclesiastical matters only. In 1865, the Parliament was 'secularized' – the medieval four-estate system was replaced by two publicly elected houses, elected in an indirect and a direct way, respectively. Still, these 'secularizing' reforms had clear confessionalizing effects. The demands for an abolition of episcopacy, raised eleven times in parliament in the first half of the century, suddenly ceased, though a few of the bishops still played important political roles as elected members of parliament. The plans for an independent Church Synod could finally be realized, and at the local level the clergy were more and more considered as representatives of the church in social contexts.

In Denmark, full religious freedom was granted as early as in the Constitution of 1849, at the same time emphasizing that the Lutheran Church was the national so-called People's Church (folkekirke). Freedom to attend any church or use the services of any clergyman within the People's Church was launched in 1855, but the extension of individual religious freedom was not combined with any greater ecclesiastical freedom on the regional or national level. Since those years, Denmark has kept its significant combination of a strongly regulated state church and individual religious freedom. Since religious freedom had already been introduced by law, the parallel and gradual development of religious freedom and loosening church–state relations, so significant to Sweden, never became relevant in Denmark. The state church was democratized along with the state, and not – as in Sweden – by its own institutions.

A startling liberty was provided at the local level, with the dioceses as a rather weak middle–level in between. The Danish system might seem to be totally monistic, if it is observed only from the national level, but at a local level it is obvious that both the rights of the parishes (or, rather, the congregations) and those of the individuals imply that the system was much more diversified when regarded from this side. In 1868 a law, made permanent in 1873, granted twenty families in a parish the right to constitute a *valgmenighed* (gathered congregation) around a clergyman of the People's Church. He was recognized by the state and under episcopal supervision, but the congregation paid all the costs.[49] This liberty facilitated the appearance of a dualistic confessional pattern at the local level, with distinct local cultures of Grundtvigian or Home Mission colour. These confessional cultures were clearly connected to the church–state relations, since it was the congregational system at a local level that made it possible for two distinct confessional groups to have their own separate congregations, schools and so on within the same church fellowship. Thus, we encounter a strong, diversified confessionalization at the local level of organization, within a common, monistic state Lutheran framework at the national level.

Recent research has underlined the importance of confession to identity. Hugh McLeod has emphasized the history and context of one's own tradition: French Protestants and English Nonconformists were, from their early childhood, conscious of their descent from martyrs and that they were a minority group – even among children. This created a special attitude towards authorities: 'they were very "law-abiding"', but their role-models were 'radical people who were prepared to give up things in order to do what they saw as the will of God'.[50] This could be an apt description of the mentality in separatist groups, like the Swedish Covenant Mission Church, as well.

According to the first Norwegian Constitution of 1814, the Lutheran religion was to continue as 'the public religion of the state'. Significant to the continuing development is that Norway, despite the union with Sweden, was hardly affected by the Swedish changes in church–state relations. Diversification developed, not in the parishes as such, but in the many missionary societies that organized laymen's work in the parishes.

The Lutheran Church in Finland was guaranteed a considerable amount of inner freedom by the Church Law of 1869; on a popular level, the Finnish development of the continuing nineteenth century, with its strong awakening movements, led by the clergy within the Lutheran Church, meant a diversified confessionalization in theology, as well as in popular tradition and lay organizations.

As Lars Österlin has pointed out in his book on Anglo–Nordic relations, the most remarkable aspect of the developments was that the Home Mission societies and evangelical revivalism remained almost entirely within the framework of the Lutheran state churches of Denmark, Norway and Finland, whereas in Sweden the conflict became much more radical, with large groups of evangelicals forming their own denominations.[51] These denominations created a new, alternative confessional culture and a Free Church mentality that still, in the twenty-first century, is an actual reality in Sweden. A theological answer from the Church of Sweden to the great challenge from the Free denominations, and their claims of having the only congregations organized according to the New Testament, was a still heavier emphasis on the historical, national Church as a divine institution. But in Sweden, the *folkkyrka*, a word of somewhat later origin than the Danish *folkekirke*, never got any popular acceptance as a designation for the Established Church. Consequently, a popular definition of state church in Sweden has been 'non-Free Church', especially 'without Free Church mentality'. In present times, when sociologists speak about the Roman Catholic church as the biggest Free Church of Sweden, or about the Church of Sweden as a Free Church since its separation from the state in the year 2000, on a popular level this is pure nonsense, since the Free Church is defined more by its mentality than by its actual model of organization.

An important prerequisite for this was the severe legislation on religion of the 1720s and 1730s, and the conflicts about the new Prayer Book of 1811. In particular, the new liturgy of baptism and its mixture of promise and moralism was criticized from a strict Lutheran standpoint among the so-called new readers in the north of Sweden. In the critical interpretation of these readers, children were baptized not into the covenant of Christ, but into the covenant of Moses. Of more serious importance to the ecclesiastical unity was their criticism of the new liturgy of common confession and absolution, and their wish to return to the old, more orthodox, order. Since taking part in this separate service was compulsory for communicants, the result sometimes became separatist, private communion services. This had purely doctrinal reasons, but the consequences were social. To arrange separatist communion services was to question one of the most important foundations of the local community. The separatists turned the social order upside-down, which paved the way for diversification, and some of the separatists later became Baptists.

Just like the differences between Roman Catholics and Protestants in Germany, or between Grundtvigians and Home Mission people in Denmark, the differences between a state church awakening mentality and a Free Church revivalist mentality in Sweden may be explained only partly from theological differences. This is exemplified by the different use of religious images in private homes. Catholic motifs of German origin, such as the heart of Jesus or the Virgin Mary, were never used in Free Church homes, but could be present in more or less pietist homes within the Church of Sweden, together with pictures of Luther and Melanchthon, as well as photographs of ministers in the parish. In Free Church homes, images were accepted gradually, and they were, preferably, biblical scenes. Another difference is revealed in the placing of images. In Lutheran homes, religious images were placed in the bedrooms, for the personal edification and instruction of their residents, while pictures of Luther and clergymen found their place in the living room. In Free Church homes the attitude to image-placing seems to have been more ambivalent, with an increasing emphasis on religious images in the living room, as an evangelizing act of confession.[52]

Other examples are found in doctrinal motivations for ethical differences. Not only did the Free Church mentality include a religiously motivated teetotalism, but a state church awakening mentality, with certain other pietist elements, could include a moderate consumption of spirits as a religious duty, to avoid self-righteousness and self-made regulations.[53]

Confessionalization could be implemented by individualizing revival movements, but it could also be promoted by quite opposite endeavours. Just as leading Catholics on the Continent did not want any Roman Catholic to become a Protestant, so the bishops of the Church of Sweden did not encourage any of its members to leave the church for other denominations recognized by the state. A somewhat illogical position was held by the Roman Catholic Church, claiming freedom of religion on a liberal basis in countries with a Protestant majority, without accepting this liberty in Catholic countries.[54] The notorious expatriation from Sweden of six female converts to the Roman Catholic Church in 1858 was, on the other hand, used by various groups of liberals, evangelicals and radicals to create a new and more 'progressive' Protestant identity in Sweden, critical of state church legislation.[55]

Confessionalization and nationalism

In the reshaping of the Scandinavian map from 1809 to 1814, the Swedish province of Finland was lost to Russia, though with a certain amount of independence in home affairs, and Norway was released from Denmark and forced to enter into a rather loose union with Sweden. In two of the countries, Finland and Norway, there consequently was much debate about what it meant to be a Finn or a Norwegian, respectively, and about the meaning of being a nation. A cultural nationalism was created from the 1830s onwards.[56]

In Finland, a national mentality from the 1850s was closely linked to the Lutheran clergy, and to the awakening movements. Finnish researchers speak of the 'fennomanization' of the clergy. In contrast to the former, official use of the Swedish language and the increasing use of the Russian language, the use of the Finnish language, an emphasis on the new-found

Finnish cultural identity, and Finnish Lutheranism were united. The church was regarded not only as the church for the Finnish nation, but also as an expression of the religious character of the Finnish people.[57]

Thus, Finnish confessionalization was closely linked to nationalization, with Lutheranism as the significant Finnish religion, while the Orthodox religion at that time was regarded as Russian. The diversified confessionalization, on a theological and popular level, within the Lutheran Church strengthened the national front-line. In the last decades of the nineteenth century, the Orthodox religion was used by Russian authorities as an important symbol of Russian nationality, and the Lutheran religion became a stronghold of Finnish nationalism as well.[58]

In Denmark, Nikolai Fredrik Severin Grundtvig and his exceptionally strong emphasis on the Apostolic creed and the 'living' word of God exemplifies another variant of confessionalization. The whole Grundtvigian culture, with its views on nation, history, church and people, its church hymns and folk-songs, its schools on different levels, and its wide cultural visions and ambitions, may be regarded as one of the most extensive efforts to confessionalize a whole nation during the second age of confessionalization. And still, the ideal Danish imagined community, in the words of Benedict Anderson, is not the somewhat more abstract 'nation', but the people, the 'folk'.[59] The actual phrase 'state church' has not been much used in Denmark, and never found popular acceptance. The emphasis is totally on the *folkekirke* or People's Church, like the Danish emphasis on *folk* in designations in many other areas of life, for example, in schools (*folkeskole*) and parliament (*folketinget*).

The first Norwegian attempts to link nation and religion came from the followers of the Danish theologian Grundtvig, but there was no breakthrough of national religiousness until the Union conflict in 1905, when the union with Sweden was dissolved and Norway got its full independence. The mainstream of theology and church life had separated from the national and democratic movement, and withdrawn from the political arena: 'Christianity and nationality were seen as competing identities.' The exception was the national religious outburst that followed on the break-up of the union. Here, national religion served the purpose of unifying the people and legitimizing the new government.[60] Though the union between Sweden and Norway had had almost no effects on theology and church life in these countries, the break-up of the union inspired national religious movements, such as the Young Church movement in Sweden.

In Sweden, the concept of nation at the cultural level gradually became a substitute for the church. Religion was nationalized, and made into an ideology.[61] This change of emphasis from confessional culture to national culture was partly inspired by the Swedish philosopher Christoffer Jacob Boström, who – around the middle of the nineteenth century – stated that the state was the highest form of church, and that the church was the state constituted in its religious guise.[62] Within the Church of Sweden, the Young Church movement from 1907 onwards launched the nationalist vision of the Swedish people as a Christian people, partly as a religious response to theological modernism, partly as a reaction to the Free Church claims of having the only real Christian congregations. Instead of the old confessional state church concept, we got the theological vision of a national People's Church, but with different accents from the Danish *folkekirke*. It could have been named a 'nation-state church'. In the words of the Swedish theologian Kjell Blückert, 'the nation became the highest form of church'. This led to a process of 'inner secularization' in the Lutheran Church of Sweden, which was parallel – though not identical – to the secularization of the Swedish state.[63] When Olaf Blaschke says that nationalism was not able to pacify the tumult of the confessions, he is clearly right, but when he states that nationalism was split by confessionalism,[64] this is somewhat complicated in the case of Sweden. The differences between state church and Free Church did have hardly any splitting effects on nationalism, though the Young Church Movement tried to monopolize the national language, not least in historiography. Simultaneously, the common anti-Catholic attitude from both state and Free Church excluded Roman Catholics from the national heritage and fellowship. Thus, the second confessional age was not over with the victory of nationalism, but the national element became dominant at the expense of pluralism.

On another level, this shift may be observed in the altered regulations on national registration. Since the end of the seventeenth century, national registration had been identical to the pastoral records of the Church of Sweden. The law of Dissent from 1860 allowed the so-called foreign denominations the right to keep their own pastoral registers as civil registration. This authority was used by Roman Catholic and Jewish congregations. It may be regarded as an example of diversified confessionalization. However, this diversified system was sometimes questioned, and in 1910 it was finally abolished. A new uniformity was introduced, followed by the secularization of the legislation of marriage in 1915.[65] The point is that the return of all pastoral registration to the Church of Sweden meant no confessional strengthening of this Church. The new uniformity meant no reconfessionalization. It is, rather, an example of the 'inner secularization' of the Church of Sweden, where the pastoral registers were instrumentalized to be, first and foremost, registers for common interests.

In Finland, the situation was quite the reverse. Here, the pastoral records of the Lutheran Church and the Orthodox Church, respectively, acted also as national registration after the national breakthrough, and in 1917, following the Russian Revolution and the Finnish declaration of national independence, these were completed with a civil registration that, at least partly and in a limited respect, worked as a third confession.

Confessionalization and conversion

If we are looking for a significant keyword of nineteenth-century Scandinavian church history to explain some of the religious dynamics in the confessionalization process, something of a sign of the times, it should be *conversion*. To the Roman Catholics, individual conversion became essential to their transition from an exceptional body of foreigners into a church with Scandinavian members, recognized by the state. Thus, conversion was a condition for the involvement of the Roman Catholic Church in the confessionalization. To the Jews, on the other hand, conversions remained a continuing problem, since emancipation was reachable, more or less, only, or at least in the easiest way, by way of conversion to Lutheranism. Here, confessionalization became a way to avoid further conversions, since diversified confessionalization meant recognition and acceptance without conversion. With the neo-orthodox Lutherans, conversion was emphasized as a daily and life-long personal project in the Church, often in sharp contrast to the Methodist concept of a sudden life-changing experience. These two different concepts of conversion formed two opposite, confessional mentalities, each of them in opposition to the popular, half-secularized mentality of being a Christian only by baptism, correct church attendance and a certain moral behaviour, without any conversion at all. In these different definitions and attitudes to conversion we approach consequences such as proselytism and other reactions on different levels. And to the great project of foreign mission, conversion was, of course, the main breach-point between church-founding missionaries, with conversion as a long-lasting pedagogical project, and evangelizing activities concentrating on sudden individual conversions.

If individual conversion is significant to the second confessional age, aversion and de-conversion, so typical of conversion processes of the nineteenth century, could even be applied as a general pattern in the whole second age of confessionalization. According to John D. Barbour, de-conversion has different variations, with four common characteristics: denial of the truth in a system of faith; moral criticism of the way of living; emotional revolution; and rejection of one's former fellowship.[66] The convert will be marked for life by his or her earlier religious experiences. This is made visible in that partly ambivalent attitude to his former context that is revealed in 'the converting work of interpretation'.[67]

Here we encounter some of the most important contrasts to the first age of confessionalization, where aversion towards other confessions had been as strong as in the second confessional age. In the latter, individual conversion became an actual possibility, either as a change of confessional belonging, or as a personal change within the same confessional body. Aversion led to deconversion, and confessionalization to pluralization.[68] Like the first age of confessionalization, the second one was, from the point of ordinary people in everyday life, a practical and cultural matter, more than a doctrinal one, but on that level it was much more dramatic, diversified and questioned than in the former period.

Notes

1   Paper presented at the Fourth Colloquium of CIHEC at the University of Exeter, 23 July 2003, produced with support from the Bank of Sweden Tercentenary Foundation.
2   Hartmut Lehmann, *Von der Erforschung der Säkularisierung zur Erforschung von Prozessen der Dechristianisierung und der Rechristianisierung im neuzeitlichen Europa*, in *(Säkularisierung, Dechristianisierung, Rechristianisierung im neuzeitlichen Europa. Bilanz und Perspektive der Forschung.* Hg. Hartmut Lehmann. (Göttingen, 1997), p. 13.
3   Olaf Blaschke, 'Das 19. Jahrhundert. Ein Zweites Konfessionelles Zeitalter?' In *Geschichte und Gesellschaft*, 26, Jg. 2000 / Heft 1 Katholizismusforschung, 44.
4   See, for example, Yvonne Maria Werner, *Kvinnlig motkultur och katolsk mission. Sankt Josefsystrarna i Danmark och Sverige 1856–1936* (Stockholm, 2002).
5   Friedrich Wilhelm Graf, 'Dechristianisierung. Zur Problemgeschichte eines kulturpolitischen Topos' in Hartmut Lehmann, *Protestantische Weltsichten. Transformationen seit dem 17. Jahrhundert* (Göttingen, 1998), p. 62.
6   Blaschke, 60 ff.
7   Ibid. 63, Olaf Blaschke, 'Der "Dämon des Konfessionalismus"'. Einführende Überlegungen, *Konfessionen im Konflikt. Deutschland zwischen 1800 und 1970: ein zweites konfessionelles Zeitalter* Hg. Olaf Blaschke. (2002), 19.
8   Olaf Blaschke, 'Vorwort', in *Konfessionen im Konflikt*, p. 8.
9   Olaf Blaschke, 'Der "Dämon des Konfessionalismus"', p. 66. 'Konfessionsblindheit' is quoted from Dieter Langewiesche, Nation, Nationalismus, Nationalstaat: Forschungsstand und Forschungsperspektiven. In: NPL, Jg. 40, 190–236, quotation 216.
10 Blaschke, 'Der "Dämon des Konfessionalismus"', p. 20, quoted from Heinrich Richard Schmidt, Konfessionalisierung im 16. Jahrhundert (1992), XI.
11 Hartmut Lehmann, Säkularisierung, Dechristianisierung, Rechristianisierung im neuzeitlichen Europa. Forschungsperspektiven und Forschungsaufgaben (Säkularisierung,

Dechristianisierung, Rechristianisierung ... Hg. Hartmut Lehmann. 1997), p. 315. However, I do not understand confessionalization to be so specific as Lehmann does.

12 Especially by Helmut Walser Smith in the *GHI Bulletin*, vol. 25 (2003), 105.

13 See Martin Greschat, 'Anmerkungen aus deutscher protestantischer Sicht', in Hartmut Lehmann (ed.), *Säkularisierung, Dechristianisierung, Rechristianisierung im neuzeitlichen Europa* (Göttingen, 1997), 81.

14 Hugh McLeod, *Secularisation in Western Europe, 1848–1914* (London, 2000), pp. 287, 289.

15 Ibid., p. 88.

16 Anders Jarlert, *Romantikens och liberalismens århundrade, Sveriges kyrkohistoria*, 6 (Stockholm, 2001), p. 64.

17 Göran Malmstedt, *Bondetro och kyrkoro. Religiös mentalitet i stormaktstidens Sverige* (Lund, 2002), p. 195.

18 Erik Sidenvall, *Change and Identity: Protestant English Interpretations of John Henry Newman's Secession, 1845–1864*, BHEL, 44 (Lund, 2002).

19 Blaschke, 'Der "Dämon des konfessionalismus"', p. 34.

20 Holsten Fagerberg, *Bekenntnis, Kirche und Amt in der deutschen konfessionellen Theologie des 19. Jahrhunderts* (Uppsala, 1952), p. 24.

21 Nicholas Hope, *German and Scandinavian Protestantism 1700–1918* (Oxford, 1995), p. 482 ff.

22 See Lars Österlin, *Churches of Northern Europe in Profile. A Thousand Years of Anglo-Nordic Relations* (Norwich, 1995), p. 110 ff.

23 Martin Friedrich, Das 19. Jahrhundert als 'Zweites Konfessionelles Zeitalter'? Anmerkungen aus evangelisch-theologischer Sicht (Konfessionen im Konflikt ... 2002), p. 98.

24 Ibid., p. 107.

25 Blaschke, 'Der "Dämon des konfessionalismus"', p. 34, Friedrich: Das 19. Jahrhundert ..., p. 111.

26 Göran Gustafsson, Tro, samfund och samhälle. Sociologiska perspektiv (1997), ch. XII.

27 José Casanova, *Public religions in the modern world* (1994), p. 65 ff.

28 Casanova, *Public religions*, p. 5.

29 John C. Sommerville, 'The destruction of religious culture in pre-industrial England', in *Journal of Religious History*, 15 (1988), 77.

30 McLeod, *The Secularization of Western Europe*, p. 285 ff.

31 Ibid., p. 287.
32 Eva M. Hamberg, 'Utbud och efterfrågan på religiösa "marknader"' (Religion och sociologi. Ett fruktbart möte. Festskrift till Göran Gustafsson. Red: Curt Dahlgren, Eva M. Hamberg, Thorleif Pettersson. Religio 55. 2002), 139 ff.
33 Blaschke, 'Der "Dämon des konfessionalismus"', p. 26.
34 Kjell Blückert, *The Church as Nation. A Study in Ecclesiology and Nationhood* (Frankfurt, 2000), p. 112.
35 See Carl Axel Aurelius, *Luther i Sverige. Svenska Lutherbilder under tre sekler* (Skellefteå, 1994).
36 Jarlert 2001, ch. 2.
37 Pål Repstad, 'Religious power in a pluralist society. The difficulties of governing denominations as sects' (Religion och sociologi . . .), 237.
38 Blaschke, 'Vorwort', p. 7; Margaretha Balle-Petersen, Det andliga storskiftet. Om väckelse och vardagsliv i Danmark (Väckelsen och vardagslivet. Västsvensk väckelse ur nordiskt perspektiv). (1995), 47, 53.
39 Frances Knight has observed an equivalent shift from quarterly communion in favour of a monthly service in the Church of England after 1830, see Frances Knight, *The Nineteenth-Century Church and English Society* (Cambridge, 1995), p. 80 ff.
40 P. G. Lindhardt, *Vaekkelser og kirkelige retninger i Danmark* (København, 1951), 105 ff.
41 Elisabeth Reuterswärd, 'Nyheter från predikstolen', in Kyrkohistorisk årsskrift 2002, 38 ff., 41 ff. Cf. Elisabeth Reuterswärd, *Ett massmedium för folket. Studier i de allmänna kungörelsernas funktion i 1700-talets samhälle* (Lund, 2001); Bill Widén, *Predikstolen som massmedium i det svenska riket från medeltiden till stormaktstidens slut* (Åbo, 2002).
42 Thomas Nipperdey, *Religion im Umbruch* (1987), p. 141.
43 Leif Jonsson and Martin Tegen, 'Musiklivet privat och offentligt', *Musiken i Sverige. Den nationella identiteten 1810–1920* (1993), 188, 122 ff.
44 Mika Nokelainen, 'The Orthodox and the Lutherans in Finland 1809–1923', in Ingmar Brohed (ed.), *Church and People in Britain and Scandinavia* (1996), p. 303.
45 Eino Murtorinne, *Finlands kyrkohistoria. 3, Autonomins tidevarv 1809–1899* (Skellefteå, 2000), p. 222.
46 Ibid., p. 224.
47 Ibid., p. 251 ff.
48 Lars Eckerdal, 'Om Svenska kyrkan som trossamfund'. Svenska

kyrkans beteckning, bestämning och benämning i svensk lagstiftning, in Kyrkohistorisk årsskrift (1988).

49   P. G. Lindhardt, in J. L. Balling and P. G. Lindhardt, *Den nordiske kirkes historie. Fjerde omarbejdede udgave* (København, 1979), p. 231.

50   McLeod, *The Secularization of Western Europe*, p. 219 ff.

51   Österlin, *Churches of Northern Europe*, p. 224.

52   Anders Gustavsson, 'Religiösa bilder inom väckelserörelser', *Meddelanden från Kyrkohistoriska arkivet i Lund* 18 (Lund 1984), 3–7. Cf. Blaschke, 'Der "Dämon des konfessionalismus"', p. 52 ff.

53   Katarina Lewis, 'Måttlighetsidealet inom schartauanismen', *Kulturforskning kring alkohol i Norden. Föredrag vid ett nordiskt symposium i Uppsala.* Red. Anders Gustavsson (Uppsala, 1993).

54   Yvonne Maria Werner, *Världsvid men främmande. Den katolska kyrkan i Sverige 1873–1929* (Uppsala, 1996), p. 91 ff.; Blückert, *The Church as Nation*, p. 113.

55   Erik Sidenvall, 'Tolkningen av "katolikmålet" 1858 i ett internationellt perspektiv', in *Kyrkohistorisk årsskrift* (2002), p. 100.

56   Dag Thorkildsen, 'Church and nation in the 19th century – the case of Norway', in Ingmar Brohed (ed.), *Church and People in Britain and Scaninavia*, p. 253.

57   Eino Murtorinne, 'Den fennomanska rörelsen och Finlands kyrka 1850–1914', *Kyrka och nationalism i Norden. Nationalism och skandinavism i de nordiska folkkyrkorna under 1800-talet* (Lund, 1998), pp. 384–91.

58   Nokelainen, 'Orthodox and Lutherans', p. 302.

59   Benedict Anderson, *Imagined Communities* (London, 1991).

60   Thorkildsen, 'Church and nation', pp. 262 ff., 266.

61   Blückert, *The Church as Nation*, p. 85 ff.

62   Ibid., p. 116.

63   Ibid., p. 320.

64   Blaschke, 'Der "Dämon des konfessionalismus"', p. 41.

65   Werner, pp. 56–62, 64 ff.

66   John D. Barbour, *Versions of Deconversion. Autobiography and the Loss of Faith* (Charlottesville, 1994), p. 2.

67   Ibid., p. 167 ff.

68   See further Anders Jarlert, 'Konversion och konfession – om konversionsliknande övergångar hos Henric Schartau och F. G. Hedberg i relation till en andra konfessionaliseringsperiod', in *Kyrkohistorisk årsskrift* (2003); abstract in English: 'Conversion

and confession – religious transitions similar to conversion in Henric Schartau and F. G. Hedberg, related to a second confessional age'.

10

England, Englishmen and the Church of England in the Nineteenth-century United Kingdom of Great Britain and Ireland: Nation, Church and State

KEITH ROBBINS

The United Kingdom of Great Britain and Ireland existed as a state from 1801 to 1922. Professor S. J. Brown has recently described it, at the moment of its inception, as a 'semi-confessional Protestant State'.[1] Its subjects, as he puts it, were expected to conform to the worship and discipline of the Established Church in whichever of the three historic kingdoms they resided in. Prior to the Irish Act of Union, the state of Great Britain had contained two of these national Church establishments – in England and Scotland respectively. Although it could be claimed that 'the Established Churches were fundamental to the constitution of the State' and represented the state 'in its religious aspect', the very fact that there were two such bodies and that they both made a claim that was 'national', was in itself a recognition that 'in its religious aspect' this United Kingdom embraced different 'nationalities'. There was an overarching 'Protestantism' but that had no single ecclesiastical embodiment. There was no common subscription to a single confession – hence the 'semi-confessional' state. This duality, of course, reflected the substantially different ecclesiastical histories of England and Scotland since the sixteenth-century Reformations. In the new constitutional settlement of 1707 the new British state had accepted, in its two constituent kingdoms, churches that differed from each other substantially with regard to doctrinal standards, forms of worship and forms of government. As 'Supreme Governor' of the Church of England, Queen Victoria had no intention of tampering with this duality by any actions of her own. It seems that she regarded the Episcopal Church as a disaster for

Scotland. No one dared to suggest to her that as the leading Anglican lay person she ought to attend a service of the Anglican Church in Scotland. Amidst much ecclesiastical clucking, she took the sacrament at Crathie Church according to the practice of the Church of Scotland.[2]

If we take the turn of the century as our point of departure, it is not easy to arrive at a straightforward assessment of what all this amounted to in considering 'church, state and nation'. It has been Linda Colley's case that throughout the eighteenth and nineteenth centuries, not to speak of later, external pressures and imperatives made the fact that Britain had 'an overwhelmingly Protestant culture' relevant and compelling in what she calls 'a quite unprecedented way'. Until 1815 it had been with 'Catholic France' that Great Britain had been involved in a succession of dangerous wars. Protestantism became 'a unifying and distinguishing bond as never before'. More than anything else, she has concluded, it was this shared religious allegiance, in an age of recurrent wars, that 'permitted a sense of British nationality to emerge, alongside of, and not necessarily in competition with older, more organic attachments to England, Wales or Scotland, or to county and village'. Protestantism determined 'how most Britons viewed their politics'; uncompromising Protestantism was the foundation on which the British state was explicitly and unapologetically based. Previous historians have perhaps failed to emphasize this absolute centrality because they have not wished to be accused of stating the obvious. The internal rivalries within the Protestant community she concedes to have been abundant and serious, but in her view they should not obscure the most striking feature in the British religious landscape, namely the gulf between Protestant and Catholic.[3]

Jonathan Clark, on the other hand, has declined to be seduced by that simple dichotomy, arguing that it is too easy to assume that Protestant and Catholic were 'simple, antithetical ontological identities'. Both terms, rather, should be seen 'as political labels, generated in a tactical context', and therefore necessarily full of tactical subtlety. 'Protestantism' was not a 'fixed, unambiguous concept which could be used to explain that ambiguous one, national identity'. He writes that one cannot simply 'read off' national identity or patriotism from religious identity. He therefore re-emphasizes the diversity and argues that the differences which existed within Protestantism cannot be reduced to a matter of finer optional points, since both the seventeenth and eighteenth centuries had shown that such differences could issue in profoundly different political and constitutional conceptions. He instances, further, work that shows the disinclination of many Protestant Irish in the late eighteenth century to advocate union with Great Britain, even though Great Britain was engaged in war with a Catholic power. Above all, however, he instances, from his own work, the American Revolution, which he characterizes as 'a civil war among Protestants' that changed anglophone history irreversibly and fundamentally. He adds that before 1776 the Dissenting sects of the Thirteen Colonies had played no clear role in generating a shared American identity.[4]

In stating that subjects of the Crown were 'expected to conform', Professor Brown is of course correct, but that expectation had, perforce, been modified. What conformity actually amounted to has, in turn, been the subject of varying emphases. Referring, perhaps a little oddly, to 'British Catholics' from the late seventeenth century until 1829, Professor Colley emphasizes the scale of their exclusion and the extent to which, in law, they were 'treated as potential traitors, as un-British'. She does, however, add the rider 'if not always in fact', but does not enlarge on the extent to which what might have happened 'in fact' was a substantial mitigation of their legal position.[5] She is emphatic, however, that the legal position of Protestant Dissenters after the 1689 Toleration Act was 'utterly different' from the position of Catholic Dissenters. She leaves the impression, in observations which may be taken to apply to the eighteenth century as a whole, that Protestant Dissenters suffered little exclusion and that 'in practice' English and Welsh Protestant Dissenters 'were able to penetrate almost all levels of the political system up to and including Parliament itself'. She adds 'so too were Scottish Presbyterians' – though, of course, they were not Dissenters. There is, of course, always a difficulty in determining, with regard to both Roman Catholic and Protestant Dissenting communities, how far practice did indeed diverge from the law – any generalization needs to be made on the understanding that its validity depends upon particular local circumstances and relationships, taken in the context of the prevailing political climate in any particular year. In the 1760s and 1770s James Bradley sees on the part of Protestant Nonconformity 'an increasingly coherent opposition', dissatisfied with its own status and developing an alternative political/ecclesiastical vision.[6] Michael Watts identifies at the end of the eighteenth century what he calls 'a swelling chorus of Anglican clerics', who were demanding restrictions on Dissenters' freedom to preach.[7] In fact, in the decade after 1801, culminating in Lord Sidmouth's abortive bill, Dissenters were successfully able to resist a Tory/Anglican attempt to curb their activities and prevent their numerical expansion. It is worth noting, too, that the restrictions on them, which were further eased, were to some extent motivated by an anxiety that otherwise there was a real danger that Protestant Dissenters would join with Catholics in opposing all religious tests imposed by the state. Watts does note that as late as 1838 two inhabitants of Llanelli were sent to prison for not attending their parish church. The gulf between 'Protestant' and 'Catholic', then, on certain matters, was indeed a significant feature of the religious landscape, but arguably, after 1801, it was matched by the different and deepening gulf between those committed to the principle of 'established religion' and those committed to explicit ecclesiastical pluralism and the elimination of national Established Churches – a free church in a free state.

The Irish Act of Union inevitably brought a fundamental challenge. The issue of ecclesiastical/national alignment had to be directly addressed in the enlarged state. In Ireland, the opponents of the Protestant Ascendancy had turned to France for help. The attempted French invasion of 1796 and the rebellion of 1798 had convinced Pitt that he had to press ahead with Union. Ireland was the Achilles heel of the British war effort. Union would remove the ability of the Protestant minority to mis-rule in Ireland, but also assuage its fears by incorporation within a state in which Protestants were clearly in the majority. The Duke of Portland, who was responsible for British Irish policy, took the view that the new state would be 'an Empire in reality and have it so much more in our power to give stability and security to . . . the other powers in Europe and to hold that balance which cannot be safely held by any other hands than our own'.[8] It was likely, however, that this gratifying expression of British enlightened disinterestedness would require matching reassurance to Catholics, who undoubtedly constituted the majority in Ireland, as they did not in the other two kingdoms. It is well known, however, that Pitt failed to overcome the opposition of George III. He had tried to explain that Catholic Emancipation in Ireland would

> conciliate the higher orders of the Catholics, and by furnishing to a large class of your majesty's Irish subjects a proof of the good will of the United parliament, afford the best chance of giving full effect to the great object of the Union, – that of tranquillizing Ireland, and attaching it to this country'.[9]

Behind the obduracy of the monarch lay that swath of opinion which could be mobilized by the Church of England party. The 'Catholic Question' led to Pitt's downfall, though arguably he could have played his cards more adroitly. The one single palliative which could have made possible the consensual consolidation of the new state was missing at the very outset.

We should, of course, be careful in referring to 'Acts of Union' in 1707 or in 1801. We should not assume that the resulting structures of government and administration conformed to a common template and produced complete uniformity within this United Kingdom. The existence of the two national churches in England/Wales and Scotland, amongst other matters, testifies to this fact. However, the realities in the distribution of power between England and Scotland at this juncture applied no less in the ecclesiastical sphere than they did elsewhere. The Church of Scotland, for example, had no official representation at the coronation of the British monarch, a ceremony which remained firmly Church of England. There was no place in the House of Lords for its annually appointed Moderator amidst the continuing galaxy of Anglican bishops. There was no sense in which the two churches were 'equal' in the eyes of a state which continued to be predominantly Anglican. This should not, however, be seen solely as a deliberate exclusion. It also reflected a continuing Presbyterian insistence on the church's independence from the state in spiritual matters. Moreover, the degree of 'distance' from the heart of the British state enhanced the Church of Scotland's capacity to claim to 'speak for Scotland' in a Scottish polity now bereft of its own parliament.

At the beginning of the nineteenth century, both English and Scottish national churches could reasonably claim that their numerical strength entitled them to be seen as 'representing' their national communities. That clearly could not be said about the condition of Anglicanism in Ireland. However, properly speaking, as Professor Brown puts it, what was created under clause V of the Act of Union was 'one Protestant Episcopal Church', whose 'doctrine, discipline and government' were to 'remain in full force for ever'.[10] Four Irish bishops could attend the House of Lords in London. However, as he says, the idea of a single Protestant Church embracing England and Ireland was in reality more a project for the future than an existing reality. Indeed, though it was the case that eighteenth-century Protestant bishops in Ireland were largely English or Anglo-Irish (a difficult term to define), the number of Englishmen appointed to Irish sees thereafter declined.[11] One obvious accompaniment of political union could be to launch a 'Second Reformation' in Ireland. If it were to be successful, it would remove the Irish 'anomaly' – as it were – and make 'Great Britain and Ireland' a fully Protestant state in all its constituent parts. As Brown demonstrates, it was an ambition attempted with enthusiasm and commitment over the next couple of decades by some churchmen in Ireland, but to no general avail. There were, however, some converts from Roman Catholicism who gloried in the capacity of the Church of Ireland, as they saw it, 'to blend England with all their dearest, their holiest, their most ennobling recollections'. There was nothing to be ashamed of in gladly acknowledging England as the fountain of the well-ordered freedom of the Church of Ireland.[12] On the other hand, James Doyle, the Roman Catholic Bishop of Kildare and Leighlin, though he had earlier ambitiously flirted with the notion of a union of the Roman Catholic Church with the Church of Ireland, believed that the 'New Reformation' so enthusiastically endorsed by William

Magee, the Protestant Archbishop of Dublin, was the gasp of an Established Church 'flushed in her decline'.[13] The idea of a confessional state had had its day.

It was necessary to accept, in other words, that the emerging liberal United Kingdom, insofar as it could be clearly discerned, would be, to use a modern expression, 'a union of multiple identities'. The repeal of the Test and Corporation in 1828, the Catholic Emancipation Act of 1829 and the Reform Act of 1832 were thus linked as harbingers of a new political and ecclesiastical order, which might yet take time to emerge, but which was irreversible. Brown clearly demonstrates how, despite the vigour and enthusiasm of church leaders in England, they found the modestly more representative Parliament less and less supportive of their goals. It would not provide, in any part of the United Kingdom, that additional public investment on the scale that would have been needed to enable the Established Churches to cope effectively with the rapidly expanding population. The 1830s were to prove the crucial decade which would determine the nature of the United Kingdom and, in the event, would destroy the notion that it was an essentially unitary Protestant state.

While we may agree, however, that the United Kingdom was not 'essentially' such a state, it may be more difficult to say what the state, in turn, had 'essentially' become, or was becoming. The rupture of church and state, however protracted it was to be – and it has not yet finally occurred in either England or Scotland – raised questions concerning identity and allegiance involving church, state and nation in the United Kingdom which were not resolved in the nineteenth century.[14] Frances Knight has rightly drawn attention to other 'landmarks', besides those already alluded to, as the Church of England uneasily and uncomfortably had to accept the loss, or at least the attenuation, of its national pretensions. She has concluded that 'by 1870 the Church of England could no longer claim to be the Church of the English nation'.[15] Perhaps, however, she might have said 'justifiably claim', for neither in 1870, nor for many decades subsequently, did prominent Anglican figures, both clerical and lay, abandon that claim. Perhaps we should put it differently by suggesting that while no churchman could plausibly by 1914 ignore the reality of ecclesiastical pluralism and the numerical strength of both Protestant and Catholic Dissent, as compared with what that strength had been in England a century earlier, there still remained a widely prevalent opinion that the intimacy between church, state and nation in England was profound and pervasive.[16] Randall Davidson, writing in 1912 as Archbishop of Canterbury, continued to believe that the Church of England was the national church and could claim to be 'the religious mouthpiece of the Nation, and the chief Executive force of its religious life'.[17] Indeed, commenting on the first half of the twentieth century, Ross McKibbin stresses that while it might not have been a national church, 'it was certainly an official one. It was the Established Church of the kingdom of England and was thus conspicuously a part of the state and its rituals' – though we may wonder whether a 'kingdom of England' exists.[18]

'The English Church', wrote Mandell Creighton, historian and Bishop of London, in 1898, 'must be the religious organ of the English people.'[19] In his primary charge he had deplored talk of 'freeing the Church from the bondage of the State'. To speak in this way was to represent the state as something inherently unholy and something stifling to spiritual aspirations'. It was his opinion that it would be deplorable if what he called 'the English State' divested itself of its religious character – for that would be what Disestablishment would mean.[20] What he called the 'general trend' of the Church had to be regulated by the wishes of the English people. Edward King, Bishop of Lincoln, spoke at the turn of the century of his belief that 'the truth as we have it in the Church of England is the secret of England's highest happiness and of England's power'.[21] 'We English', wrote the veteran Christian Socialist Dr Llewellyn Davies (bearer of names not invariably linked with Englishness), in his introduction to the volume of essays by Hensley Henson published in 1908 under the title *The National Church*, 'have not found it difficult to confess and worship the Father of the Crucified Son of man as the God of our fathers and of our country'. The feeling encouraged in its pages was that 'of a godly English patriotism, which honours the nation as having a Divine calling, and can look upon its history with pride'. The true Englishman would throw back with secure confidence the reproaches of a Church that would excommunicate and stamp 'nationalism' as a heresy.

It would not be difficult to find the expression of similar sentiments in other contemporary quarters. Henson himself spoke of

> the repugnance which an ancient Christian nation cannot but feel when it is urged to disown its most sacred traditions, unlearn the language of its saints and patriots, strike the Cross of Christ from the Crown of its Monarch, and silence the voice of prayer in the Council Chambers of its empire.[22]

Thus, while at one level it might indeed no longer be convincing, on a head-count basis, to see the Church of England as the church of the English nation, it was still being strongly urged that the English nation would lose a vital element of its own identity if either the state detached itself from the church or the church detached itself from the state. English politics, Creighton thought, gained enormously from the existence of a national church. Disestablishment would work a more abrupt change in the principles on which national cohesion rested than would any other alteration in the English system. 'I think it is deplorable', wrote the Anglo-Catholic priest Arthur Stanton in 1874 to an undergraduate, 'when any young Englishman becomes a papist and associates himself with a system which can never be English or liberal. It blights his whole life, and the freshness of his character goes'.[23] In that same year, when the Marquess of Ripon, a prominent Gladstonian Liberal, converted, *The Times* declared in a leading article that

> a statesman who becomes a convert to Roman Catholicism forfeits at once the confidence of the English people. Such a step involves a complete abandonment of any claim to political or even social influence in the nation at large and can only be regarded as betraying an irreparable weakness of character.[24]

Creighton put the point slightly differently to a correspondent in 1898:

It is quite impossible that any considerable number of Englishmen should be Roman Catholics. To join yourself to that Church is simply to stand on one side and cut yourself off from your part in striving to do your duty for the religious future of your country.[25]

William Connor Magee spoke in 1885 as Bishop of Peterborough, warning of the dangers of disestablishment. He could not believe that the English people would cast away the blessings the English Church gave them 'for the vague promises of very doubtful blessings that are to come in her place'. He believed that there was still 'in the heart of the nation some reverence for the past, some love of old ways and old institutions'. This was not because of their antiquity as such, but because 'their very age proves their strength and worth'.[26] This salutary interpretation of the views of the English people came from one of the few Irishmen to occupy an English see (Peterborough) – a Disraelian inspiration. In 1891, this grandson of the Archbishop of Dublin became the first Irishman to become Archbishop of York. William Alexander (Tonbridge and Brasenose College, Oxford), Bishop of Derry, preached at this notable enthronement. The English congregation sang 'St Patrick's Breastplate', as translated by Mrs Alexander. Seven weeks later, Magee was dead.[27]

Looking at the world at the end of the nineteenth century, it was indeed difficult to discount the notion that there was an intimate relationship between the extraordinary scope of the British Empire and the strengths of 'English character'.[28] Preoccupation with the peculiarities of English character had itself been something of a national pastime since the eighteenth century. Then, Immanuel Kant had detected that it amounted to little more than 'a contempt for all foreigners, primarily because the English think they alone can boast a respectable constitution that combines domestic civil liberty with might in external affairs'.[29] Writing on holiday (in Wales) in August 1898, Creighton was still arguing that a nation existed by virtue of a particular type of character. Further, character was largely founded on religion. He deplored the fact that there was, in some quarters, an attempt to bring back religious observances of an exotic kind 'which do menace English character'. The function of the Church of England was 'to be the Church of free men'. The Church of Rome was 'the Church of decadent peoples'. It lived in the past and had no future. The Church of England had before it 'the conquest of the world. We can only succeed if we gird up our loins with the assurance that the future is ours.'[30] The South African War, which broke out in the following year, gave a jolt to this self-confidence. Edward King thought that God might be using the war 'to knock off from England some of the habits which very naturally accrue, and which has brought England to the front in the world', but even so the bishop only envisaged a temporary setback, because God might well be working, through the war, to make a great united Empire.[31]

English churchmen, as they encountered the continent of Europe in the nineteenth century, normally had the virtues of their Englishness confirmed. On Lake Como, on 3 August 1829, for example, Thomas Arnold thought tempting the prospect of 'voluptuous enjoyment' if he settled in Italy with his family, but was clear that such a life would not compensate for the abandonment of the life of usefulness and activity which he had in England. Moments of recreation abroad were welcome, but only to strengthen Englishmen for work to come. 'England', he wrote

> has other destinies than these countries, – I use the word in no foolish or unchristian sense, – but she has other destinies; her people have more required of them; with her full intelligence, her restless activity, her enormous means, and enormous difficulties; her pure religion and unchecked freedom.

Her citizens, least of all people, should not think of their own rest or enjoyment but should strive to the uttermost to do good to themselves and to the world. The beauty of foreign lakes and mountains should not be coveted. England, so entirely subdued as it was to man's uses, with its gentle hills and valleys, was best suited as an instrument of usefulness.[32] Writing from 'Chamberri' the following summer, he was struck with

> the total isolation of England from the European world. We are considered like inhabitants of another planet, feared,

perhaps, and respected at many points, but not loved, and in no respect understood or sympathized with. And how much is our state the same with regard to the Continent. How little did we seem to know, or to value their feelings, – how little do we appreciate or imitate their intellectual progress.[33]

It is perhaps not surprising, as he noted at the conclusion of another continental tour in 1841, one which left him with 'a more unfavourable impression of France than I have been wont to feel', that Arnold recorded that he was 'never for an instant tempted to live abroad; not even in Germany, where assuredly I would settle, if I were obliged to quit England'.[34] The lack of 'the holy calm of an English sabbath' upset young Richard Trench in 1834. When a nation gave up the sabbath, he thought, it gave up 'as a nation at least, having any religion'. That appeared to have happened in France.[35]

A recent author has studied these reactions closely. Marjorie Morgan has identified one important difference between the anti-Catholicism felt by Victorian travellers and that expressed prior to the nineteenth century.[36] It can be summarized by saying that fear had been replaced by repulsion and a mixture of contempt and pity. 'Intolerable smells' were widely identified as an inescapable concomitant of Roman Catholicism. However, some had encountered exceptions to this rule. In Flanders 'a very simple and pure form of the Catholic faith' was observed to go hand in hand with 'excessive cleanliness of streets, order, activity'. 'Pure' Catholicism and 'excessive cleanliness' was obviously the product of the 'Flemish character'.[37] In southern Europe, untidiness and dirt, particularly characteristic of priests, pointed to the absence of salutary wifely presences. Words beginning with 't' seemed to spring to the minds of English travellers when confronted by objects which 'littered' the churches and countryside in Catholic territories: trash, tinsel, tawdry, tasteless and trumpery.[38] Further, the propensity to spit, encountered in southern Europe, was particularly deplorable and un-English. In a church in Nice, even while adoring the Host, a priest was observed by an English visitor to turn round and spit. Frederick Faber, eager to worship on the Continent as though he were already a Roman Catholic, found in Cologne that the Catholic ritual would not do. He, too, observed priests spitting on the altar steps, and saw representations of our Blessed Lord which he found 'indecent'.[39] He felt homesick and out of place.[40] In April 1833, writing from Naples, J. H. Newman thought it right to inform his mother that southerners had 'a fashion of spitting about, too, to an excess perfectly incredible to an Englishman. They are ever at it. He had seen an elegantly dressed lady spit manfully – or rather had heard her, and then had felt obliged to turn round to watch and see her in action.[41]

Pervasive though this alien partiality apparently was, however, it would be wrong to suppose that it was the sole concern of English clerical travellers on the Continent. For some, while it was impossible not to accept that many things were 'in very bad taste', there was also much to be said in favour of continental Catholicism. One Tractarian traveller in Germany pronounced himself not blind to the many faults he found in the services he attended, but 'comparing with our own hard, cold, rationalistic service, all that I see here is infinitely preferable as a work of devotion. The people here are worshippers – is England?'[42] Writing from Prague in 1858 Brooke Westcott was impressed by the way in which the congregation joined in the chant at Mass. 'Why cannot we have the same thing in our Church?' he asked himself.[43] Observing Easter in Athens in 1847, Richard Church noted 'both more reverence and attention and more levity than in an English congregation'. However, he did not profess to understand their way of behaving. The congregation passed unpredictably and abruptly, without hesitation or concealment, from devotion to mutual salutations and smiles. The sort of orderly inattention and stealthy gossip that he had observed to go on in services in England was absent.[44] Attending Mass at Calais in 1845, W. E. Gladstone wrote to his wife that he witnessed an amazing accumulation of gestures and evolutions, almost dancing-master-like, on the part of the priests in celebrating. It never failed 'to prompt a puritanical reaction in my mind'.[45] In Sweden, Charles Wordsworth was impressed by the very good singing in the Lutheran parish church which he attended in 1833, though he was surprised to find men and women taking their places on different sides of the main aisle. It was unfortunate, however, that the minister, before leaving the pulpit, gave out a long succession of notices, taking a quarter of an hour, of the most secular kind, relating not only to births, deaths and marriages but to auctions and markets. In Berlin in the following spring he sought out the lectures of 'the acknowledged leader of the new German school of theology', Friedrich Schleiermacher, and was agreeably surprised to find that his manner was interesting and energetic, rather than solemn or impressive. Occasionally, indeed, he was facetious so as to elicit roars of laughter from his audience.[46] Schleiermacher's own contention that

> Every nation . . . which has developed to a certain height is degraded by receiving into it a foreign element, even though that may be good in itself; for God has imparted to each its own nature, and has therefore marked out bounds and limits for the habitations of the different races of men on the face of the earth

finds many English echoes.[47] Reflecting appropriately on the life of St Paul, in a sermon on the royal yacht off Malta in 1862, Arthur Penrhyn Stanley reminded his congregation: '*We* are not indolent Asiatics, but active Englishmen: we are not Mussulmans, who place their chief duty in passive resignation, but Christians, who know that the chief duty of men is the active service of God and mankind'.[48] The Prince of Wales, a member of the congregation, listened attentively.

It was not the case that new German theology was expounded to the accompaniment of roars of laughter in England. As is well known, H. J. Rose and E. B. Pusey led the revolt against it. Rose saw in the 'strange aberrations of the German Protestant Divines' strong proof of the necessity of an efficient and active system of Church discipline.[49] In the words of W. R. Ward, 'the English world of intellect, and especially of theology, had lost contact with the great developments in German theology . . . and did not want to know what had been going on'.[50] Such insular intellectual isolationism reinforced the view that the Church of England was a unique treasure which should be protected from foreign contamination. When Charles Kingsley described Germany as a wonderful country, he felt obliged to add 'though its population are not members of the Church of England'. It is not clear why he felt so obliged, since there cannot have been too many of his countrymen who laboured under a misapprehension in this regard.[51] He had no doubt, of course, that only English people could really belong to the Church of England. He told a correspondent in 1851 that it was 'wonderfully and mysteriously fitted for the souls of a free Norse-Saxon race; for men whose ancestors fought by the side of Odin, over whom a descendant of Odin now rules'. Roman elements, now being introduced into the Church of England, were 'unsuited to Englishmen, and to God's purposes for England'. How far the Roman system was best for the Italian or Spanish spirit he could not judge, but if they had been capable of anything higher, God would have given them something higher.[52]

The sense that both 'England' and the 'English Church' occupied a distinctive role in relation to Europe, both politically and ecclesiastically, was more general, though there was disagreement about the implications of this distinctiveness. Reflecting in Sicily in 1833, J. H. Newman found the state of the Church which he found there to be 'deplorable'. He was told that at Naples all the property of the Church had been lost and it lived in poverty. These countries, he believed,

> have the evils of Protestantism without its advantages – that is Anglican Protestantism; for there are no advantages in schism like Dissent, or Socinianism such as Geneva's. But here, too, they have infidelity and profaneness, as if the whole world (Western) were tending towards some dreadful crisis. I begin to hope that England after all is to be the 'Land of Saints' in this dark hour, and her Church the salt of the earth.[53]

It was, of course, a hope that he was to abandon, but it was frequently matched by others elsewhere. On his way home, a French vessel was in the harbour at Algiers but Newman records that he 'would not even look at the tricolour', and while he had perforce to stop for twenty-four hours in Paris he kept indoors the whole time.[54] France was the embodiment of a detested Liberalism. Just as England could not be 'fully European' in a political sense, so it could not be 'fully European' in an ecclesiastical sense. The 'might in external affairs', which Kant had discerned, grew ever more apparent, setbacks notwithstanding, as the nineteenth century progressed. In his famous lectures on *The Expansion of England* Sir John Seeley drew attention to the extraordinary changes brought about by 'the extension of the English name into other countries of the globe'. In his famous sentence, he wrote that England had 'conquered and peopled half the world in a fit of absence of mind'. Historians had not taken on board that in the eighteenth century the history of England had not been 'in England but in America and Asia'. It even remained the case, as he was lecturing in 1883, that Englishmen still had not ceased 'to think of ourselves as simply a race inhabiting an island off the northern coast of the Continent of Europe'. His lectures were designed to remedy this failing.

The Church of England was, of course, strongly present in the British Empire. Here again, however, 'Englishness' and 'the *British* Empire' coexisted uneasily. The establishment of legislative assemblies in colonies from the 1830s onwards steadily made it necessary for colonial bishops to come to terms with these developments. The problems that were increasingly posed led to calls for a meeting of Anglican bishops worldwide, the outcome being the first Lambeth Conference in 1867. At this juncture, the global Anglican Communion could still be said to serve the needs of English settlers. Quite apart from the contentious theological issues of the time, not far below the surface were issues of identity in the evolving colonies and the extent to which Anglican bishops, for the most part transplanted Englishmen, equated Anglicanism with Englishness. The Church of Ireland, in this context, was quoted on occasion as an example of a church that had failed because, allegedly, it had employed English bishops, not used the language of the people and appeared to be the church of the conquerors. For a time, the Church Missionary Society drew the conclusion that the Church had to be more closely integrated with indigenous cultures – without a full realization of how difficult it was to be to separate the pure gospel from its English packaging. In referring to 'the growing confusion over the relationship between the Church in the colonies and the English State', however, the historian of these developments neglects one important dimension.[55] There was no English state. There was a British state and there were British colonies. Particularly from Scotland, there were complaints about the extent to which, it seemed, only the English Church was normally regarded as being established in them. It was true that the Church of Scotland could be given land or government subsidies – as could other denominations – but it was not regarded as an equal Established Church. Constitutionally, this stemmed from the fact that the Church of Scotland recognized no sovereignty vested in the Crown. Only the Church of England possessed a Supreme Governor.[56] In practice, of course, the inhabitants of the colonies of overseas settlement came, in varying proportions in different colonies, from the United Kingdom as a whole. They were far from being new settlements that would be for ever England. Anglicans of English origins had to live alongside other denominations from the entire United Kingdom to a degree that did not apply in England itself.

Whether their mindset was 'insular' or 'imperial', however, Englishmen could not be Europeans in the sense that 'continentals' were.[57] Mandell Creighton's one-time pupil, Sir Edward Grey, studiously avoided visiting the nearby continent when he was Foreign Secretary. When he accompanied King George V to Paris in April 1914, this was his first and last foreign visit when in office.[58] In foreign policy, Robert Seton-Watson concluded his survey of the period 1789 to 1914 by arguing that Britain had occupied 'a middle path' – as had also been the case in its internal social and political development in that long century.[59] It was a stance, he thought, which naturally reflected Britain's hybrid position as part of Europe and yet, in some respects, outside it. Moreover, it also reflected the contention that Englishmen, in general, could not align themselves unambiguously with one European Great Power or another. Reflecting in 1871 on the Franco-Prussian war of 1870, for example, Dean Church could not disguise his disgust 'at French lying and vapouring and vanity' and his admiration 'at the unequalled intellectual greatness of the Prussian success', but he also felt fear, faced with 'the revival of the military barbarism of the kings and nobles of the old times'. Therefore, French wickedness, with its conceit, lies and chattering insolence, seemed almost childish beside the deliberate pride of force which he detected in the German nature.[60] It seemed that

Englishmen quintessentially faced both ways. In 1870 William Cunningham wrote in his undergraduate diary at Cambridge, 'We can only trust for the rise of an united Germany to dictate to the world', but in 1914 he was grateful for France, and even more for the United States.[61]

The Church of England could therefore be said to occupy a comparable 'middle position' in the ecclesiastical world between continental confessional Protestantism and Catholicism – and to be vulnerable to the same charge of indefiniteness. As has been pointed out, the idea that it constituted an Aristotelian mean between ecclesiastical extremes had proved particularly attractive to Hanoverian churchmen. Apologists of the *via media* could content themselves with explaining what the Church of England was not, rather than what it was. All of this was set in a cyclical theory of English church history, which claimed that a religious exaggeration in one direction was liable to produce a dangerous swing in the opposite direction. The ideal English churchman, it might almost appear, should be a disciple of the great 'Trimmer', the Marquis of Halifax.[62] Archdeacon Denison put the same notion a different way – though it hardly corresponded to his own practice – when he remarked that: 'An Englishman, when he gets up in the morning, thinks when he is shaving how many compromises he can make before breakfast.'[63] Such facility in trimming, apparently in respect to both facial hair and intellectual conviction, was perhaps an inescapable aspect of the position 'at once perilous and most precious' which Gladstone felt the Church of England to be in when he asked himself in 1875 whether it was worth preserving. She was 'in a partial but not an unreal sense, a link of union between the several fractions of the Christian body'. She sat between 'the great Latin communion' on the one hand and the 'in no way other than respectable, forms of Nonconformity' on the other.[64] In his 'Letter on the English Church', addressed to the St Asaph diocesan conference in 1884, Gladstone returned to the theme that in the Church of England 'the Reformation and the counter-Reformation tendencies were, in the order of providence, placed here in a closer juxtaposition than anywhere else in the Christian world'. It was a juxtaposition which produced stresses and strains but was also indicative of 'a course of destiny' so peculiar as to indicate, on the part of the Supreme Orderer, a peculiar purpose'.[65] This emphasis upon mediation ran comfortably alongside Gladstone's constitutional narrative. He had dwelt in 1866 on the 'pre-eminently rich and fruitful' institutions and traditions of England, but they required reform. England had inherited more of what was 'august and venerable than any other European nation', but it was also more modern than any other.[66] That paradox ran through English life and through the Church of England.

There was, therefore, still in 1914 a lingering self-image of 'Englishness' and 'Anglicanism' which was mutually supportive. A virtuous circle linked cricketing heroes, public school headmasters and bishops – and men, at appropriate stages in their lives, moved between these categories with assured frequency. The 'sporting spirit', in the opinion of Sir Arthur Conan Doyle – not an Englishman – 'was England's invention, and the chief characteristic of Englishmen'. In 1885 Randall Davidson, youthful Dean of Windsor, could scarcely contain his excitement when Harrow beat Eton at the annual cricket match.[67] It was appropriate that the Bishop of Calcutta, Winston Churchill's (though not Davidson's) headmaster at Harrow, the mentally and physically massive J. E. C. Welldon, should explain to a Japanese audience in 1906 that in the training of an Englishman, games, not as physical exercises but as moral disciplines, were more important than studies. The Japanese Minister of Education, who was present, accordingly learnt that a cricketer worthy of the name would be glad to sacrifice himself, if he could win the victory for his side by doing so.[68] Within a decade, of course, there was another kind of victory to be won. As regards that struggle, in the opinion of the Bishop of London in June 1915 the Church of England could 'best help the nation first of all by making it realize that it is engaged in a Holy War . . . Christ died on Good Friday for Freedom, Honour and Chivalry, and our boys are dying for the same things'.[69]

Bishop Welldon spoke freely about 'the whole governing class of Englishmen' who exemplified the virtues and values in which he had been reared and which he exemplified. The glorious interpenetration of Anglicanism and Englishness, honed on the playing fields of Eton, may characterize the ethos of the 'governing class' but, despite its comforting resonances, it glossed over, rather than resolved, underlying issues of identity within England itself, and even more within the United Kingdom as a whole. The predominance of England within the political structure of the United Kingdom and the concomitant preponderance of Anglicanism within its ecclesiastical portrayal frequently led to the conclusion that the content of those self-images held good for the whole United Kingdom. The secular and religious politics of the United Kingdom in the second half of the nineteenth century demonstrated, however, that this assumption was itself a source of friction.

In the very year in which Bishop Welldon drew Japanese attention to the virtues of cricket, a Liberal government won a handsome electoral victory and seemed set for a twentieth century of change. Its very composition meant that it was not representative of 'the governing class of Englishmen'. Amongst its most prominent figures, only Sir Edward Grey (Winchester and Balliol) – a real tennis champion as an Oxford undergraduate – stood out as a quintessential English gentleman and reticent, and perhaps reluctant, Anglican. Winston Churchill was a rather unusual Harrovian. He was scarcely an ardent member of the Church of England, and had taken the liberty of informing his old headmaster, now episcopally in Calcutta, that he opposed Christian missions.[70] Campbell-Bannerman, Haldane, Loreburn, Bryce and Lloyd George were neither English nor Anglican. Amongst the small band of Englishmen, Asquith, Birrell and Simon had Free Church origins. Sir Henry Fowler was a notable Wesleyan Methodist, as was Walter Runciman. Herbert Samuel and Rufus Isaacs were Jews. Clearly, much had changed since John Bright had become the first Protestant Dissenter to serve in a Cabinet when appointed President of the Board of Trade in 1868.[71] Behind these ministers stood numerous Nonconformist MPs.[72] In 1862, on the bicentenary of the 1662 ejection of some 2,000 ministers from the Church of England because they would not give unfeigned assent to the new Prayer Book, Benjamin Jowett expressed the view that it had constituted

> the greatest misfortune that has ever befallen this country, a misfortune that has never been retrieved. For it has made two

nations of us instead of one in politics, in religion, almost in our notion of right and wrong; it has arrayed one class of society permanently against another.[73]

The 'England' of the Church of England, on such an analysis, was only one element in the English nation. There was another – by definition outside 'the Establishment' and its cultivation of an image of Englishness. Dissent had been preoccupied with issues of religious equality. As has been observed, the mid-century concerns and campaigns of Dissenters left many issues unresolved in their political world-view –'not the least being the fundamental question of the very meaning of the notion of a "Christian" nation'.[74] The very terms Dissent and Nonconformity implied opposition to the hegemonic values of society. The latter decades of the century, with substantial equality achieved, forced reconsiderations. Leading figures, while continuing to assert that 'the central idea of a voluntary and congregational, not a national church' was the basis of 'primitive *ecclesia*', recognized that it could easily foster isolation, sectarianism and schism if not blended with other ideas.[75] The Annual Report of the West London Mission (Wesleyan) in 1891 stated that 'In olden times the Nonconformist Churches were small societies of godly persons . . . in spirit essentially private societies', but that was no longer good enough. The Anglican Church, 'being in fact a branch of the public service' had, of course, recognized the public duty of the Church, but the time had at last come for the Methodist and other churches 'to accept and undertake these national functions'.[76] The pecularities of Dissent had not totally disappeared in the transition to 'Free Churchmen', but as they tentatively embraced 'the nation' they also sought to ensure it should not be defined simply in terms of Anglicanism.[77] In particular, English Dissent was so permeated by Welshmen that it is going only a little too far to speak in this period of 'Anglo-Welsh' Dissent.[78]

And, to complete the Cabinet collection of Christians (if that is how they may be thought of), whatever *The Times* may once have thought about his conversion to Roman Catholicism, the Marquess of Ripon now served without difficulty as Lord Privy Seal, the final stage in a career which – post-conversion – had seen him as Viceroy of India, First Lord of the Admiralty and Colonial Secretary in the 1880s and 1890s. In short, English Anglicans were scarcely to be seen. There was clearly a disjuncture between the rhetoric of 'English Anglicanism' and the reality of a British Cabinet which, in its ethnicity, was substantially non-English and, as a body, virtually without allegiance to the Church of England.

It could be said that to highlight this divergence – normally in the later nineteenth century more apparent whenever Liberal governments were in power, given the geographical distribution of the party's support and the extent to which it had established links with Protestant Nonconformity – is to exaggerate its significance. While concern to make appropriate distinctions in employing the words England/English and Britain/British is now politically correct, contemporary usage was somewhat unpredictable. Walter Bagehot wrote *The English Constitution* (1867) long after the Constitution had ceased to be English. While Bishop Welldon was concerned with the education of an English gentleman, he could, a few lines later, refer to the qualities of the 'British race'. Sir John Seeley wrote on the expansion of England because the impetus behind empire came from England, though it had become a British enterprise. The 'Greater Britain' which he observed was, in his opinion, substantially homogeneous. From his perspective,

> if in these islands we feel ourselves for all purposes one nation, though in Wales, in Scotland and in Ireland there is Celtic blood and Celtic languages utterly unintelligible to us are spoken, so in the Empire a good many French and Dutch and a good many Caffres and Maoris may be admitted without marring the ethnological unity of the whole.[79]

But whether, 'in these islands', it was the case that 'we' were 'for all purposes one nation' was itself questionable. It seemed self-evident that in many respects, perhaps most respects, the inhabitants of 'these islands' could be held to constitute one nation. The running of the British Empire was a common enterprise in which all the peoples of the 'British Isles' came to have a part. Indeed, going further, it has recently been argued that 'Empire' was integral to Scotland's history (though Seeley bothered little with that history).[80] It was a British Army (which had come to include Catholic Irishmen) which advanced and defended it. Yet the peoples of the United Kingdom had manifestly not become one nation 'for all purposes'. If one nation had to have a religious purpose, or a religious expression embodied in a 'national church', the United Kingdom manifestly did not contain 'one nation'. If Anglicanism outside England was to thrive or survive it needed to downplay its 'Englishness'. The extent to which emphasis continued to be placed in England upon the peculiar intimacy between the 'English Church' and the 'English State' was a matter of some embarrassment to Anglicans outside England as they sought their own 'national' accommodations.

The single 'Protestant Episcopal Church' of the Irish Act of Union never took wing. Laurence Brockliss notes that 'in no sense is it possible to talk of the clergy forming an all-British profession in the first fifty years of the new British state'.[81] With two exceptions, every Anglican bishop of an English diocese in the reign of Victoria was educated at Oxford or Cambridge, though a few had also been to Scottish universities.[82] Of course, that does not mean that there were not some non-English Anglicans who made prominent careers in England (the two episcopal exceptions were products of Trinity College, Dublin, though one was an Englishman). Hugh McNeile, arguably the most formidable evangelical preacher in the Church of England, was an Ulsterman. Before his appointment as Dean of Ripon in 1868, he had exercised a major influence on the politics, ecclesiastical and civic, of Liverpool.[83] The capacity of Scotsmen, sometimes baptized in the Church of Scotland, to succumb to educational influences in England and progress to the highest offices in the *English* Church did not go unremarked.[84]

In the other direction, Englishmen were wrenched from Oxford or Cambridge common-rooms and settled in suitable sees outside England. There, whether for a short or long duration, they wrestled with the peculiarities of their new surroundings. The archdiocese of Dublin seemed a suitable location for distinguished men from England. Richard Whateley, a consistently eccentric Englishman known as the 'White Bear' of Oriel, who, inter alia, had a penchant for throwing stones at college birds but was also 'the most acute clerical mind upon the Whig side', was shunted there in 1831 and remained in office until his death in 1863.[85] Particularly in Ireland, they could not fail to be aware of the uncomfortable anomalies of their situation. It was difficult to understand what this new United Kingdom was supposed to be. Logic was Whateley's speciality and he did not find it much in evidence in the governance of Ireland. By 1861 he had lived in Dublin under thirteen vice-royalties and had come to the conclusion that the office was not only useless but also mischievous. The Union could never be complete while it existed. It was a suitable office for a distinct kingdom, or a province with a distinct legislature, but utterly unsuitable for a part of one united kingdom. As things stood the Act of Union was most emphatically a half-measure.[86] But was not the United Kingdom full of 'half-measures'? Logic had also suggested to him that it was sensible for the state to pay Roman Catholic priests and that he should become a Commissioner of National Education. These were not conclusions which appealed to the majority of his Church, although there was satisfaction that he refused permission to Pusey to preach in Dublin. If, as is suggested, there was resentment against the appointment of an Englishman, it is arguable that it was because that Englishman wilfully refused to fit into the 'fierce extremes' which he found, disliking, as he did both evangelicals and men of the Oxford Movement.[87] Irish Roman Catholics and Orangemen were, he thought, 'much more like each other than either of them to an Englishman'. The English could be turbulent, violent and unjust but – referring to a contrast with Orangemen – 'they would not go on year after year and generation after generation trampling on, insulting and tormenting a fallen foe'.[88]

Whateley was followed by Richard Chenevix Trench, a prolific and wide-ranging scholar who had, unusually, produced lectures on philology which were entertaining as well as instructive. It was, as with Whateley, the literary and intellectual pretensions of these Englishmen (allegedly beyond the taste of most Church of Ireland clergymen) which 'aroused animosity in the church'.[89] 'England', Trench did indeed write at the time of his appointment (he was then Dean of Westminster), 'is my world, the lands of all my friends, the English church seems to me to feel full of life and hope and vigour, of which I see little in Ireland.'[90] To describe him, even so, simply as 'English' begs the question. He had been born in Dublin of Irish Protestant parents (but also of considerable Huguenot descent), but was brought up in England. His contemporary at Harrow, Charles Wordsworth, thought, however, that his throwing a quoit at him in a temper during the course of a game they were having indicated that Trench possessed 'an Irish rage'. It is not revealed whether the future Bishop of St Andrews considered his reciprocal action – distinctly disturbing the arrangement of Trench's teeth – testified to a characteristic English phlegm. In 1831, after spending more than a month in Ireland, Trench wrote that it was not the place for him. He had been too long in England 'ever to account any other my country'.[91] Trinity College, Cambridge, Trench's post-ordination career had been in England. It fell to him to give leadership to a Church of Ireland which was shortly to be disestablished and he did so with some distinction, though regular visits to England were required to lift his spirits. After the 1882 Phoenix Park murders he concluded, 'Ireland, with its dreadful blood spots, is a land in which it is very difficult to take delight'. He resigned in 1884, to die in Eaton Square and be buried in Westminster Abbey.

The disestablishment of the Church of Ireland constituted a recognition, by the government of a united kingdom, that it had to come to terms with the ecclesiastical complexion of Ireland. That, of course, was not how the wife of the Bishop of Derry, Fanny Alexander, saw it. On 1 January 1871 the congregation in the cathedral sang her lines:

> Look down Lord of heaven on our desolation
> Fallen, Fallen is now our country's crown
> Dimly dawns the new year on a churchless nation.[92]

Whereas, in his stern unbending youth, Gladstone had not thought it too much to assume that what he called the imperial legislature took a sounder view of religious truth than did the majority of Ireland, in their destitute and uninstructed state, as he formed his first government in 1868 he had changed his mind. Ireland could not be treated as though it was simply another England. There is no room in this essay for detailed consideration of Gladstone's motives and the legislation itself, but several paradoxes may be noted. Disestablishment of the Church of Ireland did not mean that he was converted to disestablishment of the Church of England. Rather, the position of the Church of England in England would be strengthened if it were not associated with the defence of what was now widely thought to be indefensible in Ireland. It can also be argued, however, that only by making Ireland ecclesiastically unlike England (taken together with other measures he had in mind for land reform) could Gladstone coax a reformed Ireland into being, in other respects, more like England. When, 'unmuzzled', he at length visited Dublin in 1877 to receive the freedom of the city he argued that the three kingdoms of the United Kingdom 'should be one nation in the face of the world', but that the kingdom's government was overcentralized and more should be done locally.[93] Whether or not such a strategy would ever be successful, the fact remained that Ireland had become the only part of the United Kingdom without a 'national church' recognized by the state.[94]

When Thomas Burgess (Winchester and Corpus Christi College, Oxford), a Hampshire boy, was appointed to the see of St David's in 1803 he came to a huge diocese of the Church of England. That diocese, however, was in Wales. But what was Wales? This puny principality had not for centuries been thought to occupy any distinctive constitutional, ecclesiastical or political space in a 'three-kingdom' United Kingdom. Bishops in Welsh dioceses who were Englishmen was the norm. Wales had no 'higher education' institution. What Bishop Burgess was to found at Lampeter might perhaps be analogous to Trinity College, Dublin. He was soon to find that the whole diocese was full of Dissenters of different denominations. He was also soon to discover the reality of the Welsh language. He entered ardently and imaginatively into his new responsibilities before, in 1825, at the age of 68, he 'went home' on his translation to the see of Salisbury, in which cathedral, on his death in 1837, he was buried. He subsequently earned praise as 'the best English Prelate the Principality ever saw'.[95] He was succeeded by more Englishmen, the most distinguished of whom being Connop Thirlwall, translator of Schleiermacher and another formidable scholar. In turn, Thirlwall was to be the only bishop in the House of Lords to vote in favour of the disestablishment of the Irish Church. Although not unapprehensive about aspects of the Church of England in Wales, Bishop Burgess would probably have been astonished to have gathered that, in less than a century after his departure, English bishops were being replaced by Welsh bishops and that a disestablished Church in Wales had come into being.[96] Perhaps he would have been even more surprised by the extent to which Wales had 'reappeared' in the political and cultural landscape of the United Kingdom.[97] It has not been the purpose of this essay to explain how this came about or to analyse its implications. It has, however, attempted to give some glimpses of analogous contexts in the ambiguous and ambivalent life of the Church of England in the nineteenth-century United Kingdom to those experienced in the diocese of St David's by Thomas Burgess.

Notes

1. Stewart J. Brown, *The National Churches of England, Ireland and Scotland 1801–46* (Oxford, 2001), p. 1.
2. Owen Chadwick, 'The Sacrament at Crathie, 1873', in Stewart J. Brown and George Newlands (eds.), *Scottish Christianity in the Modern World* (Edinburgh, 2000), pp. 117–19.
3. Linda Colley, *Britons: Forging the Nation 1707–1837* (London, 1994), pp. 18–19.
4. J. C. D. Clark, 'Protestantism, nationalism, and national identity, 1660–1832', *Historical Journal*, 43, 1 (2000), 272–3: Gerald Newman, *The Rise of English Nationalism* (London, 1987), looks at 'nationalism' in this period from a more general perspective. Adrian Hastings, *The Construction of Nationhood: Ethnicity, Religion and Nationalism* (Cambridge, 1997), p. 59, argues that such 'nationalism' 'was a redirection in a situation providing heightened consciousness of something which had long existed'. See also C. Kidd, *British Identities before Nationalism* (Cambridge, 1999). This complex discussion cannot be pursued in detail here.

5   Edward Norman, referring to relief measures passed by
    Parliament from the 1770s, writes that many of the benefits
    were actually formal: legislation simply legalized practices
    which had, anyway, gone on for years. Edward Norman, *The
    English Catholic Church in the Nineteenth Century* (Oxford,
    1984), p. 35.
6   James E. Bradley, *Religion, Revolution and English Radicalism:
    Non-conformity in Eighteenth Century Politics and Society*
    (Cambridge, 1990), p. 422.
7   Michael Watts, *The Dissenters Volume II: The Expansion of
    Evangelical Nonconformity 1791–1859* (Oxford, 1995), p. 368.
8   Cited in Michael Duffy, *The Younger Pitt* (London, 2000),
    p. 196.
9   Cited in Duffy, *Younger Pitt*, p. 207.
10 Brown, *National Churches*, p. 2.
11 Complete lists of bishops of the Church of Ireland from 1534
    can be found in T. W. Moody, F. X. Martin and F. J. Byrne, *A
    New History of Ireland*, IX (Oxford, 1984), pp. 392–438.
    D. H. Akenson, *The Church of Ireland: Ecclesiastical Reform
    and Revolution, 1800–1885* (New Haven and London, 1971),
    p. 12, concludes that (though political affiliation may in fact
    have been the determining factor) of the bishops appointed
    between 1750 and 1800, twenty-seven were English, twenty-
    four Irish and two Scottish. It was sometimes suggested that
    the Catholic peasantry found the moderate principles of an
    Englishman preferable to the Protestant bigotry of a Scotsman
    or an Irishman.
12 William Phelan in 1823, cited in Brown, *National Churches*,
    p. 22.
13 The simple answer (given by Desmond Bowen) as to why the
    Irish Church Mission crusade, in particular, failed is that the
    movement was '*English*, in origin, in design, and in the goals it
    sought to achieve'. Desmond Bowen, *The Protestant Crusade in
    Ireland, 1800–70* (Dublin, 1978), p. 246.
14 See Keith Robbins, 'Religion and identity in modern British
    history' (1982), reprinted in *History, Religion and Identity in
    Modern Britain* (London, 1993), pp. 85–103, and 'Church,
    chapel and the fragmentation of faith', in *Nineteenth-Century
    Britain: Integration and Diversity* (Oxford, 1988), pp. 63–96.
15 Frances Knight, *The Nineteenth-Century Church and English
    Society* (Cambridge, 1995), p. 201.
16 It is noteworthy, however, that in pursuing *Identity of England*
    (Oxford, 2002), Robert Colls has presumably found little trace

of this intimacy – because he does not give it any attention, other than to refer to McKibbin's comments.

[17] Cited and discussed in Melanie Barber (ed.), 'Randall Davidson: a partial retrospective', in Stephen Taylor (ed.), *From Cranmer to Davidson: A Church of England Miscellany* (Woodbridge, 1999), p. 399.

[18] Ross McKibbin, *Classes and Cultures: England 1918–1951* (Oxford, 2000), p. 276.

[19] Louise Creighton, *The Life and Letters of Mandell Creighton* (London, 1913), p. 301.

[20] Cited by Hensley Henson, *The National Church* (1908), pp. 20–1.

[21] G. W. E. Russell, *Edward King: Sixtieth Bishop of Lincoln* (London, 1912), p. 254.

[22] Henson, *National Church*, p. 20.

[23] G. W. E. Russell, *Arthur Stanton: A Memoir* (London, 1917), p. 146.

[24] Cited in Adrian Hastings, *Church and State: The English Experience* (Exeter, 1991), p. 37.

[25] Creighton, *Mandell Creighton*, p. 349.

[26] C. S. Magee (ed.), *Speeches and Addresses by the late W. C. Magee D. D.* (London, 1893), p. 56.

[27] Alexander was an Ulsterman. We learn, however, that though he seldom preached in Belfast or Dublin he was in constant demand in England – where the Athenaeum club provided an agreeable home from home. W. G. Neely, 'Primate Alexander', in John R. Guy and W. G. Neeley (eds.), *Contrasts and Comparisons: Studies in Irish and Welsh Church History* (Welshpool, 1999), p. 82.

[28] Kathryn Tidrick, *Empire and the English Character* (London, 1992). She uses the term 'character' as a convenient shorthand 'for an untidy bundle of thoughts and feelings' to be found amongst the 'men in the outposts' with whom she is concerned.

[29] Cited in Paul Langford, *Englishness Identified: Manners and Character 1650–1850* (Oxford, 2000), p. 291.

[30] Creighton, *Mandell Creighton*, pp. 301–2.

[31] Russell, *King*, p. 253.

[32] There could scarcely be a better illustration of David Lowenthal's contention that in no country but England has landscape been taken to embody so clearly national virtues and a national way of life. D. Lowenthal, 'European and English landscapes as national symbols', in D. Hoosen (ed.), *Geography and National Identity* (Oxford, 1994), pp. 15–38.

33 A. P. Stanley, *The Life and Correspondence of Thomas Arnold, D. D.* (London, 1845), II, pp. 380–1.

34 Ibid., p. 440.

35 J. Bromley, *The Man of Ten Talents: A Portrait of Richard Chenevix Trench 1807–86: Philologist, Poet, Theologian, Archbishop* (London, 1959), p. 53.

36 See Colin Haydon, *Anti-Catholicism in Eighteenth-Century England c.1714–80* (Manchester, 1993).

37 F. Bennett, The Story of W. *J. E. Bennett and of his part in the Oxford Movement of the Nineteenth Century* (London, 1909) p. 154.

38 Marjorie Morgan, *National Identities and Travel in Victorian Britain* (Basingstoke, 2001), pp. 94–9.

39 Cited in Ibid., pp. 108–9.

40 Notwithstanding his subsequent founding of the Italianate Brompton Oratory, Faber wished to see a church which could be put 'before English Catholics in an English shape, translated into native thought and feeling, as well as language'. Cited in M. Heimann, *Catholic Devotion in Victorian England* (Oxford, 1995), p. 27.

41 Anne Mozley (ed.), *Letters and Correspondence of John Henry Newman during his Life in the English Church* (London, 1891), I, p. 394.

42 Bennett, *Bennett*, p. 155.

43 Arthur Westcott, *Life and Letters of Brooke Foss Westcott* (London, 1903), p. 188.

44 Mary C. Church, *The Life and Letters of Dean Church* (London, 1894), p. 99.

45 A. Tilney Bassett (ed.), *Gladstone to his Wife* (London, 1935), p. 56.

46 Charles Wordsworth, *Annals of My Early Life, 1806–1846* (London, 1891) pp. 127 and 145: Schleiermacher died in 1834. The English translation of his life and letters was published in 1860. It was not until 1893 that an English translation of his *Reden* on religion was published, translated by John Oman.

47 Cited in David Nicholls, *Deity and Domination: Images of God and the State in the Nineteenth and Twentieth Centuries* (London, 1984), p. 179.

48 Cited in Peter Hammond, *Dean Stanley of Westminster* (Worthing, 1987), p. 134.

49 Cited in Keith Robbins, *Protestant Germany through Victorian Eyes: A Complex Victorian Encounter* (London, 1993), p. 13.

50 W. R. Ward, 'Faith and fallacy: English and German

perspectives in the nineteenth century', in R. J. Helmstadter and B. Lightman (eds.), *Victorian Faith in Crisis* (Stanford, 1990), p. 55.

51 R. B. Martin, *The Dust of Combat: A Life of Charles Kingsley* (London, 1959), p. 135.

52 F. E. Kingsley, *Charles Kingsley: His Letters and Memories of his Life* (London, 1883), p. 99.

53 Mosley, *Newman*, I, p. 353.

54 J. H. Newman, *Apologia Pro Vita Sua* (London, 1892), p. 83.

55 W. M. Jacob, *The Making of the Anglican Church Worldwide* (London, 1997), p. 158.

56 Peter Hinchliff, 'Colonial church establishment in the aftermath of the Colenso controversy', in N. Aston (ed.), *Religious Change in Europe 1650–1914: Essays for John McManners* (Oxford, 1997), p. 346.

57 J. R. Seeley, *The Expansion of England* (London, 1883), p. 8.: In another aspect of his thinking Seeley also had an Anglocentric perspective; see R. T. Shannon, 'J. R. Seeley and the idea of a national church', in R. Robson (ed.), *Ideas and Institutions of Victorian Britain* (London, 1967), pp. 236–67

58 Keith Robbins, *Sir Edward Grey: A Biography of Lord Grey of Fallodon* (London, 1971).

59 R. W. Seton-Watson, *Britain in Europe 1789–1914* (Cambridge, 1945 [1937]), p. 650.

60 Church, *Church*, p. 197.

61 A. Cunningham, *William Cunningham: Teacher and Priest* (London, 1950), p. 119.

62 John Walsh and Stephen Taylor, 'Introduction: the Church and Anglicanism in the "long" eighteenth century', in John Walsh, Colin Haydon and Stephen Taylor, *The Church of England c.1689–c.1833: From Toleration to Tractarianism* (Cambridge, 1993), pp. 56–7.

63 Bennett, *Bennett*, p. 234.

64 Cited in A. R. Vidler, *The Orb and the Cross: A Normative Study in the Relations of Church and State with Reference to Gladstone's Early Writings* (London, 1945), p. 103.

65 Cited by Dean Church, 'Mr Gladstone's Letter on the English Church', in R. W. Church, *Occasional Papers* (London, 1897), II, p. 68.

66 Patrick Joyce, 'The narrative structure of Victorian politics', in James Vernon (ed.), *Re-reading the constitution: New Narratives in the Political History of England's Long Nineteenth Century* (Cambridge, 1996), p. 189. The extent to which

'modernity' was inherently 'Protestant' was much debated. *Self-Help* by Samuel Smiles was translated into Italian in 1865, and was referred to a few years later, in an Italian book on idleness in Italy, as an *opera santa*. The marvellous activity of the Anglo-Saxons was referred to in this work as being like perpetual motion. Jane Garnett, 'Catholics, Protestants, and work in nineteenth-century Europe', in R. N. Swanson (ed.), *Studies in Church History Vol. 37: The Use and Abuse of Time in Christian History* (Woodbridge, 2002), p. 261.

67 G. K. A. Bell, *Randall Davidson, Archbishop of Canterbury* (Oxford, 1952), p. 113. Davidson considered that his early pursuits had taught him instinctively to grasp the lay view 'and sometimes the sporting view on all sorts of questions'. Stuart Mews, 'Randall Davidson's attitudes to work, rest, and recreation', in R. N. Swanson (ed.), *Studies in Church History Vol. 37: The Use and Abuse of Time in Christian History* (Woodbridge, 2002), p. 387

68 Cited in W. J. Reader, *'At Duty's Call': A Study of Obsolete Patriotism* (Manchester, 1988), pp. 96–7; P. Scott 'Cricket and the religious world in the Victorian period', *Church Quarterly*, 3 (1970), 134–44.

69 George Robb, *British Culture and the First World War* (Basingstoke, 2002), p. 114. The position of the Church of England can be more thoroughly studied through Albert Marrin, *The Last Crusade: The Church of England in the First World War* (Durham, NC, 1974), and Alan Wilkinson, *The Church of England and the First World War* (London, 1978).

70 Keith Robbins, *Churchill* (London, 1992), p. 17.

71 Keith Robbins, *John Bright* (London, 1979), pp. 205–6. There was relief on the part of colleagues that his Dissent had not initially been very wide-ranging and had been limited to asking certain questions about the expenses of the royal yacht.

72 D. W. Bebbington, *The Nonconformist Conscience: Chapel and Politics 1870–1914* (London, 1982), and Stephen Koss, *Nonconformity in Modern British Politics* (London, 1975), provide detailed accounts.

73 Cited in Dale A. Johnson, *The Changing Shape of English Nonconformity 1825–1925* (New York, 1999), p. 164. For further reflections on how 1662 was viewed in 1862 see Timothy Larsen, 'Victorian Nonconformity and the memory of the ejected ministers: the impact of the bicentennial commemorations of 1862', in R. N. Swanson (ed.), *Studies in*

Church History Vol. 33: The Church Retrospective (Woodbridge, 1997), pp. 459–73.

74 Timothy Larsen, *Friends of Religious Equality: Nonconformist Politics in Mid-Victorian England* (Woodbridge, 1999), p. 267.

75 The Congregationalist John Stoughton, cited in Johnson, *Changing Shape of English Nonconformity*, p. 108.

76 Cited in J. H. S. Kent, 'Hugh Price Hughes and the Nonconformist conscience', in G. V. Bennett and J. D. Walsh (eds.), *Essays in Modern English Church History in Memory of Norman Sykes* (London, 1966), pp. 188–9.

77 H. Macleod, 'Dissent and the peculiarities of the English, *c.*1870–1914', in Jane Shaw and Alan Kreider (eds.), *Culture and the Nonconformist Tradition* (Cardiff, 1999), pp. 117–41

78 K. Brown, *A Social History of the Nonconformist Ministry in England and Wales 1800–1930* (Oxford, 1988), pp. 44–6, gives details of the Welsh contribution to the English ministry. In the city of Bristol, for example, Welshmen, by one definition or another, dominated the leading Congregational pulpits: David Morgan Thomas, *Urijah Rees Thomas: His Life and Work* (London, 1902), H. Arnold Thomas, *Memorials of David Thomas* (London, 1876), *Arnold Thomas of Bristol: Collected Papers and Addresses with a Memoir by Nathaniel Micklem* (London, 1925). Hugh Price Hughes, so closely linked with the 'Nonconformist conscience', flourished in London but came from Carmarthen. Christopher Oldstone-Moore, *Hugh Price Hughes: Founder of New Methodism: Conscience of New Nonconformity* (Cardiff, 1999).

79 Seeley, *Expansion*, pp. 49–50.

80 Michael Fry, *The Scottish Empire* (East Linton/Edinburgh, 2001), p. 498.

81 Laurence Brockliss, 'The professions and national identity', in Laurence Brockliss and David Eastwood (eds.), *A Union of Multiple Identities : The British Isles c.1750–c.1850* (Manchester, 1997), p. 22. On the other hand, it has been suggested that 'Irish clergymen began to go in increasing numbers to English parishes' by R. B. McDowell, *The Church of Ireland 1869–1969* (London, 1975), p. 1. Nigel Yates, *Anglican Ritualism in Victorian Britain, 1830–1910* (Oxford, 1999), pp. 138–40, suggests that one reason for movement was the hostility to even the mildest forms of ritualism in the Church of Ireland and the fact that the clergy were a good deal 'higher' than the laity.

82 Owen Chadwick, *The Victorian Church*, II (London, 1970),

p. 435: William Jacobson of Chester (1865–84), for example, first spent a session at Glasgow University, where it was cheaper. J. W. Burgon, *Lives of Twelve Good Men*, II (London, 1888), p. 241.

83 Kenneth Hylson-Smith, *Evangelicals in the Church of England 1734–1984* (Edinburgh, 1988), pp. 147–8

84 Archibald Tait (Edinburgh High School, Edinburgh Academy, Glasgow University, Balliol College, Oxford), Bishop of London (1856–68) and Archbishop of Canterbury (1868–82). Through his wife, Tait had connections with Anglicans in Co. Clare and, as Dean of Carlisle, he had experienced 'the very squalid poverty of a mass of people drawn in no very unequal proportions from England, from Scotland, and from Ireland'. W. Benham (ed.), *Catherine and Crauford Tait: A Memoir* (London, 1879), pp. 39–40: Randall Davidson (Harrow and Trinity College, Oxford), Bishop of Winchester (1895–1903) and Archbishop of Canterbury (1903–28); Cosmo Gordon Lang (The Park School, Glasgow, Glasgow University, Balliol and All Souls colleges, Oxford), Archbishop of York (1909–28) and Archbishop of Canterbury (1928–42).

85 Owen Chadwick, *The Victorian Church*, I (1970), pp. 42–3, 53–4.

86 E. J. Whately (ed.), *The Commonplace Book of Richard Whateley, D.D., late Archbishop of Dublin* (London, 1865), p. 269.

87 The suggestion is made by Akenson, *Church of Ireland*, p. 328.

88 E. J. Whateley, *Life and Correspondence of Archbishop Whateley*, I (London, 1866), p. 127.

89 Akenson, *Church of Ireland*, p. 328.

90 Cited in R. B. McDowell, *The Church of Ireland 1869–1969* (London, 1975), pp. 8–9.

91 Bromley, *Trench*, p. 42.

92 Cited in Neely, 'Primate Alexander', p. 79.

93 D. George Boyce, 'Gladstone and Ireland', in P. J. Jagger (ed.), *Gladstone* (London, 1998), pp. 108–11. Other pertinent aspects of the situation are discussed in Hilary Jenkins, 'The Irish dimension of the British *Kulturkampf*: Vaticanism and civil allegiance 1870–1875', *Journal of Ecclesiastical History*, 30, 3 (July, 1879), pp. 353–77.

94 Owen Chadwick speaks of there now being, for the first time, 'one part of Great Britain' which existed without an Established Church – but Ireland was not part of Great Britain. O. Chadwick, *The Victorian Church*, II (London, 1970), p. 433.

95 Cited in D. T. W. Price, *Yr Esgob Burgess a Choleg Llanbedr/Bishop Burgess and Lampeter College* (Cardiff, 1987), p. 61. the words of Rowland Williams, the most distinguished Welsh scholar of his time, who was himself later to leave Lampeter and find solace in the diocese of Salisbury.
96 Keith Robbins, 'Episcopacy in Wales' *Journal of the Welsh Religious History Society*, 4 (1996), 63–78; Paul O'Leary, 'Religion, nationality and politics: disestablishment in Ireland and Wales, 1868–1914', in Guy and Neely, *Contrasts and Comparisons*, pp. 89–113.
97 Keith Robbins, 'Cultural independence and political devolution in Wales', in H. T. Dickinson and M. Lynch (eds.), *The Challenge of Westminster: Sovereignty, Devolution and Independence* (East Linton, 2000), pp. 81–90, 'Locating Wales: culture, place and identity', in N. Garnham and K. Jeffery (eds), *Culture, Place and Identity: Historical Studies XXIII* (Dublin, 2005), pp. 23–38, and 'Wales and the "British Question"', in *Transactions of the Honourable Society of Cymmrodorion*, New Series 9 (2003), 152–61.

11

Recreating the history of the Church of England: Bishop Burgess, the Oxford Movement and nineteenth-century reconstructions of Protestant and Anglican identity

PETER NOCKLES

Bishop Burgess one used to hear of as an Apostolic Bishop. He was reputed to be a man of very simple habits, and, if I mistake not the expression 'gig bishop' arose from someone having met him making the round of the diocese of St David's in a vehicle of that sort. At Salisbury he did as his predecessors had done. In 1831 I passed some days at old Mr Stevens', the Rector of Bradfield, with whom Bishop Burgess had been staying over a Sunday not long before. The Bishop kindly preached. The church is barely half a mile from the parsonage, and the Bishop went in his carriage, with two apparitors bearing wands walking before the horses all the way, making it, as the old rector said, very like a black job.[1]

Thomas Mozley's anecdotal description of Bishop Thomas Burgess, to whom he devoted a short chapter in his somewhat quirky and unreliable *Reminiscences of Oriel College and the Oxford Movement* (1882), may only reveal a trivial or inconsequential incident amidst the confused and inconsequential ramblings of an aged former Tractarian. On the other hand, it may also indicate something of the ambivalent, if not patronizing, attitude of those who came to be labelled the 'Apostolicals' towards a preceding generation of orthodox Anglican churchmen, for whom the search for apostolical continuity as the basis of the Church of England's spiritual claims was no less important than it was for themselves. Was Burgess, for all his well-deserved reputation as a conscientious diocesan committed to the improvement of clerical theological education, being shown up to be less than 'apostolical' in his habits, and thus primitive ethos (the cardinal Tractarian virtue), than his reputation warranted? The term 'Apostolical', of course, became self-referential among the Tractarians soon after the launch of the Oxford Movement in 1833.[2] Newman's correspondence in 1833 and 1834 is littered with references to such and such an individual embracing 'Apostolical principles', becoming a 'regular Apostolical', or joining 'the Apostolical movement',[3] thereby signifying their adhesion to the principles of the Tractarians, a distinctive benchmark of which was loyalty to the supposed ethos of the primitive church. The same epithet, as previously applied to Bishop Burgess at a time when the epithet 'apostolical' (like that of 'primitive') was still a cross-bench term used by Anglican evangelicals and High Churchmen alike, was perhaps an uncomfortable reminder to the early Tractarians that they could claim no monopoly in allegiance to the practice and spirit of the primitive church. This article will explore the often-subtle ways in which Anglican churchmen such as Bishop Burgess, but most notably the leaders of the Oxford Movement, used history to further their own cause within, or on behalf of, the nineteenth-century Church of England.

The Tractarian project rested on the confident claim to be merely renewing the historic Anglicanism of the seventeenth century for a supposedly 'forgetful generation'. This claim needs examination. The Oxford Movement's opponents, no less than its proponents, used and interpreted sixteenth- and seventeenth-century English religious history (notably the English Reformation and the Laudian era) in their own distinctive, highly selective and competing senses. They were both locked into a contemporary nineteenth-century ecclesiastical agenda as to who could claim to be the most faithful heirs of the historical 'Anglicanism' of the later sixteenth and seventeenth centuries. The debate was fierce because both sides used history as a determinant of what sort of church the Church of

England ought to be. Bishop Burgess had used church history in a different, though no less polemical way, by moulding his account of ancient British church history to proclaim the early origins and continuity of the Church of England's Protestant identity.

There was a long tradition of High Church Anglican historiography, in varying degrees and at varying times both anti-Presbyterian and anti-Roman Catholic, stretching from Henry Spelman's *Concilia* (1639) to Peter Heylin's *Ecclesia Restaurata* (1676), through Jeremy Collier's eight-volume *Ecclesiastical History* (1708–14), to Christopher Wordsworth's *Ecclesiastical Institutes* (1810) and Robert Southey's *Book of the Church* (1824). This tradition, with its emphasis on the 'primitive Church' as the true model of the Church of England, viewed Puritanism and 'Popery' as challenges to that model.[4] There was another, if not counter, ultra-Protestant and Whig Low Church historiography, associated with John Foxe (the first full edition of Foxe's *Actes and Monuments*, or 'Book of Martyrs', appeared in 1563, and the ninth in 1684; thereafter, popular editions were published at intervals[5]) and Gilbert Burnet (author of a *History of the Reformation*) respectively. The writings of Bishop Burgess, like those of other early nineteenth-century Protestant High Churchmen, such as (the former Unitarian) Southey's *Book of the Church* and Wordsworth's *Ecclesiastical Biography*, with its reprints from Foxe's martyrology,[6] do not fit exclusively into either tradition but converge and retain elements of both.

According to Bishop Burgess's biographer, John Harford, writing in 1840, in his deep attachment to the apostolic mode of government, primitive ordinances and scriptural doctrines of the Church of England Burgess was, 'in this sense, a high churchman', but Harford consciously sought to offset the contemporary negative connotations of that term among many of his readership. Thus, Harford insisted that 'there was no bitterness in his orthodoxy', and that 'however uncompromising in his opinions, charity and kindness influenced his whole mode of communicating them'.[7] Harford's readers would have taken the hint. However, Mark Smith has persuasively argued that Bishop Burgess was a more rigid High Churchman than his irenic reputation, as established by his biographer, the

Anglican evangelical Harford, might have suggested. Nonetheless, Burgess's generous support for the non-denominational British and Foreign Bible Society (founded in 1804) and good relations with prominent Anglican evangelicals,[8] as well as his defences of the religious writings of that patron saint of the 'commonwealth' tradition of seventeenth-century ultra-Protestants, John Milton, would seem to separate him clearly from High Churchmen of the character of Charles Daubeny (1745–1827), Archdeacon of Sarum (from 1804). Burgess's support for the Bible Society was by implication criticized by Daubeny[9] and Herbert Marsh, Regius Profesor of Divinity at Cambridge and later Bishop of Peterborough, who on principle opposed the distribution of the Bible without the Book of Common Prayer as subversive of the Established Church. Marsh was also critical of the very title of Burgess's work in defence of the Bible Society, *The Bible and Nothing but the Bible, the Religion of the Church of England*, as, 'a very injudicious one. For it contains a proposition, which is not only false in one sense, though true in another, but is false in that sense, in which it is more likely to be understood and applied'.[10] Although Marsh was himself criticized by one High Churchman for not taking high enough ground in his appeal to apostolical tradition, his position was closer to the 'High Church' one of Daubeny and William Van Mildert than to that of Burgess.[11] Burgess took advantage of Marsh's consequent embarrassment at the hands of the Roman Catholic controversialist, the Jesuit Peter Gandolphy, who ironically congratulated him 'on renouncing the great principle of the Reformation' and 'vital principle of Protestantism'.[12] Burgess defended Marsh from what he regarded as the Jesuit's perversion of Marsh's reasoning, but also conceded that Gandolphy's charge was plausible. Although he accepted that 'the learned Professor's reasoning' had been 'perverted' by Gandolphy, Burgess implied that Marsh had left himself wide open to misrepresentation, arguing that, 'the objection to the distribution of the Bible, without the Prayer Book, is, in its principle, of so anti-protestant a complexion, that the Roman Catholics claim the chief supporter of it, as their friend, and have congratulated him on renouncing the great principle of the Reformation'.[13] Burgess, however, made clear that his support for the

Bible Society by no means implied conciliation or encouragement of Protestant Dissent. As he put it, 'The union of churchmen and Dissenters for the distribution of the Scriptures, is not
much more likely to render churchmen favourable to sectarian
principles, than it is to reconcile Dissenters to the Church'.[14]

Burgess's concern for establishing the Church of England's ecclesiastical continuity with the early church, however, was a High Church emphasis. Burgess did not get
drawn into the theological controversy in 1798–1805
between Daubeny and the Anglican evangelicals Sir Richard
Hill and John Overton over grace, free will and justification, or whether or not the Thirty-Nine Articles supported
an exclusively Calvinist or Arminian interpretation.[15] However, Burgess's own Arminianism was pronounced and
extreme, occasionally finding polemical expression. Thus,
he joined Daubeny in 1826–7 in a defence of the late
seventeenth-century Bishop of St David's, George Bull,
whose ultra-Arminian soteriology and teaching on justification were expressed in Bull's *Harmonia Apostolica*
(1669–70), against the strictures of the evangelical Archdeacon of Ely, Edward Browne, in a Charge to his archdeaconry in 1826. Burgess accused Archdeacon Browne of
having 'a strong taint of the Calvinian heresy',[16] and
condemned the Archdeacon's critique of Bull, 'author of the
celebrated tract on the *Corruptions of the Church of
Rome*', as 'erroneous and absurd' and as defeating 'itself by
its own extravagance'. Burgess commended Daubeny's refutation of the Archdeacon's attack as showing 'a zeal for the
honour of Bishop Bull, and for the doctrine which he
maintained, worthy of his younger years'.[17] 'Bishop Bull
... and his admirers', Burgess insisted, did not, as Archdeacon Browne suggested, 'confound Justification with
Sanctification, but with Hooker, they distinguish the two
meanings of Justification, which the two Apostles have
variously adopted with different views, and, therefore,
without contradiction'.[18] In defending Bishop Bull, Burgess
appealed to the testimony of the Nonjuring layman Robert
Nelson (1660–1715) and the later encomium on Bull's
Harmonia Apostolica by the High Churchman Samuel
Horsley (1733–1806), Burgess's predecessor as Bishop of St

David's.[19] Such an approach was divisive and, in fact, can be contrasted with the more inclusive line earlier enjoined by Bishop Horsley, who had tried to bridge the Arminian–Calvinist divide.

Burgess's High Church preoccupations were also evident in his sacramental views, notably on baptismal regeneration and in his hard-line position on the invalidity of Protestant Dissenters' baptism, which was exemplified in his stand during the legal case brought in 1809 by William Kemp against an Anglican clergyman, John Wight Wickes, for refusing to bury a child who had been baptised by a Dissenter.[20] When Sir John Nicholl gave a judgment in favour of the complainant in the Court of Arches, Burgess published a critique claiming that the judgment, implying 'that a lawful minister is not essential to baptism', misinterpreted the rubric and tended 'directly to the subversion of the Established Church'.[21] Nonetheless, Burgess's somewhat narrowly legalistic and establishmentarian, rather than purely sacramental, ground of concern at the judgment is clear from his own explanation:

> A churchman's objection to sectarian baptism does not declare such baptism to be null and void for the purposes of sectarian discipline; it does not even deny it the name of a Christian office; it only declares it to be not lawful according to the laws of the Church of England; to be null, as to the Church, and therefore not entitled to the privileges of church baptism.[22]

Burgess's orthodoxy was also manifested in his polemical writings against Unitarianism, which preoccupied him as much as his anti-Catholic works, and earned him a reputation for 'high church bigotry' in these quarters, with one Unitarian lay seceder in 1814 describing the bishop's arguments as 'far better adapted to the state of Christendom in the twelfth century, or to the meridian of Spain at the present moment, than to the enlightened age and country in which we live'.[23] However, his passionate concern for the defence of orthodox Trinitarian doctrine against Unitarians was one shared by Anglican evangelicals. Burgess's High Churchmanship also manifested itself in more positive ways. His spirituality was fed on the devotional classics of Caroline, Nonjuring and eighteenth-century

High Church divines, such as Nelson's *Practice of True Devotion*, Law's *Serious Call* and Bishop Thomas Wilson's *Sacra Privata*.

Colin Kidd has argued that by the second half of the eighteenth century, the rise of Enlightenment and end of confessional warfare had encouraged a decline in the British identity of the Church of England.[24] This may have held true for political discourse, but it was manifestly not the case in Anglican theological discourse. Far from paying mere 'lip-service' to earlier ecclesiastical rhetoric, Bishop Burgess made the issue of the ancient British church a key feature of his opposition to Catholic Emancipation. In Burgess's works, such as *The First Seven Epochs of the Ancient British Church* (1813), *Christ and not St Peter, the Rock of the Christian Church* (1814) and his *Tracts on the Origins and Independence of the Ancient British Church* (1815), anti-Catholicism was the overarching theme. These works drew on a tradition of Anglican apologetic exemplified by Isaac Basire's *Ancient Liberty of the Britanick Church* (1661), Edmund Stillingfleet's *Origines Britannicae* (1685) and works by William Cave; a tradition which the historian Glen Burgess has characterized as a 'patriotic antiquarianism', which extended to claims of ancient origins for legal, constitutional and parliamentary, as well as ecclesiastical, institutions.[25] They used history to demonstrate a supposed continuity of the Church of England with origins in an ancient British Christianity which was non-Roman, and to claim, in Bishop Burgess's words, that papal jurisdiction was 'not established till the twelfth century, and then only by violent usurpation',[26] and that consequently 'Romanism' in Britain was akin to 'schism'.[27] For Bishop Burgess, 'the Church of Britain was a Protestant church nine centuries before the days of Luther'. He argued that the Reformation allowed the Church of England to 'resume her primitive character' and 'ancient independence'. 'Popery' was portrayed as 'an intruder upon the Church of England and not the Church of England upon Popery'.[28] More controversially, Bishop Burgess's historical labours led him to conclude that 'our ancestors not only rejected Popery, as early as the beginning of the seventh century, but made a public and indignant protest against the authority of the Pope, as well as the corruptions of his Church'[29] – a conclusion which put him

239

in conflict with the very different reading of Anglo-Saxon Christianity propounded by the English Catholic clerical historian, John Lingard,[30] Lingard contending 'that the rock on which the Bishop of St David's has built his British church, is no better than a hillock of sand'.[31]

In the context of later assumptions about High Churchmanship being but a halfway house or approximation to Roman Catholicism, it is significant that in the immediately pre-Tractarian era it was Whig latitudinarians or Low Churchmen, such as Henry Bathurst (1744–1837), Bishop of Norwich, rather than extreme High Churchmen, such as Daubeny, who displayed tolerant attitudes towards English Roman Catholics; the 'ultra-Tory' Burgess actually took issue with Bishop Bathurst for apparent over-leniency towards Roman Catholicism. Burgess even approvingly cited the Erastian arguments against Catholicism expounded by the notorious Low Churchmen Benjamin Hoadly (1676–1761),[32] the object of William Law's famous strictures in the so-called Bangorian controversy, and Francis Blackburne (1705–87), Archdeacon of Cleveland, in his *Considerations on the Present State of the Controversy between the Protestants and Papists* (1767).[33] Blackburne's virulent anti-Catholicism from a 'rational' latitudinarian perspective had led him to assail even that acknowledged ornament of Anglican orthodoxy (and later something of an oracle for the Tractarians) Joseph Butler for alleged Catholic tendencies.[34] In citing Hoadly and Blackburne, of whose latitudinarianism he disapproved, Burgess's anti-Catholicism seemed to have got the better of his own anti-latitudinarianism.

A few pre-Tractarian High Churchmen, however, were more irenic towards the Church of Rome. The High Churchman Samuel Wix, Rector of St Bartholomew-the-Less, City of London,[35] engaged in controversy with Bishop Burgess in 1818–20 over Wix's controversial proposals for reunion with a reformed Church of Rome, apparently modelled on proposals of Archbishop William Wake for a *rapprochement* with the Gallican Church in 1718. Unlike Burgess, Wix stressed Anglican apostolical continuity, in a way which emphasized the shared inheritance of both Churches. To Burgess's evident dismay, Wix maintained that, 'no solid objection prevails against the Church of England attempting a union with the Church of Rome; since the Church of Rome is acknowledged by the Church of England to be a true apostolical church'.[36]

Wix disdained temporal emoluments and privileges as the ground of attachment to the Established Church, an anti-Erastian emphasis which drew explicit inspiration from works of the Nonjurors, such as Thomas Brett's *Account of Church Government* and William Law's *Three Letters to the Bishop of Bangor* (1717), and led him to eulogize the non-established Scottish Episcopal Church.[37] It was an emphasis which like-wise prefigured that of the Tractarians in the 1830s. Signifi-cantly, Wix also defended various apostolical practices, such as prayers for the dead (later to be propagated by the Tractar-ians), by reference to the later Nonjuring defences of disused primitive usages, as set forth in George Hickes's *Christian Priesthood*, Thomas Brett's *Tradition Necessary* and Thomas Deacon's *Complete Collection of Devotions* (1734),[38] in a way which pre-dated the teaching of the Tractarians. In his defence against what he claimed were Burgess's 'misrepresentations' of his own views and proposals, Wix protested that he yielded 'to no one in his just abhorrence of the errors, of the delusions of the Church of Rome'; but he also appealed to the sentiments of Caroline divines, such as Richard Montagu, Jeremy Taylor and Herbert Thorndike, in favour of the lawfulness of such cus-toms, including the invocation of saints, citing Laud's first biographer, Peter Heylin, in the introduction to his *Cyprianus Anglicanus* (1668): 'nothing that was apostolic, or accorded primitive, did fare the worse for being Popish'.[39]

With disarming irenicism, Wix maintained that, 'the Roman Catholics, it is believed are greatly misunderstood and cruelly calumniated. Truth requires this statement. With respect to their errors, it well becomes Protestants to guard against irritating and confirming them in their errors by misrepresenta-tion'.[40] The implication was that the Bishop was guilty of this mistake. Wix complained about what he regarded as the Bishop's misquotations from Jeremy Taylor on the subject of the supposed 'idolatry' of the Church of Rome. He himself cited various Caroline divines, notably Montagu and Thorn-dike, to clear the Church of Rome from this charge, even citing Thorndike's bold argument that they 'who justify the Reformation by charging the Pope to be Anti-Christ, and the Papists Idolators' were themselves 'schismatics before God'.[41] In a passage that prefigured (and even went further than) Newman's later argument in Tract 90, Wix rebutted Burgess's claim that the Catholic practice of invocation of saints was idolatrous, by appealing both to the Anglican Homily against Idolatry and to the Catechism of the Council of Trent, insisting that:

> The Church of Rome positively disclaims any honour to the Creature which is due to God only. Consequently, the words of the Homily do not apply to Invocation, as directed by the Roman Church, with whatever truth they may apply, and too justly, I fear they do apply, to the practices of certain individuals.[42]

Moreover, Wix argued that discrepancies in the doctrine of the Eucharist between the British and Roman churches reflected 'different shades of opinion', and suggested that even on the 'fundamental error of Transubstantiation', a conference with Roman Catholics might clear up misunderstandings and 'lead to mutual concession and unity of sentiment'.[43]

Such irenic overtures in the direction of Rome were anathema to Bishop Burgess. For Burgess, anyone who thought the declaration against transubstantiation for office-holders to be an 'unfounded calumny' or held the 'worship of the Church of Rome not to be idolatrous' could not be 'Protestants, whatever they may profess to be'.[44] Whereas Wix minimized differences between the Church of England and Rome on the Eucharist by reference to the irenic position of various Laudian divines of the 1630s, Burgess emphasized the gulf. He conceded that individual divines such as Montagu and Thorndike had appeared to deny that practices such as invocation were idolatrous (at least under qualification), but he appealed to Stillingfleet's *Discourse on Idolatry* as conclusive on the matter. He cited approvingly Stillingfleet's words: 'I cannot see why the authority of some very few persons (Thorndike, Montagu, etc.) though of great learning, should bear sway against the constant opinion of our Church ever since the Reformation'.[45] Burgess identified closely with the anti-Catholic polemic works of Anglican divines from the era of that earlier constitutional crisis of the 1680s. These included those of Edmund Stilling-fleet (1635–99), Bishop of Worcester, and three successive Archbishops of Canterbury: John Tillotson, author of *A Discourse against Transubstantiation* (1684), and Thomas Tenison, both Whig Low Churchmen, and William Wake, author of *A Discourse of the Holy Eucharist* (1688) and a Whig High Churchman, of sorts. He cited favourably Tenison's comment (from his translation of Placete's *Six Conferences*) that the Roman Catholic 'doctrine of the eucharist overthrows the proofs of the Christian religion'[46]. He also cited Wake's view, in his *Preservative against Popery* (1687), that on the Eucharist, 'we are at the farthest distance from one another'[47].

There was a defensive tone to Harford's references to the Bishop's controversy with Wix. Wix was certainly dismayed by the ferocity of Burgess's critique of his pamphlets favouring reunion with the Church of Rome on strictly limited conditions. Wix made a veiled charge against the Bishop of anti-Catholic bigotry suggesting that this blinded Burgess to the reality of his own modest proposal:

> The truth is, that so excessive are the prejudices of the amiable Bishop of St David's against the Church of Rome, that he cannot separate the proposal as to the expediency of a Council, to consider whether measures may be adopted to prevail with the Romanists to remove their errors, as the way to Christian union, from a disposition to unite with those errors.[48]

Wix even hinted at the malign influence of the Bishop's support for the Bible Society and the resulting need to placate its evangelical supporters:

> No bishop has more distinctly stated the constitution of the Christian Church, than the Bishop of St David's has done . . . yet, from a goodness which allows him not to suspect evil of others, his Lordship gives countenance to a Society, whose tendency is to neutralise all the exterior forms, as well as the peculiar doctrines of Christianity.[49]

Wix's antipathy to the Bible Society as 'the grand modern engine of religious schism and insubordination'[50] was a characteristic contemporary High Church trope and mirrored the view of Daubeny, Mant, Marsh, Van Mildert and others. Wix clearly felt that the Bishop's theoretical strictness of churchmanship was being compromised in practice by his readiness to work with Anglican evangelicals, and even Protestant Dissenters, as a consequence of an over readiness to oppose anything savouring of 'Popery'. Certainly, as late as 1835, in his last discussion with the Bishop, Harford was able to cite what other High Church-men might have regarded as Burgess's over-generous acknowl-edgment of the Wesleyan Methodists' attachment to the Established Church. According to Harford, Burgess 'spoke with much esteem of that community of Christians'.[51] That Burgess was prepared to regard the Church of England as closer to Protestant Dissent than to the Church of Rome, and at least temporarily to cast aside the question of antiquity of apostolical lineage, was made explicit in one of his responses to Wix's irenic pamphlets:

> Would it not be much more natural and charitable and Christian-like, to devise some means, if possible, of recovering to the Church the various denominations of Dissenters in England and Ireland, and of the Kirk of Scotland? Mutual concessions might be more practicable with them, than with the Church of Rome, a very large portion of the Dissenters being what are called orthodox Dissenters, and none of them having to look higher for their origin than the sixteenth century, and a very small proportion of them differing from us in the essentials of their Faith.[52]

For a High Churchman, this was a rather unusual argu-ment, especially as evangelical Calvinist Dissenters were, by implication, being embraced. For Burgess, in this instance, novelty was seemingly being privileged over antiquity. It marked a reversal of Burgess's more general concern to establish the Church of England's supposedly ancient ori-gins when arguing directly against Roman Catholic claims. Burgess, however, got round the usual High Church con-cession (as expounded by a consensus of the Caroline Divines) that the Church of Rome, for all its doctrinal corruptions, was a true church, on account of its apostolic foundations. For Burgess,

> If a church be Apostolical in its discipline, and not in its doctrines, it is not the true church, and if it be Apostolical in its doctrines and not in its discipline, it is not the true church ... A church, therefore, to be a true church, must be Apostolical in its outward form and its internal principles – in its discipline and its doctrines.[53]

Some High Churchmen in the 1790s, such as Bishop Samuel Horsley, had conceded (to his temporary ally, the Roman Catholic Bishop John Milner) that Socinianism was then a far worse threat to the Established Church than that posed by Catholicism.[54] In contrast, Burgess would not admit Wix's contention that the errors of Protestant sectaries, even those of Socinians, Anabaptists and Quakers, were more serious than the errors of 'Popery'.[55] Burgess even linked Socinian and Catholic errors together, citing a 'very curious work entitled *Roma Racoviana et Racovia Romana*'. He concluded,

> But of the other sects is there any one guilty of idolatry? And can any thing be more alarming than the idolatrous doctrine of Transubstantiation, the adoration of the Host, the Invocation of Saints, etc? Can anything be more alarming than the idolatry of those, who believe that every consecrated wafer which they eat, contains the whole power of the Godhead.[56]

Burgess's hard-line position partly derived from an influential Protestant view dating back to the Reformation era, and later expounded, among others, by Bishop Thomas Newton in his *Dissertation on the Prophecies* (1762). Burgess was at one with some High Churchmen (though with notable exceptions, such as Bishop Horsley), as well as Anglican evangelicals in the era of later Revolutionary and Napoleonic Europe, in identifying St Paul's 'Man of Sin' with the Antichrist, and 'applied their united character to the Pope and the Church of Rome'[57]. This prophetical interpretation enabled Burgess to assert that while the Church of Rome was 'apostolical in origin and in doctrine and practice for at least the first three centuries', thereafter, from the commencement of 'the Papal Apostasy', 'it was a very heretical, and unapostolical church for many centuries before the Reformation, in a very large portion of its doctrines and usages . . . Truth of character must require something more than authenticity of origin, or external form'.[58]

Wix seems to have been an exception to the well-attested trend among Anglican High Churchmen towards anti-Catholicism after 1801.[59] He got into trouble, not only with Bishop Burgess, but with the editor of the High Church *Anti-Jacobin Review* in 1818 (significantly, the title of this journal had been given the addition of the *Protestant Advocate* by this date). A letter from Wix to the editor was attacked in a long article. Wix's publications were denounced as 'favourable to Popish interests' and as being designed 'to show the expediency of attempting a conciliation with men who were . . . avowedly thirsting for the blood of our sons, our daughters, and ourselves'.[60] However, whether or not it was under the influence of Burgess's strictures on his reunion proposals, Wix himself came to modify his irenic sentiments towards Catholicism in later writings. Many passages in his *Plain Reasons why political power should not be granted to Papists* (1822) adopted Burgess's own line of reasoning against the Catholic claims. For example, Wix now argued, in apparent contradiction of his earlier expressed view, that:

> The acknowledgment of Papal Supremacy by the Roman Catholics, circumstances them, towards the British Constitution, very differently from any description of our Protestant Dissenters. This is that peculiarity in them, as a political religious body, which should never be forgotten by Englishmen: though it is apprehended, that in the desire . . . of perfecting religious liberty, it has been overlooked by many good persons. What, politically, might perhaps be safely conceded to Dissenters, who acknowledge no foreign head, in church or state, could not, on the same terms, be granted to Roman Catholics.[61]

Wix had embraced the very tenets of Protestant constitutionalism which his erstwhile adversary Bishop Burgess had relentlessly been expounding.

As in the case of Bishop Burgess, the Oxford Movement's appeal to history was concerned with proving the apostolical continuity of the Church of England with the primitive church. The Tractarians were at one with Bishop Burgess's insistence that the Church of England's origins should not be sought in the era of the Reformation. However, after its early phase, the Oxford Movement's anti-Catholic overtones came to be increasingly muted, greater weight being given to the undivided church as the ultimate source of authority and model of unity. Tractarian historicism was less narrowly insular than Bishop Burgess's or Southey's, and was less concerned with 'British' ancestry. Moreover, in not subscribing to Protestant theories of an era of papal apostasy and papal Antichrist,[62] it accorded much greater respect to the Middle Ages. The Movement's deference to Christian antiquity, according to the rule of catholic consent enunciated by St Vincent of Lerins in the fourth century, echoed the same appeal made by Wix in the irenic pamphlets which so irritated Bishop Burgess. In both cases, this appeal to antiquity had a dynamic quality which distinguished it from the more restricted and selective character of Bishop Burgess's use of the primitive church in his controversial writings. In particular, in even their mutedly anti-Catholic works, the early Tractarians consciously avoided the 'rationalistic' or anti-supernatural tone of Anglican polemic against transubstantiation, as expounded by Stillingfleet, Tillotson, Tenison and Wake in the late seventeenth century and by Bishop Burgess early in the nineteenth. In Tract 71, Newman hinted that he found such polemic irreverent. Transubstantiation was to be opposed because it was apparently not to be found in antiquity, not because it was irrational. On the contrary, transubstantiation was erroneous because it was itself a form of rationalism, and an 'innovation' on the teaching of the early church.[63]

For Newman and the Tractarians, it was important to convince contemporary churchmen that they had Anglican as well as patristic history on their side, and to harmonize the two sources of historical testimony. As Newman put it in his *Lectures on the Prophetical Office of the Church* (1837): 'We have a vast inheritance, but no inventory of our treasures. All is given in profusion; it remains for us to catalogue, sort, distribute, harmonize, and complete'.[64] Newman did not regard the Oxford Movement as a passive legatee of the whole Anglican inheritance. He looked beyond and behind the English Reformation and its formularies, in a way which Bishop Burgess might have regarded as almost treasonable. Newman's agenda involved the seventeenth-century divines being called into service, not so much to support, but to reinterpret the sense or amend the deficiencies of their sixteenth-century predecessors.

The Tractarians found the religious history of the Church of England to be something of a Noah's Ark, full of beasts clean and unclean. Although Pusey for a long while remained loyal to the English Reformers, they soon came to hold no place of honour in the Tractarian theological canon, largely due to the influence of Hurrell Froude and his published *Remains* (1838–9), as edited by Newman and Keble. Froude privately labelled Bishop Jewel, author of the classic *Apologia Ecclesiae Anglicanae* (1562), a text hitherto sacred to old High Churchmen as well as to Anglican evangelicals, as 'what you would call in these days an irreverent Dissenter'. He denounced the Reformation as 'a limb badly set – it must be broken again in order to be righted'.[65] Froude's role was crucial in disconnecting the Oxford Movement from the cause of the English as well as continental Reformation. In an influential article in the *British Critic* in 1841 Frederick Oakeley extended the attack on Jewel and the Reformers.[66] Under Froude's influence, Newman had for some time privately distanced himself from the Reformers, especially Cranmer.[67] His role as editor and part-author of the preface to the *Remains* had been a liberating experience. By 1841, in expressing sympathy for Oakeley's line, he could confide to Pusey: 'I fear I must express a persuasion that it requires no deep reading to dislike the Reformation. "A good tree cannot bring forth evil fruit" . . . Whence all this schism and heresy, humanly speaking, but for it?'[68]

In his pre-Tractarian days, Keble had identified with Cranmer and Ridley, and regarded the writings of the Reformers to be as important as those of the Fathers.[69] However by 1835, under Froude's influence, he maintained that 'Hooker wrote many things in order to counteract in a quiet way the Ultra Protestantism of . . . Cranmer and his school'.[70] By 1836, he regarded the Reformers as of 'the same class with the puritans and radicals'.[71] In his preface to the third volume of Froude's *Remains*, Keble agreed with Froude that contemporary churchmen had to make a choice between adherence to the principles of antiquity and a catholic consent of Fathers on the one hand, and to those of the Reformers on the other'.[72] For Keble, Hooker was a 'middle term between Laud and Cranmer, but nearer the former' and 'in a transition state when he was taken from us; and there is no saying how much nearer he might have got to Laud, if he had lived twenty years longer'.[73] Moreover, Hooker had

> his full share in training up for the next generation, Laud, Hammond, Sanderson, and a multitude more such divines: to which succession and series, humanly speaking, we owe it, that the Anglican church continues at such a distance from that of Geneva, and so near to primitive truth and apostolical order.[74]

For the Tractarians, reverence for Hooker and his apparent successors made it easier for them to ditch the Reformers. When the Tractarians were in danger of becoming embarrassed by a scheme to erect a Martyrs' Memorial at Oxford in 1838, perceived as being directed against them, Keble, like Newman, refused to countenance the idea, maintaining that 'anything which separates the present church from the Reformers, I should hail as a great good'.[75]

For the Tractarians, 'Anglicanism' represented the teaching of a narrow range of divines covering the period from the 1600s to the 1680s, with Hurrell Froude dating the rise and extinction of what he called the Church of England's 'genus' of 'Apostolical divines' from the beginning of the reign of King James I until the Revolution of 1688–9 and the separation of the first Nonjurors (that is, the period from Saravia to Bishop Ken).[76] Froude placed the key shift of theological gear in a catholic direction to Bishop Bancroft's St Paul's Cross sermon in 1589, in which he apparently preached up *jure divino* episcopacy.[77] Froude's anti-Erastianism fuelled an extreme historical reversal of alliances: he sympathized with the Elizabethan Puritans in their controversy with Whitgift because he argued that the former, unlike the latter, upheld 'a *jus divinum*, though not the true one'. Froude admired the 'mar-prelate' polemicist John Penry, and even considered writing 'An Apology for the early Puritans'.[78]

The Tractarian abandonment of the Reformers and even the English Reformation marked a discontinuity from the historiography of the older High Church tradition, according to which Cranmer and Jewel remained exemplars, and notably from that of the Protestant-minded Bishop Burgess and Southey. Some historians within the 'High Church' tradition, such as Heylin and Collier, had sharply criticized sacrilege, spoliation and loss of church wealth,[79] while even Bishop Burnet, exponent of a parallel Whig Low Church history of the Reformation, had conceded Henry VIII's 'great enormities'.[80] Thus, Bishop Burgess was not being especially controversial when he condemned the means by which 'the tyrant Henry' introduced the Reformation as 'most violent and oppressive',[81] or lamented that for many, nobles under Edward VI it was the lure of church wealth rather than 'love for religion' which 'promoted the reforming scheme'.[82]

In High Church historiography, the English Reformation itself was defended as canonical and an orderly restoration, rather than a revolution.[83] Burgess, though, differed from some High Churchmen in his almost Erastian emphasis on the origins of the Reformation lying not so much in the theological upheaval of the sixteenth century as in a late medieval rising 'abhorrence of a foreign jurisdiction',[84] symbolized by the Statutes of *Praemunire* and finally enshrined in the first 'Protestant Acts of Parliament' in the 1530s. As Burgess put it,

> The long series of statutes against the papal encroachments, created prior to the Reformation, during the 14th and 15th centuries, is of great importance in distinguishing the political danger of Popery from the religious corruptions of the Church of Rome; and in showing that the Church of England's rejection of Popery at the Reformation, did not originate with Luther, or in the sensualities of Henry VIII (as the Papists pretend) but was the ultimate result of the national abhorrence of a foreign jurisdiction.[85]

In contrast, the Tractarians were as hostile to the political as they were to the theological character of the English Reformation. Tractarian discourse, with its antipathy to what Newman called the 'Law Church' of Henry VIII and

William of Orange and the constrictions on catholicity implied in the notion of a 'national church', represented a repudiation of Bishop Burgess's line of apologetic.[86] Burgess's acceptance of the Erastian and political background to the English Reformation and defence of the Restoration state's imposition of a Declaration against Transubstantiation as a condition of civil office was not designed to appeal to Tractarian anti-Erastian sensitivities. Moreover, the Tractarian assault on the character and principles of the Reformers themselves, and not merely greedy courtiers, represented a departure from earlier High Church apologetic against Anglican evangelicals of a preceding generation – an apologetic which had been based on the assumption that High Churchmen and Arminians, rather than Anglican evangelicals and Calvinists, were the true heirs of the English Reformers.[87] The Tractarian exaltation of the seventeenth-century divines was also at the expense of those of the eighteenth century as well as of the mid sixteenth.

For most Tractarians, especially Froude and Newman, eighteenth-century Anglicanism represented the Church in the desert, a view which Bishop Burgess would have found incomprehensible. In Tractarian polemic, the Hanoverian Church was condemned for an apparent neglect of the 'sounder divinity' (that is, Laudian) of the seventeenth century. Tractarians and Anglican evangelicals were at one in denigrating the coldness, latitude and doctrinal aridity of the 'orthodox' and not so orthodox divines of the very late seventeenth and eighteenth centuries, such as John Tillotson, Samuel Clarke, William Warburton and John Jortin. Both espoused a historiography of doctrinal corruption and lowered theological temperature in the eighteenth century, but each gave it a different twist and explanation. For the Tractarians, the litmus test of orthodoxy was patristic and sacramental, rooted in a 'catholic consent' of the Fathers; for Anglican evangelicals, the litmus test was more narrowly 'scriptural' and rooted in the 'fathers of the Reformation'. The Tractarians blamed a decay of patristic and sacramental orthodoxy on the political and constitutional compromises of the post-Revolution Church of England – the very compromises of which Bishop Burgess so thoroughly approved.[88] They also blamed those compromises for the emergence of ultra-latitudinarian divines, such as Benjamin Hoadly and Francis Blackburne. On the other hand, Anglican evangelical revivalists had tracked a supposed decline of Reformation doctrine (as reputedly enshrined in the Thirty-Nine Articles as well as doctrinal views of the Reformers) past the Restoration to Laud and the Laudians, arguing that Arminianism or 'the free-will heresy' had set off a causal chain which led on to latitudinarianism and outright infidelity.[89]

If the Reformation was a weak point in the Tractarian armoury, they would seem to have been on much firmer ground in appropriating seventeenth-century Anglican divinity. Newman, however, was interested in the Fathers, whom he had discovered through Joseph Milner's writings while an evangelical,[90] before he became familiar with the Caroline divines. His reading of the Caroline divines prior to 1833 was sketchy and unsystematic.[91] This helped subordinate the Caroline divines to the Fathers in his theological method. Moreover, while Keble's knowledge of and reverence for the seventeenth-century divines was clear, until Newman introduced him to them in 1829 Pusey, who was then already Regius Professor of Hebrew at Oxford, had little acquaintance with the Caroline divines.[92] Old High Churchmen argued that it was the relative ignorance and misunderstanding of seventeenth-century Anglican teaching on the part of the Tractarian leaders which ultimately blew the Movement off-course.[93] Charles Wordsworth, later Bishop of St Andrews, maintained that the Tractarians 'threw themselves into the study of the Fathers without the steadying guidance which that study pre-eminently requires'. Apart from Keble in the case of Hooker and Newman in the case of Bishop Bull, Wordsworth maintained that the Tractarians made no deep study of the leading seventeenth-century divines. He found it significant that the *Library of Anglo-Catholic Theology*, designed to propagate the teaching of those divines, was only set up in 1841, in belated response to the anti-Tractarian *Parker Society*, and five years after the commencement of the *Library of the Fathers*.[94]

The *Library of Anglo-Catholic Theology* attracted the suspicion of anti-Tractarian propagandists because the majority of the committee were deemed to be either authors of the *Tracts for the Times* or closely allied to them.[95] The Tractarian component included the first editor, William Copeland, and the treasurer and secretary, Charles Crawley, who soon became dissatisfied with the content and tone of some authors whose works they edited.[96] Newman privately made clear that the project was 'no plan of mine', and that 'neither Pusey nor I was warm about it'.[97] His unease partly stemmed from a reluctance to tie the Movement too much to the teaching of earlier Anglican divines per se, even to those of the seventeenth as well as of the sixteenth century. As he confided to Charles Crawley in January 1841: 'For myself, I have never had any desire, or made any effort to manage our divines – I do not want to make them better than they are – I do not wish to bring the early Church to their judgement seat – Really I think one can bear to differ from them.'[98] Newman preferred a reversal of this methodology – he wished to take such later Anglican writers to the judgement seat of the early church. Newman went along with the project only as a way of countering the rival Cambridge and Low Church-inspired *Parker Society* (which he labelled an 'Opposition Society') and his fears that it would 'inundate us with Protestantism pure and undiluted'.[99] Newman only reluctantly agreed to promote the Library unless less catholic authors were excluded.[100] In short, the writings of the Caroline divines had to be packaged.

After his conversion to Rome in 1845, Newman reacted strongly against criticism from High Churchmen and even some former Tractarian allies, such as James Mozley, that he had only ever paid lip-service to the teaching of the Caroline divines, and had never been a truly faithful son of the Church of England.[101] Paul Elmer More, in his *The Spirit of Anglicanism* (1935), conceded Newman's expressions of loyalty to the seventeenth-century divines but questioned its basis – affection, rather than intellectual conviction.[102] More recently, Frank Turner has argued that in his pursuit of an ideal ascetical Catholicism, Newman sat loosely to all theological traditions, both Anglican and Roman Catholic, and as Tractarian leader acted on a sectarian principle in thought as well as practice. For Turner, Newman in his *Apologia* sought to impose an orderly theological development on his Tractarian career, which, Turner argues, was singularly lacking at the time.[103] However,

Newman's later defence of his religious motivation deserves to be taken at face value. Newman was candid enough in the *Apologia* when it came to explaining his relationship to the older Caroline tradition in Anglicanism. The arguments which he employed against the French divine Abbé Jager in 1834–5, Newman later admitted, 'were not mine, but the evolution of Laud's theory, Stillingfleet's etc. which seemed to me clear, complete and unanswerable'.[104] It is only when viewed in retrospect and with benefit of hindsight that Newman's *via media* can be presented as a temporary staging-post in a long religious odyssey, with the Caroline divines tied into a schema of his own devising. George Herring recently has applied an interesting parallel with the approach (obviously, not the doctrine) of Martin Luther. As Herring argues, like Luther three centuries earlier, Newman was 'personally testing the beliefs, formulas and practices of the ecclesiastical body in which he had been born; did they answer the needs of both his intellect and spirit? Like Luther he would need time, but the emerging answer was just as negative'.[105]

In his Tractarian apologetic, Newman sought to complete the 'inheritance' of seventeenth-century Anglicanism. As he confided to his old High Church friend Hugh James Rose in 1836, 'the Anglican system of doctrine is in matter of fact not complete – there are hiatuses which have never been filled up – so that, though one agrees with it most entirely as far as it goes, yet one rather wishes for something more'.[106] By appealing directly to antiquity, Newman aimed to supplement perceived lacunae in the Anglican doctrinal and disciplinary system by the reintroduction of disputed points of primitive faith and practice, including a form of monasticism. Nonetheless, while this position represented a radical divergence from that of orthodox churchmen, such as Bishop Burgess, it was not a wholesale departure from the approach of at least the more advanced Laudians, and was certainly in line with the later Nonjuring method. Caroline and later High Church apologists could be more rigid about their positions in their day than Stephen Sykes and Paul Avis, with their emphasis on the 'liberal spirit' of the Caroline divines, allow.[107] The Tractarians poured scorn on the notion of the 'middle way' being historically synonymous with 'moderation'.[108]

The Laudian phase in the history of the Church of England was crucial for the construction of the Tractarian claim to historical legitimation as the true exponent of 'Anglicanism'. For the Tractarians, Laud stopped the Church of England 'just in time, as she was rapidly going downhill, and he saved all the Catholicism which the reign of Genevan influence had left her'.[109] They welcomed Laud's breach with the Calvinist sense of the Thirty-Nine Articles, but the Tractarians were less concerned with this issue than their immediate High Church predecessors had been, and were more preoccupied with the sacramental and ecclesiological implications of the 'school of Geneva'. Newman, especially, felt that Arminianism, as mediated through the Dutch theologian and jurist Hugo Grotius (1583–1645), had a long-term tendency towards rationalism and depreciation of the sacraments. In a revealing review article of Charles Le Bas's *Life of Archbishop Laud*, in the April 1836 number of the *British Critic*, Newman blamed 'our reunion with foreign Protestantism' at the Synod of Dort for the introduction of what he called the 'plague' of 'latitudinarian indifference', while he exempted Laud from responsibility for the trend. As Newman explained:

> Hales, who accompanied Sir Dudley Carleton to the Synod of Dort, made acquaintance there with Episcopius, the disciple of Arminius, brought back his doctrines to England, and communicated them to Chillingworth. We have evidence in history of the great disquiet which this importation gave to Laud, who prevailed on one of these two divines to abandon or conceal his opinions. However, the contagion ran its course; in the next reign it gave rise to a school in Cambridge, under Tillotson and others, diffused itself through the nation in the writings of the celebrated Mr Locke, which drew upon him the condemnation of Laud's own university, and evinced its inbred hatred to the Church, by co-operating in the separation of the Nonjurors, in the erection of the Presbyterian Kirk, and in the ascendancy of Hoadly and his party.[110]

In adopting this historiography, Newman was reverting to a Protestant genre of tracing the history of doctrinal error and corruption, while turning it on its head at the expense of Protestantism. He also appears to have been influenced by his favourite late Caroline divine (as well as Bishop Burgess's favourite), George Bull (1634–1710), Bishop of St David's and celebrated author of a *Defence of the Nicene Faith* (1685) and also of *Harmonia Apostolica* (which for Bishop Burgess was almost a sacred text), as well as by the views of Hurrell Froude on the subject. Froude sought to distinguish Laud and his friends as the 'Apostolical party' from those known as 'Arminians', with whom they were only in partial and contingent agreement and alliance, concluding: 'from the restoration of Charles II to the present day, Calvinism, Erastianism, and Arminianism, have, like Herod and Pontius Pilate, been made friends together to carry on a joint war against Apostolical Christianity.'[111]

Newman maintained that the apparently rationalizing virus introduced by Dutch Arminianism had infected even the High Churchmanship characteristic of the eve of the Oxford Movement. Like Froude, Newman admired Calvinism for asserting that church authority was from God and for holding to a higher sense of supernatural order and the transcendent than that which characterized 'high and dry' pre-Tractarian High Churchmanship. In a striking passage in his *Autobiographical Memoir* when referring to the Oxford of the 1820s, Newman observed: 'a cold Arminian doctrine, the first stage of liberalism, was the characteristic ... both of the high and dry Anglicans of that day and of the Oriel divines'.[112] Newman's Tractarian friend Samuel Wood made a similar point. On Newman's prompting, Wood in May 1837 proposed an article for the *British Critic* in which, as Wood explained, he would:

> point out that the Arminianism ... which succeeded the Calvinism of the Reformation and was its reaction, and which assumes to itself ... the name of Orthodoxy, is just as non-catholic and more Rationalistic, and as far removed from the Mysterious and True System as Calvinism.[113]

One wonders how far this verdict might have been applicable to the staunchly Arminian Bishop Burgess.

Arminianism was deemed to have had a detrimental effect on other aspects of Anglican doctrine. One mid-nineteenth-century High Churchman argued that in the seventeenth century the highest doctrine of the Eucharist emanated from Calvinist as much as from classical Laudian divines, and traced the revival of Zwinglian eucharistic doctrine (and consequent erosion of the Laudian doctrine of real presence tied to worthy reception) in the eighteenth-century Church of England to the influence of Dutch Arminianism on Anglican latitudinarian divines such as Burnet, Tillotson and Tenison.[114]

Newman's private verdicts on individual Caroline divines could be as critical as any of Hurrell Froude's on the Reformers. Froude himself, as early as 1834, had criticized Newman for printing the Laudian John Cosin's *History of Popish Transubstantiation* in number 27 of the *Tracts for the Times*, because of what Froude regarded as its unacceptable Protestantism.[115] Newman came to regard William Chillingworth, one of Bishop Burgess's heroes, as the patron of later latitudinarianism, on account of his celebrated maxim, 'the Bible only is the religion of protestants',[116] a view which mirrored the way in which Chillingworth had been presented and claimed by the school of Hoadly and Blackburne and its heterodox tail.[117] In contrast, Edward Churton in 1836 planned a new edition of Chillingworth's works in order to demonstrate that Chillingworth was 'a good churchman and a good loyalist', whose views had been misinterpreted by, and were far removed from, later ultra-latitudinarians.[118] Newman also found fault with statements in the writings of Henry Hammond and Jeremy Taylor, asking Churton rhetorically in 1837: 'how come Taylor to be so liberal in his *Liberty of Prophesying*? And how far is Hammond tinctured as regards the Sacraments with Grotianism?'[119] While he recommended Taylor's spiritual writings to his younger sister in a letter of June 1837, he proceeded to describe him as, 'a writer essentially untrustworthy – i.e. if some external attraction meets him, he cannot resist it . . . The necessity, for example, of seeming an anti-Papist will draw all his nails out'.[120]

As Newman's *via media* construct began to unravel after the initial doubts which his reading of Wiseman's famous article in the *Dublin Review* in 1839 induced,[121] the Anglican devotional tradition became even more important for Newman as a residual mark of Anglican catholicity. Newman urged those in danger of seceding to Rome to immerse themselves in what he regarded as the spiritual treasures of the Caroline tradition, notably the devotional writings of Lancelot Andrewes, Jeremy Taylor, John Cosin and Thomas Ken. In this, Newman was in line with Bishop Burgess's own earlier regard for such writings, as illustrated in John Harford's biography of the Bishop.[122] Newman's interest in propagating this devotional tradition had been illustrated in 1836 by Tract 75, in which he virtually canonized Bishop Ken in an anniversary service which he composed on the lines of the Roman breviary,[123] and was continued in 1840 by his translation and arrangement of the Greek Devotions of Bishop Andrewes in Tract 88.[124] Frederick Faber's 1838 edition of Laud's *Private Devotions*, first published in 1667, and his 1839 edition of Laud's *Autobiography* had the hagiographic and polemical purposes of appropriating the Laudian devotional heritage at the expense of contemporary evangelical religiosity.[125]

Some individual Caroline divines were more amenable to Tractarian packaging than others. Pusey, like Henry Manning, came to have a special regard for Herbert Thorndike (1598–1672), Prebendary of Westminster, because as Pusey put it, Thorndike had 'seen further than others'.[126] Significantly, in explaining a shift in his own position, Pusey commented to Manning in 1845: 'It was Thorndike who first broke in upon the acquiescence which I had ever yielded to our hereditary maxim that a particular church had a right to reform itself. A misgiving, expressed by him, raised the question in my mind'.[127] In his *Just Weights and Measures* (1662), while adhering to the standard Anglican controversial line of blaming Rome for the breach in church unity at the Reformation, Thorndike argued that should the Church of England move in a more Protestant direction in order to conciliate or comprehend Puritans and Presbyterians, then the incidence of guilt for the schism might shift.[128] Tractarians also identified with Thorndike's advocacy of a restoration of penitential discipline and primitive practices, such as prayers for the dead. In a Chichester archidiaconal Charge of 1841, Manning appealed to Thorndike's *Just Weights and Measures* to support his call for a practical restoration of the Church's powers of the keys through auricular confession, approvingly citing Thorndike's assertion: 'the Church is founded upon the power of the keys. And therefore when that power is not in force . . . then it is a Church in hope rather than in deed and being'.[129]

Old High Churchmen, initially supportive of the Tractarians, questioned Newman's assumption, as expressed in Tract 38, that 'in the seventeenth century the theology of the body of the English Church was substantially the same as theirs'. As proof, the author of the Tract had professed, in stating the errors of Rome, to 'follow closely the order observed by Bishop Hall in his *Treatise on the Old Religion*'.[130] Rejecting this claim, the High Church Bishop of Exeter, Henry Phillpotts, in an episcopal Charge of 1839, pointedly commented that the writer might have followed the order of Bishop Hall's anti-papal treatise of 1628, but had departed widely 'from his truly Protestant sentiments on more than one article'.[131] Phillpotts proceeded to enumerate the Tract writer's palliation of the invocation of saints, honour paid to images, prayers for the dead, and reluctance to engage in controversy with Rome over transubstantiation – all points which Bishop Burgess would, along with Bishop Hall, have denounced as 'Romish idolatries'.

Old High Churchmen also disputed Pusey's claim of sanction for the eucharistic teaching of his Oxford sermon of 1843, *The Holy Eucharist, a Comfort to the Penitent*, from seventeenth-century Anglican divines such as Andrewes, Overall, and Bramhall,[132] a sermon condemned by six Oxford Doctors of Divinity. When Bishop Sumner of Winchester in 1842 refused to ordain Keble's curate, Peter Young, to the priesthood, for failing to deny the real presence, 'excepting in the faithful receiver' (the standard Cranmerian doctrine, which also was widely regarded as Hooker's position), Keble likewise appealed to Andrewes, Taylor, Ken and Wilson, in support of what he claimed was the Church of England's leaving of the nature of the presence an open question. In article 18 of his formal letter of protest to Bishop Sumner in March 1842, Keble was explicit in his appeal to a narrowly particular period in the doctrinal history of Anglicanism, stating that the Bishop's ground of refusal was wrong:

Because if any one generation of Divines were to be specified whose views of the meaning of our Formularies might well be considered binding on their successors it would be that of the Revisers of the Prayer Book after its restoration in 1660: and three of those at least, Bishop Cosin, Bishop Sparrow, and Mr Thorndike, have recorded their judgement to be substantial.[133]

Newman employed the testimony of the Caroline divines in a particularly controversial way in Tract 90.[134] That Tract was the fruit of Newman's shift in interest from the apostolicity of the Church of England, which had been shaken by Wiseman's article, to that of its catholicity. It was important now for Newman to present a 'catholic' interpretation of the Thirty-Nine Articles, partly to offset the crisis of Anglican allegiance emerging among his younger followers,[135] and again he selectively used Anglican doctrinal history to bolster his case. Exploiting the 'catholic latitude' which Laud, in reaction against prevailing Calvinist rigidity, had won for later interpreters of the Articles, Newman claimed that Bramhall, Laud, Taylor, Bull and Stillingfleet, had allowed 'of much greater freedom in the private opinions of individuals, subscribing them, than I have contended for'.[136] Edwin Abbott observed in the 1890s that Newman: 'seemed to assume that every opinion, however extreme in the direction of Rome, that had been once expressed by any one high church bishop or divine, and had not been authoritatively censured, at once became part of justifiable Anglican doctrine'.[137] According to Newman's sister-in-law Anne Mozley, he selected 'here a teacher, there an authority', but accepted 'them no further than they fell in with his views'. She felt that he snatched at 'every chance saying of any of our Divines', even though 'the whole tenor of the work has no weight with him'.[138] Newman's selectivity was shown in his readiness to abandon Hooker when formulating his own doctrine of justification. For in his *Lectures on Justification* (1838), Newman concluded: 'since we are not allowed to call any man our master on earth, Hooker, venerable as is his name, has no weight with any Christian, except what is agreeable to catholic doctrine'.[139] This, of course, begged the question. While anxious to enlist Hooker as a patron of catholic views and 'in the great point of the sacraments' as 'almost or entirely with us', Keble treated him in similarly selective fashion. He admitted that Hooker's 'notion of Regal, or rather State, power' and 'dislike to anything approaching to Justification by inherent grace' separated him from the Tractarians, and conceded that Hooker was 'not my master, as I have dared to differ widely from him in my Preface [to Hooker's *Works*]'.[140] The problem in this case was that Newman's presentation of a 'via media' doctrine of Justification rested upon the teaching of only post-Restoration Caroline divines over a mere thirty-year period, from which such notable Anglican apologists as Hooker, Andrewes and Hall were necessarily absent.[141] On the question of justification, Newman was forced to be even more selective with seventeenth-century Anglican testimonies than on other doctrinal issues. Yet even on the Eucharist selectivity was practised. When in the 1850s Keble came to alter his own eucharistic views in favour of an 'objective' real presence, he was shamelessly selective in citing earlier Anglican authorities, claiming: 'I see no disingenuousness in adopting words, from Ridley (e.g.) or any other, to express one's own view, without stopping to inquire whether, on other occasions, the same author might not have employed different or even contradictory language.'[142]

James Mozley and Frederick Oakeley perfected the art of selective citation in the cause of what Oakeley called 'unprotestantizing' the Church of England. In an article in the *Quarterly Review* in 1842, William Sewell aimed to settle the then-raging party conflict provoked by Tractarianism, by looking back 'to the old standard Theology of the English Church, and to ascertain the sentiments of our acknowledged great Divines on some of the debated questions of the present day'.[143] The seventeenth century was called in to adjudicate on the theological conflicts of the nineteenth. In response to Sewell's anti-Tractarian use of Caroline testimonies, James Mozley in the *British Critic* in 1842 conceded what he regarded as faults in the controversial temper of the Caroline divines, but maintained that they went as far as the Tractarians, if one but separated 'their real spirit from their controversial phraseology'. Mozley countered the claim of old High Church contemporaries that they, rather than the Tractarians, were the true heirs of the Laudian mantle, highlighting the affinity between the dynamic characters of both the Laudian and Tractarian movements. Just as the Tractarians were reviled as innovators in the 1830s, so had the Laudians been in the 1630s. Against Sewell, Mozley justified the apparent Tractarian breach of earlier parameters of High Churchmanship by appealing to the precedent of the Caroline divines, insisting that 'our church divinity has been . . . a progressive, not a stationary one. The Laudian school was as clearly a new development of the church, in its day, as history can show it'.[144] Sewell was faulted for not distinguishing between the primarily Calvinistic Jacobean and the later Caroline divines.[145]

In his defence of Tract 90 Frederick Oakeley, by then on the 'Romanizing' wing of the Movement, defended Newman's interpretation of the Thirty-Nine Articles by reference to seventeenth-century history. Like Newman, Oakeley appealed to the precedent of the English Franciscan friar and chaplain to Queen Henrietta Maria, Christopher Davenport, alias Franciscus a Sancta Clara, for an earlier attempt to bridge the gap between the Thirty-Nine Articles and Roman Catholic teaching.[146] Davenport had argued his case by frequent reference to the high sacramental teaching of the then-contemporary Anglican divines Andrewes and Montagu, in a way which prefigured Newman's and Oakeley's historical interpretation of the Thirty-Nine Articles.[147] Drawing on the apparent evidence of the seventeenth-century Anglican historians such as Peter Heylin, Oakeley went further than Newman by arguing that the Thirty-Nine Articles were drawn up with the deliberate intention of comprehending Roman Catholics as well as Protestants, rather than being merely 'patient' of a catholic interpretation.[148] Oakeley also made use of extracts from the seventeenth-century bishops Forbes and Montagu, and Thorndike, in favour of eucharistic adoration, the invocation of saints, reverence for images and the doctrine of an intermediate state of purification, as support for a catholic interpretation of the Articles.[149] This mirrored the similar appeal to Caroline authors made by Samuel Wix against Bishop Burgess's contrary interpretation. Selectivity and one-sided citation could cut both ways.

In correspondence with Oakeley over the second edition of his *The Subject of Tract XC Historically Examined* (1845),

Manning undermined the historical basis of Oakeley's argument, arguing that subscription to the Thirty-Nine Articles by English Catholics early in Elizabeth's reign entailed mere concession or surrender to the governing powers of the Reformation state.[150] However, in his historical defence of Tract 90, Oakeley reproduced the details of the case of Bishop Montagu, who in 1625 had been assailed by Puritan parliamentary opponents for apparently contravening in his writings the Protestant interpretations of the Thirty-Nine Articles. Oakeley found parallels with the contemporary outcry against Tract 90 and drew a pointed analogy between those who now sought to exclude Tractarian teaching and 'the Puritans of former times' who had sought to exclude similar teaching in the 1620s.[151] Moreover, a manuscript tract by Montagu entitled 'Concerning Recusancie of Communion with the Church of England', recently edited by Anthony Milton and Alexandra Walsham, and published by the Church of England Record Society, appeared to be designed to entice English Catholics to conform by minimizing the differences between Rome and Canterbury. It included an acknowledgement of the power of the keys, the sanctity of holy places, altars, the eucharistic real presence and sacrifice, extreme unction and penance in absolution, and an avowal that between the two churches, 'the differences are not great, nor should make a separation'.[152] Samuel Wix's pamphlets in 1818–20 advocating conciliation and reunion with the Church of Rome under strict conditions, which so antagonized Bishop Burgess, can be placed in the same irenic tradition. Wix approvingly cited the Laudian Peter Heylin's lament (in his *History of the Reformation*) that English Catholics after the 1560s, 'might have stood much longer to their first conformity, if the discords brought in by the Zwinglian faction, together with the many innovations both in doctrine and discipline, had not afforded them some further ground for desertion'.[153]

Oakeley himself was candid in conceding that citations from the seventeenth-century divines could be used against as well as in favour of Tractarian teaching. He explained that 'all that *catenae* necessarily show, and all that, as a matter of fact, they are genuinely intended to show, is that certain doctrines are not new'. The object of such citations as being:

not to justify the Caroline Divines, any more than to ground particular doctrines upon their authority, but merely to show what they have felt themselves at liberty to say without protest. And this fact has its own weight, whatever these divines may chance to have said elsewhere.[154]

Any contradictions between Caroline and Tractarian teaching could safely be ignored, because there was no need to press the Caroline divines 'into our service beyond the point for which they are here claimed'.[155]

While some Anglican evangelical critics of the Oxford Movement equated Tractarianism and Laudianism as related manifestations of the Antichrist,[156] many of them laid claim to a Jacobean or early Caroline theological inheritance, identifying with the episcopalian Calvinist school of Ussher, Davenant, Carleton and Hall. Anglican evangelicals, such as William Goode, and Protestant churchmen, such as James Garbett and George Stanley Faber, by appealing to the same seventeenth-century historical sources, sought to refute the Tractarians on their own ground, in order to prove that the controversy was not one between the 'Catholic' and 'Genevan' schools of doctrine but one between orthodox Protestantism and 'semi-Romanism'. Goode's *Divine Rule of Faith and Practice* (1842), according to one reviewer, exposed the Tractarians as guilty of 'a convenient process of misquotation, and accumulating catenae of later Divines, simply by detaching passages from the context and applying them in a manner diametrically opposite to that which their authors designed'.[157]

Garbett and others cited Laud, Andrewes, Bramhall and a litany of Caroline authors to refute Pusey's interpretation of Anglican eucharistic doctrine based on their testimony.[158] Anglican evangelical critics also accused the Tractarians of deception in their *catenae patrum* on the theological questions of justification and sanctification, though they conceded that Newman's favourite Anglican divine, Bishop Bull, supported the Tractarian theory of an infused, as distinct from an imputed, righteousness.[159] The Anglican evangelical Henry Fish in his *The Jesuitism of the Oxford Tractarians* (1842) was particularly critical of Pusey for citing Hooker and Andrewes 'in confirmation of Mr Newmans views of Justification:

whereas the views of both those men were the very reverse of Mr Newmans'.[160] Moreover, the strength of the Anglican evangelical argument was conceded by Newman's Tractarian friend, Samuel Wood. Wood warned Newman of the danger of resting his teaching on justification on earlier Anglican precedent: 'Is not the 'peculiar' [that is, evangelical] view of justification in some sense their stronghold, inasmuch as it is only false as being partial and distorted, and has there not been a great school on that side ever since the Reformation?'.[161] Moreover, Goode similarly appealed to earlier Anglican historical authorities in order to refute Tractarian teaching on the necessity of apostolical succession and authority of tradition.[162]

Even old High Churchmen, however, were troubled by the apparent plausibility of Goode's arguments and evidence. After anxious consultation with William Howley, Archbishop of Canterbury in 1842, Archdeacon William Rowe Lyall conveyed to Bishop Bagot of Oxford Howley's concern that:

> if Dr Pusey and Mr Newman believe their opinions to be founded on the authority of the Ancient and Anglican Fathers . . . it is for them to make good their opinions by showing that Mr Goode is guilty of the fault with which he charges others'.[163]

Tractarian polemicists stepped forward, notably Pusey in his monumental *Letter to the Archbishop of Canterbury on the Present Crisis in the Church* (1842), but the controversy was not resolved conclusively.

Significantly, some of those High Churchmen and Tractarians who seceded to Rome after the Gorham Judgment in 1850 acted not only out of anti-Erastian objections to the nature of the outcome of the Gorham Judgment. They left the Church of England also partly because they concluded that Anglican evangelicals, such as Goode, had had the better of the purely historical argument. The Gorham controversy in 1849–50 over baptismal regeneration, provoked by Bishop Phillpotts's refusal to institute George Cornelius Gorham as Rector of Brampford Speke, Devon, found High and Low Churchmen battling over rival interpretations of the Anglican formularies and appealing to the views of the Reformers and Elizabethan divines.[164] Gorham provoked Phillpotts by appealing to a long line of Anglican testimonies in support of Gorham's 'charitable hypothesis' understanding of regeneration in the baptismal service.[165] Some Tractarians concluded that Gorham's Anglican evangelical supporters had the better of the historical argument.[166] The conversion of several Tractarians to Rome was aided by their perception that Goode had exploded the High Church assumption that the doctrine of unconditional baptismal regeneration was the only doctrine allowed by the Church of England. To the embarrassment of High Churchmen but the delight of Goode, Phillpotts's chaplain, William Maskell, while seceding to Rome on the rebound from the Gorham Judgment, came down in favour of the evangelical representation of Anglican teaching on baptism, based on the Thirty-Nine Articles and known opinions of the English Reformers and Elizabethan divines. To the dismay of High Churchmen in 1850, the High Church Maskell conceded that the Caroline divines ultimately had failed in the controversial uses to which not only Tractarians, but a preceding generation of High Churchmen, had put them. As Maskell candidly admitted:

> catenae are useful enough, within their proper and reasonable limits; they create difficulties sometimes whilst they seldom suffice to establish a conclusion: employed, however, as they have been, of late years by own [High Church] party, they are not merely a packed jury, but a jury permitted only to speak half of their mind.[167]

Newman himself had reached a similar conclusion by the eve of his conversion to Rome in 1845; his earlier confidence in the seventeenth-century divines evaporating as 'he read the Fathers more carefully, and used his own eyes in determining the faith and worship of their times'.[168] The different paths to Rome for Maskell in 1850 and for Newman in 1845 had been smoothed by a common sense of betrayal and of having been, in Newman's words, 'taken in' by the Caroline divines, whose language he had adopted, to the sacrifice of his own words.[169]

Conclusions

The Tractarians related themselves to the history of the Church of England primarily in ways which suited their contemporary polemical purposes; Bishop Burgess had given a reading of the earlier history of the British church in a similarly polemical and present-centred way. Burgess used the High Church argument of apostolical continuity to construct or support an explicitly Protestant identity for the historic Church of England, its lineage rooted in a non-Roman ancient British church. Burgess's reconstruction of the history of the early British church as proto-Protestant and one from which the Church of England could claim lineal descent was partly dictated by the exigencies of rebutting Roman Catholic claims for emancipation in the 1810s and 1820s. In contrast to Newman's polemic, with its assumption as to the unhistorical and modern origin and nature of Protestantism, for Bishop Burgess 'primitive' was equated with 'Protestant'. Tractarian polemic, on the other hand, was more in tune with that of Burgess's opponent, Samuel Wix, who applied that same apostolical emphasis in such a way as to distance the Church of England as far as possible from Protestant Dissent, while trying to build bridges with the Church of Rome.

Burgess's virulent anti-Catholicism was characteristic of the High Churchmanship of the immediately pre-Tractarian period, and can be contrasted with the much more moderate attitude towards Catholicism that marked many 'Claphamite' evangelicals in the same era.[170] In his acceptance of the Reformation doctrine of the Pope as the Antichrist, Burgess was heir to a Protestant eschatological tradition associated with John Foxe, Thomas Newton and others.[171] It was a tradition enthusiastically embraced by the more anti-Catholic element among Anglican evangelicals as well as by evangelical Protestant Dissenters, but one which most Laudian divines had jettisoned and which most Tractarians would abandon (though in Newman's case the process was gradual). Burgess's biographer, Harford, chose to dwell only on two examples of Burgess's controversial zeal – anti-Catholicism and anti-Unitarianism, causes which tended to unite High Churchmen and Anglican evangelicals of his generation. When compared to the Tractarians, Burgess might seem to have been 'above party', and he certainly deplored party spirit.[172] However, it is perhaps significant that Harford gave little emphasis to Burgess's marked anti-Calvinism (albeit less extreme than Daubeny's). Moreover, Burgess's pamphlet controversy with a more distinctively High Church contemporary, Samuel Wix, in 1818–20, shows how far a shared emphasis on the apostolical foundations, origins and continuity of the Church of England might be interpreted in different ways and prove highly divisive, even among pre-Tractarian High Churchmen.

The Tractarians initially opposed Roman Catholic teaching because they regarded the Church of Rome, not as authoritarian or traditional, but as innovatory in relation to the patristic era. This was only partially Bishop Burgess's position. The Tractarians differed widely from Bishop Burgess in their repudiation of 'rationalistic' polemic and raillery when arguing against transubstantiation. Consequently, with the exception of Stillingfleet (whose views varied in different works), the Revolution-era divines, such as Tillotson, Tenison and Wake, whom Burgess favoured, formed no part of the Tractarian canon of seventeenth-century Anglican divinity. Newman was privately highly critical of the mode 'in which e.g. Wake conducts the controversy with Rome', enlarging with severity on what he called 'Revolution Protestantism'.[173] The Tractarians also differed from Bishop Burgess in their anti-Erastian emphasis. Tractarian historiography regarded the Revolution of 1688 as debilitating in its long-term religious consequences, by strengthening the influence of the Civil Power in favour of latitudinarian compromise. On the other hand, for Bishop Burgess, the 1688 settlement represented the constitutional completion of the work of the Reformation.[174]

As a Protestant Tory, not least in speeches in the House of Lords in the 1820s, Burgess defended the Protestant Constitution as immutable,[175] and the Established Church as a fulcrum of national and political as well as religious identity. The Protestant Constitution guaranteed what for Burgess were the sacred principles of the nationality and independence (from Rome) of the Established Church. Its effective collapse in 1829 helped pave the way for a High Churchmanship unfettered by state concerns and which sought a new identity under the guise of the old. The Tractarian polemic, unlike that of Bishop Burgess, thus involved the construction of a self-conscious 'catholic' identity for the historic Church of England, designed to supersede an alternative 'national' and 'establishment' as well as Protestant identity which had been rendered problematic by the constitutional revolution in church and state of 1828–32. To achieve this end, the Tractarians engaged in a deliberate rewriting of Anglican history to support their well-attested assault on 'ultra-Protestantism'; an anti-Protestantism which was not merely a negative repudiation of evangelicalism but which was informed by an appeal to the theology and spirituality of the Laudian as well as the patristic period. Of course, there was nothing new in the Tractarian recreation of an Anglican past; the later perception of a 'High Church' Hooker, Isaak Walton's Hooker, as founder of 'Anglicanism' partly stemmed from a self-conscious historical reconstruction, dictated by the political exigencies of the Restoration Church of England.[176] Even Burgess himself, no less than pre-Tractarian High Churchmen, such as Daubeny, when locked in conflict with Calvinistic evangelicals, had privileged an early, supposedly non-'Calvinist' phase of the English Reformation over the more Calvinistic Elizabethan era in the Church of England.[177] However, the Tractarians took historical reconstruction to new lengths. The English Reformation was an embarrassment and either sidelined or discredited, or at best regarded as only completed or corrected in theological terms by the Restoration settlement of 1662.[178] However, unlike old or pre-Tractarian High Churchmen, Froude and the Tractarians did not try to rescue the good name of the English Reformers by throwing the blame on to a foreign party or the returned Marian exiles, who had picked up 'Genevan' habits.[179]

For all its rhetoric of Anglican continuity and 'rediscovery' of a neglected tradition, the Oxford Movement as it gained momentum, after at least the 1840s, represented a discontinuity in the history of Anglicanism. Whereas the Caroline Divines and eighteenth-century High Churchmen had defended a middle way between *extreme* forms of Protestantism and Roman Catholicism, and Bishop Burgess had identified the Church of England with orthodox Protestantism, the Tractarian *via media* was a new concept in Anglicanism, a 'middle way' between Protestantism and Roman Catholicism. In short, if Bishop Burgess's theological principles fell short of the high water mark of Laudianism, then those of the Tractarians overshot that mark. Burgess had combined High Churchmanship with 'ultra' Protestantism, in the sense of implacable opposition to the Catholic claims. In contrast, the leaders of the Oxford Movement came to disown what they labelled 'ultra-Protestant', though in Tractarian parlance the term necessarily ceased merely to denote strident opposition to Catholic Emancipation, which had been conceded, but became interchangeable with 'Genevan' and was invested with doctrinal connotations which Burgess himself would have repudiated. While there is evidence that even some pre-Tractarian High Churchmen prized the title of 'Catholic' above that of 'Protestant',[180] the Tractarians went further – they became embarrassed by the term 'Protestant' per se. William Palmer (1811–79) of Magdalen College, Oxford, who as a deacon strove hard to put the 'branch theory' to the ultimate test by (in vain) demanding a right as an 'English Catholic' to communicate with the Russian Church on his own terms in the 1840s, went so far as to 'anathematise the principle of Protestantism as a heresy'.[181] Newman, in the preface to his posthumous edition of Palmer's *Notes of a Visit to the Russian Church, in the Year 1840, 1841* (1882), described Palmer's attempt to put into practice his view that the Anglican, Latin and Greek branches of the Church Catholic were separated only by 'the external accident of place, as one of realizing 'the formal teaching of Anglicanism'.[182] The Caroline divines, however, had never made catholic truth dependent on geographical location in this way. John Cosin, a Laudian divine (Bishop of Durham after the Restoration) notoriously chose to communicate with the French Calvinist Church rather than with the French Roman Catholic Church when in exile in Paris in the 1650s, a fact of which Bishop Burgess triumphantly reminded Samuel Wix.[183] For Palmer of Magdalen, as for many who were more formally 'Tractarians', the 'seemingly double character of the established church' as both 'Protestant' and 'Catholic' was an uneasy source of tension which had to be resolved one way or the other. These were concerns far removed from Bishop Burgess's self-confident Protestant High Church ecclesiology.

There was a family link between one of the Tractarian converts to Rome and Bishop Burgess (the Bishop was the great uncle of the hymn-writer Edward Caswall).[184] However, an ideological divide opened up between Tractarianism, with its perceived 'Romanizing' tendencies (real or imagined), and Burgess's brand of orthodox Protestant churchmanship. Burgess deplored party divisions and remained on good terms with leading Anglican evangelicals, such as Hannah More.[185] He regarded the account of the last illness and death of Charles Simeon, the leading Cambridge evangelical, as it appeared in the evangelical *Christian Observer*, as a spiritual model as he prepared for his own demise.[186] Yet an example of Burgess's own 'high church bigotry', belied by the evidence of his apparently cordial relations with Protestant Dissenters and Anglican evangelicals, and studiously overlooked by his biographer John Harford, was exemplified in his uncompromising attitude against the validity of Dissenters' baptism in the Kemp versus Wickes case in 1809. Burgess's stand in this case somewhat prefigured Newman's similarly hard line in the Jubber case in 1834, when he refused to bury a Protestant Dissenter, though in Burgess's case the objection was primarily legal, rather than sacramental. More positively, Burgess and Tractarians such as Newman and Keble shared a common love for the devotional side of the 'Laudian' tradition. One of Keble's favourite devotional texts, Wilson's *Sacra Privata*, had also been one of Burgess's favourites.[187] The aged Burgess certainly welcomed some early numbers of the *Tracts for the Times*. He had a reputation for a certain asceticism in his devotional life, and this aspect of Tractarian teaching may have had an appeal. Significantly, he *informed* Pusey in a letter of February 1834 that he had read his Tract (No. 18) on Fasting, 'with great pleasure, concurring most cordially with its sentiments'.[188] Although a large number of the Tracts had appeared by the time of Burgess's death in 1837, there is no record of his view of Pusey's more controversial Tracts (67–9) on Baptism, and the Bishop did not live long enough to add his voice to the crescendo of episcopal criticism of the Tracts which emanated from the bench from 1841 onwards. It was perhaps just as well.

The Tractarians not only largely abandoned the old High Church defence of the Reformation as a conservative, orderly settlement, or restoration of primitive Christianity, as Bishop Burgess contended, but appealed to the Caroline divines in a subtly different way from that of orthodox churchmen of Burgess's stamp: eventually, more as polemical support in defence of their own position within the Church of England and for long-disused or disputed points of faith and practice, such as prayers for the dead and private confession, rather than primarily as polemical support in defence of the Church of England as an institution against her denominational adversaries. They tended to play off the Caroline divines against the Reformers, regarding the former as a corrective of the latter. An 'Anglo-Catholic' writer summed up this attitude in 1879 with a bold claim:

> It is then to the Caroline prelates and divines that the Anglican Church owes its theology, almost its existence as a Church. They had inherited a position they would never have voluntarily chosen, and did their best, under terrible disadvantages, to improve it. From the nature of the case, their work was reactionary and reconstructive: 'to gather up the fragments that remained'.[189]

Contrary to Newman's hopes and aims, post-Tractarian Anglo-Catholicism arguably became sectarian in a way in which pre-Tractarian Anglicanism had never been, and which early Tractarianism had not intended. Any residual consensus within the Church of England as to what 'Anglicanism' stood for or which Bishop Burgess might have recognized, broke down. Newman sought a doctrinally rigid synthesis, which appeared to run counter to the underlying diversity of Caroline divinity, but arguably some Laudians had done the same. Neither Tractarians nor Laudians rested content with an inherited orthodoxy, but both sought to redefine and remould the Church of England of their day in order to carry forward their own agenda; both were engaged in a struggle for their own vision of Anglicanism. Before they were forced to settle for a mere right to observe certain catholic doctrines and practices within the widening comprehensive fold of Anglican teaching – a compromise which Newman was not prepared to make – the Tractarians had sought the removal of evangelical or 'ultra-Protestant' doctrines from the Church of England's formal polemic. This uncompromising, anti-moderate position was exactly in line with that of those Laudians, such as Montagu, who had sought the removal of Calvinist doctrines from the Church's formal polemic two centuries earlier.

Later Tractarianism or Anglo-Catholicism was only tolerated by the establishment, rather than owned as the authoritative teaching of a living church speaking with one voice, as the Movement of 1833, and especially Newman, had envisaged. In short, Anglo-Catholicism was saved only by that very tolerance of difference which was the hallmark of the comprehensive Anglicanism against which the Oxford Movement under Newman's leadership had originally risen up in protest.[190] Comprehensiveness in practice had been extended in a 'catholic' direction well beyond the parameters of what Bishop Burgess might have approved.

Tractarian reinterpretations of Anglicanism, however, had a long pedigree, and anti-Tractarians employed the same technique of a selective reading of the past. The Oxford Movement may have exacerbated, but it did not create, internal party divisions within the Church of England, based on divergent interpretations of her foundation documents and the teaching of her seventeenth-century divines, as the earlier controversy between Bishop Burgess and Samuel Wix illustrated. The seventeenth-century divines served very different, often contradictory, rhetorical and controversial purposes for competing parties within the nineteenth-century Church of England, as well as between that church and other denominations. The protean quality of the texts of seventeenth-century Anglican divinity allowed them to be given varying degrees of Protestant and anti-Protestant gloss; on the one hand, by Bishop Burgess and his opponent Samuel Wix, and later by Tractarians and their Anglican evangelical opponents. The disputed legacy of this Anglican inheritance served to check Tractarian efforts to appropriate the Caroline divines definitively in support of all the Oxford Movements doctrines and practices and to pass them off as the Church of England's 'official' teaching. Just as Bishop Burgess's historical reconstruction of the Church of England's 'primitive' Protestant origins was not always convincing, the Oxford Movement's historical reconstruction of Anglicanism was also bound to be partial and incomplete.

Notes

1   T. Mozley, *Reminiscences of Oriel College and the Oxford Movement*, 2 vols (London, 1882).

2   P. B. Nockles, *The Oxford Movement in Context: Anglican High Churchmanship in Britain, 1760–1857* (Cambridge, 1994), pp. 33–43, (p. 35).

3   Hurrell Froude coined the term 'Apostolicals' to distinguish followers of the nascent Oxford Movement from their more conservative or old High Church supporters, whom he labelled 'Zs'. *Remains of the Late Richard Hurrell Froude*, ed. J. Keble and J. H. Newman, 4 vols (I, i-ii, London, 1838; II, i-ii, Derby, 1839), I, i, p. 329.

4   See A. Gardiner, 'Swift and the idea of the primitive Church', Sustaining Literature: Essays on Literature, History and Culture, 1500–1800. Commemorating the life and work of Simon Varey. Edited by Greg Clingham (Lewisbury, Pa., 2007), pp. 109–26.

5   See P. B. Nockles, 'The reception of Foxe's "Book of Martyrs" in the nineteenth century' (forthcoming); A. Penny, 'Foxe's Victorian reception', *Historical Journal*, 40, 1 (January, 1997), 111–142 (115–16).

6   C. Wordsworth, *Ecclesiastical Biography: or Lives of eminent men connected with the history of religion in England, from the commencement of the Reformation to the Revolution. Selected and illustrated with notes*, 6 vols (London, 1810). Significantly, Wordsworth's memoir of Cranmer, which comprised volume III, was transcribed almost verbatim from Foxe's *Acts and Monuments*. For Wordsworth (p. xxii), Foxe was 'one of the most faithful and authentic of all historians'.

7   J. S. Harford, *The Life of Thomas Burgess, D. D. . . . late Lord Bishop of Salisbury* (London, 1840), p. 179. John Scandrett Harford (1787–1865) was associated with the moderate Anglican evangelical 'Clapham Sect'.

8   Harford, *Life of Thomas Burgess*, p. 484. See Mark Smith's chapter in this volume. See n. 185 below for examples of Burgess's cooperation with the evangelical Hannah More. Grayson Carter also makes the point that Burgess regularly ordained moderate evangelicals. G. Carter, *Anglican Evangelicals. Protestant Secessions from the Via Media, c.1800–1850* (Oxford, 2001), p. 42. However, for Burgess's

hard line against the irregularity of the eventual seceder William Tiptaft, see Carter, *Anglican Evangelicals*, pp. 287–90. Nigel Yates has characterized Burgess as a 'strong' High Churchman. N. Yates, *Anglican Ritualism in Victorian Britain 1830–1910* (Oxford, 1999), p. 184.

9   C. Daubeny, *Reasons for Supporting the S.P. C. K. in Preference to the New Bible Society, Partly Given in a Charge to the Clergy of his Archdeaconry at his Visitation in 1812* (London, 1812), esp. p. 19.

10   H. Marsh, *A Comparative View of the Churches of England and Rome*, 2nd edn (London, 1814), p. 287. Marsh even exclaimed (p. 288): 'surely a Bishop should not forget, that the rejection of the Prayer Book in the time of Charles I, was the very thing, which overturned the Church'. Another High Churchman, Henry Handley Norris, even likened the Bible Society to the Scottish Presbyterian Solemn League and Covenant of the late 1630s. H. H. Norris, *A Practical Exposition of the Tendency and Proceedings of the British and Foreign Bible Society, Begun in a Correspondence between the Rev. H. H. Norris, and J. W. Freshfield, Esq. Relative to the Formation of an Auxiliary Bible Society at Hackney*, 2nd edn (London, 1814), p. 359.

11   Philodike, *Strictures on the Rev. G. Glover's 'Remarks on the Comparative View of the Churches of England and Rome by Dr Herbert Marsh Lord Bishop of Peterborough'* (London, 1821), pp. 62–3.

12   P. Gandolphy, *A Congratulatory Letter to the Rev. Herbert Marsh . . . on his Judicious 'Inquiry into the consequences of neglecting to give the Prayer-Book with the Bible'* (London, 1812), esp. p. 6.

13   T. Burgess, *A Charge delivered to the Clergy of the Diocese of St David's in the Month of September 1813* (Durham, 1813), p. 23. Marsh would have been embarrassed by Burgess's conceding (p. 28) that Gandolphy's charge that 'this vital principle of Protestantism' had been surrendered, was 'plausible'.

14   Ibid., p. 26.

15   See P. B. Nockles, 'A disputed legacy: Anglican historiographies of the Reformation from the era of the Caroline Divines to that of the Oxford Movement', *Bulletin of the John Rylands University Library of Manchester*, 83, 1 (Spring, 2001), 125–6.

16   C. Daubeny, *A Vindication of the Character of the Pious and Learned Bishop Bull, from the Unqualified Accusations Brought Against it, by the Archdeacon of Ely, in his Charge Delivered in the Year 1826* (London, 1827), p. 10.

17 T. Burgess, *A Charge Delivered to the Clergy of the Diocese of Salisbury at the Primary Visitation of the Diocese, 1st August 1826* ([Salisbury]), pp. i-ii.

18 Ibid, pp. xxv-xxvi.

19 [T. Burgess], *A Review and Analysis of Bishop Bull's 'Exposition of the Doctrine of Justification', by Robert Nelson, Esq. Extracted from his Life of Bishop Bull* (Bath, 1827), pp. vi-vii. On Bishop Horsley's irenic approach to the question, see F. C. Mather, *High Church Prophet: Bishop Samuel Horsley (1733–1806) and the Caroline Tradition in the Later Georgian Church* (Oxford, 1992).

20 See *The Judgment Delivered, December 11th, 1809, by the Rt Hon Sir John Nicholl, Knt. LLD. Official Principal of the Arches Court of Canterbury, upon the admission of articles, exhibited in a cause of offence promoted by Kemp, against Wickes, Clerk, for refusing to bury an infant child of two of his parishioners, who had been baptised by a Dissenting minister* (London, 1810). For a more detailed discussion of this controversy, see Mark Smith's chapter in this volume.

21 Bishop Burgess's comments appended to *The Judgment*, p. ii.

22 Ibid, p. v.

23 *A Letter to the Bishop of St David's on Some Extraordinary Passages in a Charge Delivered to the Clergy of his Diocese, in September 1813. By a Lay Seceder* (London, 1814), p. 24. Burgess's Unitarian opponent contrasted (pp. 16–18) Burgess's 'bigotry' with the tolerant and irenic attitude towards rational Dissent by other Anglican divines, such as 'Dr Peckard and Bishop Law, and his son Dr John Law', concluding (p. 19), 'the right of private judgement . . . has still enlightened advocates among the prelates of the Established Church'.

24 C. Kidd, *British Identities before Nationalism: Ethnicity and Nationhood in the Atlantic World 1600–1800* (Cambridge, 1999), p. 121.

25 G. Burgess, *The Politics of the Ancient Constitution* (Houndmills, 1992), pp. 102–3.

26 T. Burgess, *The Protestant's Catechism on the Origin of Popery, and on the Grounds of the Roman Catholic Claims; To Which are Prefixed, the Opinions of Milton, Locke, Hoadly, Blackstone, and Burke. With a Postscript on the introduction of Popery into Ireland by the Compact of Henry II and Pope Adrian in the Twelfth Century* (Dublin, 1818), p. iii.

27 See T. Burgess, *Tracts on the Origin and Independence of the Ancient British Church and on the Supremacy of the Pope*

(London, 1815); T. Burgess, *The English Reformation and Papal Schism* (London, 1819); T. Burgess, *Primary Principles of Christianity: A Charge delivered to the Clergy of the Diocese of Salisbury* (Salisbury, 1829).

28 Burgess, *Protestant's Catechism*, p. iii.
29 T. Burgess, *The First Seven Epochs of the Ancient British Church: A Sermon Preached at St Peter's Church, Carmarthen, on the Second of July, 1812, at the Anniversary Meeting of the SPCK and Church Union in the diocese of St David's* (London, 1813), p. 4.
30 See E. Jones, *The English Nation: The Great Myth* (Stroud, 1998), ch. 6: 'John Lingard and modern historiography'; E. Jones, *John Lingard and the Pursuit of Historical Truth* (Brighton, 2001), pp. 133–4, 138.
31 J. Lingard, *A Collection of Tracts on Several Subjects Connected with the Civil and Religious Principles of Catholics, Examination of certain opinions, advanced by the Right Rev. Dr. Burgess, bishop of St. David's, in two recent publications, entitled 'Christ, and not Peter, the Rock', and 'Johannis Sulgeni versus hexametri in laudem Sulgeni patris', originally published in 1812* (London, 1826), p. 379.
32 *A Letter to the Bishop of Norwich, from the Bishop of St David's* (Salisbury, 1830), p. 8.
33 Ibid., p. 5. Burgess actually praised the notorious Low Churchman Blackburne as a 'very acute writer' and his *Considerations* as 'admirable'. Burgess especially recommended the 'Appendix of important Documents respecting Popish idolatry and breach of faith towards heretics'.
34 On anti-clerical antipathy to Bishop Joseph Butler, see C. Cunliffe, 'The "spiritual sovereign": Butler's episcopate', in C. Cunliffe, ed., *Joseph Butler's Moral and Religious Thought: Tercentenary Essays* (Oxford, 1992), pp. 37–61 (pp. 45–7).
35 P. B. Nockles, 'Samuel Wix', *Oxford Dictionary of National Biography* 59 (Oxford, 2004), pp. 917–8.
36 S. Wix, *Christian Union without the Abuses of Popery* (London, 1820), pp. 16–17.
37 S. Wix, *An affectionate Address to those Dissenters from the Communion of the Church of England, Who Agree with Her in the Leading Doctrines of Christianity. With a Postscript to the Rev Samuel Newton, occasioned by his Address to the Author, entitled 'The Dissenter's Apology'* 2nd edn (London, 1820), pp. 23–4.
38 S. Wix, *Reflections Concerning the Expediency of a Council of the Church of England and the Church of Rome Being Holden, With a View to Accommodate Religious Difficulties, and to*

Promote the Unity of Religion in the Bond of Peace (London, 1818), pp. 40–78.

39 S. Wix, *A Letter to the Bishop of St David's, Occasioned by his Lordship's Misconceptions and Misrepresentations of a Pamphlet Entitled 'Reflections concerning the expediency of a Council of the Church of England and the Church of Rome being holden, with a view to accommodate religious difficulties, and to promote the unity of religion in the bond of peace'* (London, 1819), p. v.

40 Wix, *Reflections*, p. vii.

41 Wix, *Letter to the Bishop of St David's*, p. 44. Likewise, in his controversy with Burgess, the Catholic historian and apologist Joseph Lingard also cited the Laudian Henry Hammond as having conceded, while denying the papal supremacy, that 'St Peter was appointed by Christ to be the rock of the Christian church'. J. Lingard, '*Examination of certain opinions*', p. 360.

42 Ibid., p. 38.

43 Wix, *Reflections*, p. 20.

44 Burgess, *Protestant's Catechism*, p. 45.

45 T. Burgess, *Popery Incapable of Union with a Protestant Church, and Not a Remedy for Schism, Nor an Exemplar of Unity, Sanctity, or Christian Verity: A Letter in Reply to the Rev Samuel Wix, containing 'An Examination of the subjects intended in the Parliamentary Declarations against Popery, and a view of Papal Schism'* (Carmarthen, 1820), p. 203. As late as 1835, in a pamphlet protesting against the pro-Catholic policy of Lord Melbourne's Whig administration, Burgess cited a long *catenae patrum* of Anglican divines, which included even Andrewes and Taylor, as well as Jewel, Bilson, Davenant and Downham, in support of the notion of idolatrous character of the Church of Rome. T. Burgess, *A Letter to the Rt. Hon. Lord Viscount Melbourne, on the Idolatry and Apostasy of the Church of Rome* (Salisbury, 1835), p. 7.

46 Burgess, *Popery Incapable of Union with a Protestant Church*, p. 51.

47 Ibid., pp. 51–2.

48 Wix, *Letter to the Bishop of St David's*, p. vii.

49 Ibid., p. xii.

50 Wix, *Reflections*, p. vii.

51 Harford, *Life of Thomas Burgess*, 2nd edn (1841), p. 471.

52 Burgess, *English Reformation and Papal Schism*, p. 52.

53 Burgess, *Primary Principles of Christianity*, p. 45.

54 On Horsley's relatively pro-Catholic stance in the 1790s, see

P. B. Nockles, 'The Difficulties of Protestantism: Bishop Milner, John Fletcher and Catholic Apologetic against the Church of England in the era from the first Relief Act to Emancipation, 1778–1830', *Recusant History*, 24, 2 (October, 1998), esp. 205–10.

55 Wix, *Reflections*, p. 6.

56 Burgess, *Popery incapable of union with a Protestant Church*, p. 58.

57 Ibid., pp. 86–7. Burgess supported the application to the Papal See of the prophetic passage from Revelations (18: 4): 'Come out of her, my people, that ye be not partakers of her sins, and receive not of her plagues'. *Letter to the Bishop of Norwich from the Bishop of Salisbury*, p. 14. On theories of the Antichrist among Anglican churchmen of the period, see W. H. Olliver, *Prophets and Millennialists: The Use of Biblical Prophecy in England from the 1790s to the 1840s* (Auckland, 1978), pp. 50–1; A. Robinson, 'Identifying the Beast: Samuel Horsley and the problem of the papal Anti-Christ', *JEH*, 43 (October, 1992), 592–607; J. A. Oddy, 'Eschatological prophecy in the English theological tradition, *c.*1700–*c.*1840', unpublished, Ph.D. thesis, University of London, 1982, ch. 3.

58 Ibid., p. 55.

59 See J. J. Sack, *From Jacobite to Conservative: Reaction and Orthodoxy in Britain c.1760–1832* (Cambridge, 1993), ch. 9.

60 *Anti-Jacobin Review and Protestant Advocate*, 104 (1818).

61 S. Wix, *Plain Reasons why Political Power Should Not be Granted to Papists*, 2nd edn (London, 1822), p. 15. Burgess seems to have forced Wix on to the defensive. Wix expressed regret that he had not 'adopted terms more expressive of my reprobation of Romish delusions', but complained to Burgess: 'Had your Lordship done me the favour to point out the deficiency of my terms, instead of writing me an angry note, charging me with a disposition generally to popery, I might, in the second edition, have adopted terms of disapprobation more appropriate to the subject.' Wix, *Letter to the Bishop of St David's*, pp. 92–3.

62 Newman was something of an exception, but by the later 1830s he had gradually abandoned his earlier belief in a papal Anti-Christ. See P. Misner, 'Newman and the tradition concerning the papal Antichrist', *Church History*, 42 (1973), 375–88. As late as 1838, in Tract 20 (p. 3), Newman linked Rome with Antichrist. In his *Apologia* (1st edn, 1864, p. 219), he cited passages even from his Tract 85, 'Advent sermons on

Antichrist', as showing that, though he was 'feeling after some other interpretation of prophecy instead of his [Newton's] . . . Bishop Newton was still upon my mind even in 1838'.

63 As Newman put it, 'the arguments to be urged against Romanism ought to be taken from such parts of the general controversy as bear most upon practice, and at the same time kept clear of what is more especially sacred, and painful to dispute about'. *Tracts for the Times. By members of the University of Oxford. Vol. III. For 1835–6*, 71 [J. H. Newman], 'On the controversy with the Romanists', new edn (London, 1840), p. 5.

64 J. H. Newman, *Lectures on the Prophetical Office of the Church Viewed Relatively to Romanism and Popular Protestantism* (London, 1837), p. 30.

65 *Remains of the late Richard Hurrell Froude*, I, i, p. 379.

66 See [F. Oakeley], 'Bishop Jewel, his character, correspondence, and apologetic treatises', *British Critic*, 30, 54 (July, 1841), 1–46.

67 By 1838, Newman was privately expressing relief that he no longer needed 'all sorts of fictions and artifices to make out Cranmer or others Catholic'. J. H. Newman to T. Henderson, 9 December 1838, HEN 2/4/3, Pusey House Library (hereafter PHL), Oxford.

68 J. H. Newman to E. B. Pusey, 13 August 1841, *Letters and Diaries of John Henry Newman* (hereafter *LDN*), VIII, ed. G. Tracey (Oxford, 1999), pp. 242–3.

69 J. Keble to A. P. Perceval, 16 February 1830, Liddon bound volumes (hereafter LBV), PHL.

70 J. Keble to J. H. Newman, 21 January 1835, LBV 9/38, PHL.

71 J. Keble to T. Keble, 14 November 1836, Keble Papers, Keble College Library (hereafter KCL), Oxford.

72 *Remains of the late Hurrell Froude*, II, i (Derby, 1839), pp. xxi-xxii.

73 J. Keble to R. H. Froude, August 1835, J. T. Coleridge, *A Memoir of the Rev. John Keble, M. A. late Vicar of Hursley*, 3rd edn (London, 1870), p. 201.

74 *The Works of that learned and judicious divine, Mr Richard Hooker: with an account of his life and death by Isaac Walton. Arranged by the Rev. John Keble, M. A. late Fellow of Oriel College, Oxford*, 3 vols in 4, 3rd edn (Oxford, 1845 [1836]), I, p. cvii.

75 J. Keble to E. B. Pusey, 18 January 1839, LBV 50/16, PHL.

76 *Remains of the late Hurrell Froude*, I, ii, p. 381.

77 Froude commented (Ibid., I, i, p. 327): 'It seems to me that Saravia and Bancroft are the revivers of orthodoxy in England'.

78 Ibid.

79 J. Collier, *Ecclesiastical History of Great Britain*, 9 vols, new edn (London, 1840), V, pp. 587–8.

80 Cited in A. Starkie, 'Gilbert Burnet's *Reformation* and the semantics of popery' (forthcoming).

81 Burgess, *Protestant's Catechism*, p. 9.

82 Ibid., p. 11.

83 P. B. Nockles, 'Anglican historiographies of the Reformation', pp. 135–8.

84 Burgess, *Protestant's Catechism*, p. vii.

85 Ibid., p. 55.

86 Newman confided in 1836: 'I mourn over a "Law Church" . . . the creature of Henries and Williams's. I cannot love the "Church of England" commonly so designated . . . its very title is an offence . . . for it implies that it holds of the state'. J. H. Newman to H. J. Rose, 23 May 1836, *LDN*, V, ed. T. Gornall (Oxford, 1981), pp. 301–2. In contrast, Burgess gloried in the fact that the 'first act of the Reformation' was to reunite 'the ecclesiastical and civil authority' which had been separated by the 'policy of the Church of Rome, since its assumption of ecumenical supremacy'. *A Letter from the Bishop of Salisbury to the Duke of Wellington* (London [1829]), pp. 5–6.

87 P. B. Nockles, 'Anglican historiographies of the Reformation', 121–67 (125–8).

88 Pusey's historical comment on the period was typical of the Tractarian viewpoint: 'The last century every one readily condemns as the deadest and shallowest period of English theology. And this could be traced . . . to the line which men took in resisting James's evil.' E. B. Pusey, *Patience and Confidence the Strength of the Church. A Sermon Preached on the 5th of November before the University of Oxford at St Mary's, Oxford* (Oxford, 1837), p. 44.

89 J. Walsh, 'Origins of the evangelical revival', in J. Walsh and G. V. Bennett, *Essays in Modern Church History in Memory of Norman Sykes* (London, 1966), p. 149.

90 J. H. Newman, *Apologia Pro Vita Sua*, 1st edn (London, 1864), p. 62.

91 T. M. Parker, 'The rediscovery of the Fathers in the seventeenth-century Anglican tradition', in J. Coulson and A. M. Allchin (eds.), *The Rediscovery of Newman* (London, 1967), pp. 41–5. Cf. H. D. Weidner (ed.), *The Via Media of the*

Anglican Church by John Henry Newman (Oxford, 1990), pp. xxi-xxv. Newman himself conceded that when he came to study the Caroline divines, 'the doctrine of 1833 was strengthened in me, not changed'. Newman, *Apologia*, p. 121.

92 D. Forrester, *Young Dr Pusey: A Study in Development* (London, 1989), p. 85.

93 Edward Churton criticized the writings of ultra-Tractarians such as John Mason Neale, one of the founders of the Cambridge Camden Society, because they 'are perfectly ignorant of what our best divines of the seventeenth century have said, who were able to break the heads of a hundred such writers as these'. E. Churton to W. Gresley, n.d. [1846], Gresley Papers, GRES 3/7/59, PHL.

94 Chas. Wordsworth, *Annals of My Early Life: 1806–1846* (London, 1891), p. 343.

95 *Remarks on a Late Advertisement from Oxford (With Some Notice of an Extensive and Valuable Article in the 'Quarterly Review' Published in March last). By an Aged Layman* (London, 1842), p. 4.

96 C. Crawley to J. H. Newman, 16 January 1841, *LDN*, VIII,. ed. G. Tracey (Oxford, 1999), p. 18. Newman explained that the works of the Caroline divines which Copeland 'took pleasure in were for the most part gone [already published] – and he was forced upon such as he did not merely not like, but could not tolerate'. J. H. Newman to C. Crawley, 14 January 1841, *LDN*, VIII, p. 16.

97 J. H. Newman to F. Rogers, 10 January 1841, *LDN*, VIII, p. 10; J. H. Newman to E. B. Pusey, 12 January 1841, *LDN*, VIII, p. 14.

98 J. H. Newman to C. Crawley, 14 January 1841, *LDN*, VIII, p. 17.

99 Ibid.; J. H. Newman to F. Rogers, 10 January 1841, *LDN*, VIII, p. 10; J. H. Newman to E. B. Pusey, 12 January 1841, *LDN*, VIII, p. 14; J. H. Newman to Miss Holmes, 12 February 1841, *LDN*, VIII, p. 33.

100 Pusey likewise cautioned on the need for careful editing: 'one might have catholic and uncatholic works from the same writer, as Hall, Ussher, Beveridge . . . I thought it would be unjust to our divines, not to reserve to the editor, the right of explaining ambiguous phrases in a catholic sense, with a benign interpretation'. E. B. Pusey to J. H. Newman, 8 January 1841, *LDN*, VIII, pp. 13–14.

101 For Mozley's critique, see *English Review*, 4 (December, 1845),

especially 390. Cf. *British Magazine*, 30 (July, 1846), 61. For Newman's pained, private response, see J. H. Newman to Ambrose St John, 8 January 1846, *LDN*, XI., ed. C. S. Dessain (London, 1961), p. 87. See also E. Sidenvall, *Change and Identity: Protestant English Interpretations of John Henry Newman's Secession, 1845–1864* (Lund, 2002), p. 71.

102 Paul Elmer More and Frank Leslie Cross (eds), *Anglicanism: The Thought and Practice of the Church of England, Illustrated from the Religious Literature of the Seventeenth Century.* (London, 1935), pp. xxx-xxxi.

103 F. M. Turner, *John Henry Newman: The Challenge to Evangelical Religion* (New Haven, 2002), especially pp. 1–11.

104 J. H. Newman to H. Wilberforce, n.d. [27 January], 1846, *LDN*, XI, p. 100.

105 G. Herring, *What was the Oxford Movement?* (London, 2002), p. 62.

106 J. H. Newman to H. J. Rose, 1 May 1836, *LDN*, V, pp. 291–2.

107 For Sykes's argument that Newman created 'the myth of a unique Anglicanism', see S. W. Sykes, 'Newman, Anglicanism and the fundamentals', I. Ker and A. G. Hill (eds.) *Newman after a Hundred Years* (Oxford, 1990), pp. 365–6; H. L. Weatherby, 'The encircling gloom: Newman's departure from the Caroline tradition', *Victorian Studies*, 12, 1 (September, 1968), 57–8.

108 See Frederick Faber's comment on both Laud and the Revolution of 1688/9, echoing a theme of Newman's: 'he might remember, that the moderate party in Arian times was popular, and yet not safe, neither did it prevail. And had he lived forty-four years from his Martyrdom, he would have seen some of that church history carried out at home. Moderate men are not tall enough to throw a shade over posterity, nor of sufficient integrity of heart and purpose to project their influence on after-generations.' F. W. Faber (ed.), *Autobiography of Dr William Laud, Archbishop of Canterbury and Martyr. Collected from his 'Remains'* (Oxford, 1839), p. xvi. As Anthony Milton has observed, for the Laudians, the *via media* symbolized 'a determined exclusivity' rather than concept of 'moderation'. A. Milton, *Catholic and Reformed: The Roman and Protestant Churches in English Protestant Thought, 1600–1640* (Cambridge, 1995), pp. 531, 538–40.

109 [J. B. Mozley], 'Archbishop Laud', *Christian Remembrancer*, 9, 47 (January, 1845), 299–300.

110 [J. H. Newman], 'Le Bas's Life of Archbishop Laud', *British Critic*, 109, 88 (April, 1836), p. 368.

111 *Remains of the Late Richard Hurrell Froude*, II: i (Derby, 1839): 'Fragments' – 'The Arminians'; pp. 394–5. For Bull's critique of Limborch and Episcopius, see R. Nelson, *The Life of Dr George Bull, Late Lord Bishop of St David's. With the History of those Controversies in Which He was Engaged*, 2nd edn (London, 1714), pp. 370–7.

112 *John Henry Newman. Autobiographical Writings*, ed. H. Tristram (London, 1956), p. 83.

113 S. F. Wood to J. H. Newman, 29 May 1837, *LDN*, VI, ed. G. Tracey (Oxford, 1997), p. 77.

114 H. C. Grove, *The Teaching of the Anglican Divines of the Time of King James I and King Charles I, on the Doctrine of the Holy Eucharist, Extracted from their Writings, with an Introduction, Containing Remarks on the Late Works on that Subject by Dr Pusey and Mr Keble* (London, 1858), pp. 6–7, 15–16.

115 R. H. Froude to J. H. Newman, January 1835, *LDN*, V, p. 18.

116 Newman, 'Le Bas's Life of Laud', 368.

117 The deist Edward Gibbon acknowledged a debt to Chillingworth. *Gibbon's Autobiographies*, ed. J. Murray (London, 1896), p. 112.

118 E. Churton to W. J. Copeland, 12 April 1836; 21 May 1836, Churton Papers, Sutton Coldfield (private possession); E. Churton, *The Church of England a witness and keeper of the Catholic tradition* (London, 1836), p. 13. Churton insisted (p. 38) that Chillingworth's views 'had been much misunderstood by writers of the school of Locke and Hoadly'.

119 J. H. Newman to E. Churton, 14 March 1837, *LDN*, VI, p. 41.

120 J. H. Newman to Mrs J. Mozley, 4 June 1837, ibid., p. 81.

121 See Newman, *Apologia*, pp. 208–213. Newman famously related (p. 213) that he 'had seen the shadow of a hand upon the wall'.

122 Harford, *Life of Thomas Burgess*, pp. 181–2.

123 *Tracts for the Times. By members of the University of Oxford. Vol. III for 1835–6* [J. H. Newman], *No. 75: On the Roman Breviary as embodying the substance of the Devotional Services of the Church Catholic*, 6. 'Mattins Service for March 21. Bishop Ken's Day', new edn (Oxford, 1840), pp. 135–45.

124 [J. H. Newman], *Tracts for the Times . . . Vol. V for 1838–40*, No. 88, *The Greek Devotions of Bishop Andrewes, translated and arranged*, 3rd edn (London, 1843), pp. 1–96.

125 *The Private Devotions of Dr William Laud, Archbishop of*

Canterbury, and Martyr. Edited by the Rev. Frederic W. Faber, BA, Fellow of University College, Oxford (Oxford, 1838), pp. vii-viii; Faber (ed.), *Autobiography of Dr William Laud*, pp. xvi-xvii.

[126] E. B. Pusey to H. E. Manning, 9 July 1844, LBV, PHL.

[127] E. B. Pusey to H. E. Manning, 12 August 1845, LBV, PHL.

[128] T. A. Lacey, *Herbert Thorndike, 1598–1672* (London, 1929), p. 114. On Manning's debt to Thorndike, see J. Pereiro, *Cardinal Manning: An Intellectual Biography* (Oxford, 1998), pp. 16, 57.

[129] H. E. Manning, *A Charge Delivered at the Ordinary Visitation of the Archdeaconry of Chichester in July 1841* (London, 1841), p. 27.

[130] J. H. Newman, *A Letter to the Rev. Godfrey Faussett, D. D. Margaret Professor of Divinity, on Certain Points of Faith and Practice*, 2nd edn (Oxford, 1838), pp. 19–20.

[131] *A Charge Delivered to the Clergy of the Diocese of Exeter, by the Rt. Rev. Henry Phillpotts, Lord Bishop of Exeter at his Triennial Visitation in the Months of August, September, and October 1839* (London, 1839), p. 78.

[132] A. Härdelin, *The Tractarian Understanding of the Eucharist* (Uppsala, 1965), p. 213.

[133] *LDN*, VIII, Appendix 6, p. 595. For details of the Young case, see H. P. Liddon, *The Life of Edward Bouverie Pusey*, 4 vols (London, 1893–4), II, pp. 30–4.

[134] See P. B. Nockles, 'Newman, Tract 90, and the Bishops', D. Nicholls and F. Kerr, (eds), *John Henry Newman: Reason, Rhetoric, and Romanticism* (Bristol, 1991), pp. 28–87.

[135] J. H. Newman to T. Mozley, 7 March 1841, LDN, viii, p. 58. Newman privately made clear that Tract 90 'was necessary to keep people either from Rome or schism or an uncomfortable conscience'. J. H. Newman to A. P. Perceval, 12 March 1841, *LDN*, VII, p. 68.

[136] J. H. Newman to R. W. Jelf, 15 March 1841, *LDN*, VIII, pp. 85–7.

[137] E. A. Abbott, *The Anglican Career of Cardinal Newman*, 2 vols (London, 1892), I, p. 250.

[138] [A. Mozley], 'Dr Newman's Apology', *Christian Remembrancer*, 8 (July, 1864), p. 178.

[139] J. H. Newman, *Lectures on Justification* (London, 1838), p. 442.

[140] J. Keble to H. H. Norris, 13 November 1837, MS Eng. Lett. C. 469, fo. 92, Bodleian Library, Oxford.

[141] A. McGrath, 'John Henry Newman's *Lectures on Justification*: the high church misrepresentation of Luther', *Churchman*, 97, 2 (1983), p. 112.

[142] Cited in W. H. Mackean, *The Eucharistic Doctrine of the Oxford Movement* (London, 1933), p. 126.

[143] W. Sewell, 'The Church of England divines of the seventeenth century', *Quarterly Review*, 69 (March, 1842), 472.

[144] Mozley, 'Development of the Church in the seventeenth century', p. 344.

[145] Ibid., pp. 334–5. In order to justify his selectivity, Mozley cited (p. 345) the precedent of Bishop Tomline's selectivity when making his historical case for the anti-Calvinism of the Church of England: 'See how Bishop Tomline, in his controversy with Scott, is obliged to apologise for the divines before that [Laudian] time.'

[146] F. Oakeley, *The Subject of Tract XC Historically Examined*, 2nd edn (London, 1845), p. 11.

[147] Rev. Frederick George Lee (ed.), *Paraphrastica exposito articulorum confessionis Anglicanae: the Articles of the Anglican Church paraphrastically considered and explained, by Franciscus a Sancta Clara (Dr Christopher Davenport), to which are prefixed an introduction and sketch of the life of the author.* (London, 1865), p. 58.

[148] F. Oakeley to H. E. Maning, 27 January 1845, Manning Papers, MS Eng. Lett. C. 654, fo. 88, Bodleian Library; Oakeley, *Subject of Tract XC*, p. 29.

[149] Ibid., pp. 53–71; J. B. Mozley, 'Extracts from Divines of the seventeenth century', *British Critic*, 32, no. 114 (October, 1842), esp. pp. 360–1.

[150] H. E. Manning to F. Oakeley, 25 January 1845, Manning Papers, MS Eng. Lett. C. 654, fo. 75, Bodleian Library.

[151] Oakeley, *Subject of Tract XC*, (2nd edn), p. x.

[152] [Richard Montagu], 'Concerning Recusancie of Communion with the Church of England', [c.1635], ed. Anthony Milton and Alexandra Walsham, in Stephen Taylor (ed.), *From Cranmer to Davidson: A Church of England Miscellany* (Woodbridge, 1999), p. 93.

[153] Cited in Wix, *Plain Reasons*, p. 15.

[154] Oakeley, *Subject of Tract XC* (1st edn), pp. 3–4.

[155] Ibid., p. 31.

[156] For examples of the genre, see R. Rabett, *Archbishop Laud More than Half a Papist: Or, Laudism (After the Lapse of Two Centuries) Revived, Under the Appellation of Puseyism*

(London, 1842), pp. i-ii, 15–17; P. Maurice, *A Postscript to the 'Popery of Oxford': The Number of the Beast* (London, 1851), p. 2.

157 W. Goode, *The Divine Rule of Faith and Practice, or, a Defence of the Catholic Doctrine of Holy Scripture*, 2 vols (London, 1842), I, p. xxiii. Goode claimed (p. xxix) that the Tractarian *catenae* 'revealed a great want of acquaintance even with the works of our own great divines'.

158 J. Garbett, *A Review of Dr Pusey's Sermon, and the Doctrine of the Eucharist According to the Church of England* (London, 1843), p. ci.

159 J. Garbett, *Christ as Prophet, Priest, and King: being a Vindication of the Church of England from Theological Novelties, in Eight Lectures preached before the University of Oxford, at Canon Bampton's Lecture, in the year MDCCCXLII*, 2 vols (Oxford, 1842), I, pp. 437–8.

160 H. Fish, *Jesuitism Traced in the Movements of the Oxford Tractarians* (London, 1842), pp. 61–2; [C. P. Golightly], *New and Strange Doctrines Extracted from the Writings of Mr Newman and his Friends, in a Letter to the Rev. W. F. Hook, by One of the Original Subscribers to the 'Tracts for the Times'* (Oxford, 1841), pp. 12–13; Garbett, *Christ as Prophet, Priest, and King*, I, pp. 438–9.

161 S. F. Wood to J. H. Newman, 8 April 1837, *LDN*, VI, p. 53.

162 Nockles, *Oxford Movement in Context*, pp. 134–5, 158–9.

163 Archdeacon W. R. Lyall to Bp. R. Bagot, 14 January 1842, Bagot Papers, PHL.

164 P. B. Nockles, *Oxford Movement in Context*, pp. 228–35.

165 W. Goode, *A Letter to the Bishop of Exeter, containing an examination of his 'Letter to the Archbishop of Canterbury'* (London, 1850), p. 45.

166 J. B. Mozley, *The Primitive Doctrine of Baptismal Regeneration* (London, 1856), p. lii; *A Review of the Baptismal Controversy* (London, 1862); W. Maskell, *A Second Letter on the Present Position of the High Church Party in the Church of England* (London, 1850), pp. 1–33.

167 Maskell, *Second Letter on the Present Position of the High Church Party*, p. 16.

168 J. H. Newman to E. B. Pusey, 19 February 1844, LBV, PHL.

169 Newman, *Apologia*, p. 328.

170 Harford gave a glowingly enthusiastic account to his friend William Wilberforce of a personal audience which he had had with Pope Pius VII in 1817 on the subject of slavery. J. S. Harford,

Recollections of William Wilberforce, Esq. M.P. for the county of York during nearly thirty years. With brief notices of some of his personal friends and contemporaries, 2nd edn, (London, 1865), pp. 79–83. See esp. p. 80 where Harford commented: 'I felt highly honoured in being permitted to approach him.' See also p. 81: 'It was impossible to look at the venerable Pope without feeling sympathy for his past misfortunes, and for the firmness he had displayed in opposition to the efforts of the first Napoleon to render him the tool of his ambition.' It is unlikely that Burgess might have approved of such a statement. Harford also (p. 21) recounted his friendly relationship with the influential Vatican diplomat, Cardinal Consalvi.

[171] Burgess, *Popery Incapable of Union with a Protestant Church*, pp. 86–7.

[172] Burgess commented that 'division in the Church makes us a rope of sand'. Harford, *Life of Thomas Burgess*, p. 471.

[173] J. H. Newman to H. J. Rose, 11 May 1836, J. W. Burgon, *Lives of Twelve Good Men*, 2 vols, 4th edn (London, 1889), p. 214. Newman used the expression, he 'could not endure' Wake's mode of controversy. In response, Rose teasingly agreed to 'first formally give up Abp. Wake . . . and Revolution-Protestantism'. H. J. Rose to J. H. Newman, 13 May 1836, ibid.

[174] Burgess, *Protestant's Catechism*, p. 51.

[175] Ibid., p. 50.

[176] See J. Martin, *Walton's Lives: Conformist Commemorations and the Rise of Biography* (Oxford, 2001), ch. 5; MacCulloch, 'Hooker's reputation', esp. pp. 779–81.

[177] P. B. Nockles, 'Anglican historiographies of the Reformation', pp. 126–8.

[178] W. J. Copeland, MS. 'Narrative of the Oxford Movement', ed. W. Borlase, 2 vols., no pag., PHL.

[179] Frederick Oakeley commented: 'Is it not somewhat unfair, by whatever great names the practice has been recommended, to lay all the Protestantism of the Church of England at the door of the foreign Reformers . . . when, we ask, was this baneful influence repudiated, when was it discountenanced, when was it not really admitted?' [Oakeley], 'Bishop Jewel', p. 75.

[180] See P. B. Nockles, *Oxford Movement in Context*, p. 154.

[181] W. Palmer, *A Letter to a Protestant-Catholic* (Oxford, 1842), esp. pp. 36–7; W. Palmer, *Aids to Reflection on the Seemingly Double Character of the Established Church, With Reference to the foundation of a 'Protestant Bishopric' at Jerusalem* (Oxford, 1841).

[182] *Notes of a Visit to the Russian Church in the Years 1840, 1841. By the Late William Palmer, M.A. Selected and Arranged by Cardinal Newman* (London, 1882), p. vii.

[183] Burgess, *Popery Incapable of Union with a Protestant Church*, p. 60; W. Goode, *The Case as It is: Or, a Reply to the Letter of Dr Pusey to his Grace the Archbishop of Canterbury* (London, 1842), p. 17.

[184] N. de Flon, *Newman's 'Brother and Friend': The Life and Work of Edward Caswall* (Leominster, 2005) pp. 9–14.

[185] A. Stott, *Hannah More: The First Victorian* (Oxford, 2003), pp. 284, 288. More even claimed part of the credit for Burgess's foundation of a college at Lampeter for the Welsh clergy in 1822, significantly noting, however (ibid., p. 284): 'There will, unavoidably, to save [Burgess's] credit, be mixed with it a little too much High Church, but we must be glad to do something if we cannot do all that is wanted.'

[186] For correspondence between Burgess and Simeon on spiritual matters, see, *Memoir of the Life of the Rev. Charles Simeon, M.A. with a selection fro his writings and corresponndence. Edited by the Rev. William Cares*, 2nd edn, (London, 1847), pp. 750–5. Burgess was much impressed by the account of Simeon's last illness and death which appeared in the evangelical *Christian Observer*. Harford, *Burgess*, p. 484.

[187] Harford, *Burgess*, p. 181.

[188] H. P. Liddon, *Life of Edward Bouverie Pusey*, I, p. 282. Referring to the period just prior to his elevation to the episcopate, Harford noted of Burgess: 'At this particular period, there is reason to believe that he carried some of the habits and tastes of an ascetic life further than his better judgement afterwards approved.' Harford, *Burgess*, p. 195. Bishop Burgess, as consecrating prelate, had also been greatly impressed by Pusey's sermon preached at the consecration of Grove church, Wantage, on 14 August 1832, and urged that the sermon be printed. Ibid., pp. 220–1.

[189] *An Eirenicon of the Eighteenth Century. Proposals for Catholic Communion by a minister of the Church of England [1705]. New edition, with Introduction, Notes, and Appendices. Edited by Henry Nutcombe Oxenham M.A.* (London, 1879), pp. 8–9.

[190] P. B. Nockles, 'Introduction', *The Spirit of the Oxford Movement and Newman's Place in History. By Christopher Dawson. Introduced by Dr Peter Nockles, with a biographical note by Mrs Christina Scott*, new edn (London, 2001), pp. xxii-xxvi.

12

The Cardinal and the Archbishop: A Lost Opportunity? The Influence of J. B. Sumner's Apostolical Preaching on J. H. Newman's Concept of Justification

JULIE LETHABY

Introduction

No comprehensive discussion on the subject of justification is free from the personality of Martin Luther; this was the big stumbling block of John Henry Newman's own struggle with the thorny topic. The future Archbishop of Canterbury, John Bird Sumner, saw Luther as no such stumbling block in 1815, in his published consideration of justification in what was to become the first version of the *Apostolical Preaching*. Indeed, when the work was republished in 1850, after Sumner had assumed leadership of the Anglican Communion, his published understanding of Luther remained what it had been thirty-five years earlier. This essay seeks to set out the details of the influence of Sumner's *Apostolical Preaching* on the juvenile John Henry, and in so doing will highlight what appears to have been a missed opportunity ... or a blind spot of prejudice. As Newman has in more recent years been hailed repeatedly as a cornerstone of ecumenical potential, the bias of Newman's approach to the meteoric subject of justification deserves closer inspection.

Newman's discussion of justification acted as a catalyst for nineteenth-century Luther studies. His denigration of Luther has been attributed to the influence of Hurrell Froude's negative appraisal of the Reformation.[1] At the start of the nineteenth century no one would have questioned the description of the Church of England as 'Protestant', primarily because of the Church of England's rejection of the political and spiritual jurisdiction of the Pope, who was commonly considered to represent the Antichrist, a demonic alias accepted by Newman in his formative years. At the start of the nineteenth century the doctrine of justification by faith had a political as well as a religious value; as a result there was confusion as to what the term actually implied theologically. This confusion was reflected in Newman's *Lectures on Justification* where Luther was selected as the obvious historical and doctrinal adversary. In adopting this approach, Newman sought to follow the example of a number of the later Caroline divines, and of George Bull in particular. Bull's argument had, however, been directed at Grotius and not Luther, something Newman failed to acknowledge.

In general, the association of Luther's name with the Reformation, and in particular Hurrell Froude's refutation of that historical experience as an interruption to the truth and tradition of the Church, ignited an animosity amongst several of the principal players in the Oxford Movement, and in turn gave the impression of a united Tractarian hostility towards the Reformation. What is immediately obvious in the assumptions that Newman made about Luther – assumptions mirrored by W. G. Ward in his *Ideal of a Christian Church* – is that the subject of justification by faith as reconsidered at the Reformation was perceived to be an aberration from the orthodox (with a small 'o') experience of the Church. Newman's approach to Luther was initially naive, reflecting that of the early sixteenth century, when during the Henrician period it was common to call men Lutherans who showed any sympathy towards evangelicalism.[2] On the pretext of seeking to make the Church of England a living entity, by evoking its continuity with the pre-Reformation Church, Newman declared,

> I wrote my Essay on Justification in 1837; it was aimed at the Lutheran dictum that Justification by faith only was the Cardinal doctrine of Christianity. I considered that his doctrine was either a paradox or a truism – a paradox in

Luther's mouth, a truism in Melanchthon's. I thought that the Anglican Church followed Melanchthon, and that in consequence between Rome and Anglicanism, between high church and low church, there was no real intellectual difference on the point.[3]

As the account of the composition of the *Lectures* has already been told many times, it is not necessary to dwell long upon the story except to provide a contextual environment for further discussion of the *Lectures*.[4]

The *Lectures* were written at the apex of Newman's confidence *in* the Church of England. The most valuable and interesting explanation of how the *Lectures* came to be written is told through Newman's own correspondence. In spite of the multiplicity of accounts on the *Lectures*, reference to Newman's personal reflections has in general been overlooked; preference has been given in the first instance to the rostrum of the *Apologia*, and, in the second, to the dais of the *Parochial and Plain Sermons*.

The *Lectures* were born from Newman's defence of Pusey's *Tracts on Baptism*, characterized by their stress on the ambiguous status of post-baptismal sin. The staunchly Protestant periodical, the *Christian Observer*, had censored Pusey for this rigorous opinion of baptismal regeneration. In return Newman wrote to the editor C. S. Wiles, but was discouraged by the response he received, or, more precisely, by the way in which his apology was embellished with editorial comment. Newman directed,

> My present notion is to publish what will be almost a book on Justification and perhaps in the Preface to allude to the Christian Observer. Or if the editor does not publish the rest of my letter, *which I wish*, then I would publish it with such alterations as are necessary . . .[5]

This threat he duly carried out, and his intended third letter to Wiles became, after a time, his published work, the *Lectures on Justification*. Newman's *Lectures on the Prophetical Office*, written two years earlier, had been relatively well received; Newman stated in the *Apologia* that the *Lectures* were intended as a continuation of his quest for Anglican clarification.[6] The positive reception of the *Prophetical Office* had created a false sense of security for what would be received as a Roman assault upon the Protestant character of the Church in the *Lectures* themselves.[7]

Newman was concerned that his letters to the *Christian Observer* had disappointed fellow Tractarians, and in particular his former pupil, Samuel Wood. Wood, in a letter to Newman, highlighted the significance to evangelicals of the coupling of the subject of justification with the Reformation. He drew attention to the subsequent 'moral or miraculous' divide on the doctrine, pointing out that to the observer the Tractarian opinion appeared to rest on a sacramental matrix that combined both the 'moral and the miraculous' (that is, works and faith respectively). This for Wood was congruent with the prized Anglican notion of the *via media*. Interestingly, in contradistinction to the line of argument that Newman chose to take in the *Lectures*, Wood accused Luther of going *further* than the Anglican Church. He claimed that his doctrine of justification by faith sought to supersede the sacraments; at the same time he also criticized the Roman dependence on the sacraments and the belief that they claimed to confer justification. Wood remarked that the discussion in the *Christian Observer* had highlighted the need for an independent Anglican definition of the doctrine. Newman proceeded to rise to the challenge, although with some trepidation.[8] Significantly, his correspondence from this period reveals that he did not consider his *Lectures* as independent from the wider aims and objectives of the Oxford Movement itself.[9] The movement, rather than the subject of justification, can therefore be seen to have set the agenda for his *Lectures*; they were not therefore intentionally objective, irenic or ecumenical.[10]

Missed opportunity or blind spot?

A review of the available evidence strongly suggests that Newman's understanding of justification in the *Lectures* stemmed from his time at Oriel during 1824–5 and, in particular, from the inferences he drew from J. B. Sumner's *Apostolical Preaching* and the implications it implied for the evolution of his concept of justification. It is clear from his personal correspondence that he had made up his mind about Luther as early as 1834.

In recent years several commentators, including Thomas Sheridan and C. S. Dessain, have sought to stress an irenic approach to the subject of justification in Newman's *Lectures*, and in particular the role of the indwelling Holy Spirit in the act of salvation. At the time of writing the *Lectures* one thought preoccupied Newman, and that was a defence of the Church of England. In this context, Newman's ideas about the means and mode of justification and its dependence on the indwelling presence of the Holy Spirit can be traced directly to his reading of Sumner's *Apostolical Preaching*, which, on the foundation of the teaching of St Paul, taught the very same thing. It was not Knox's 'Essay on Justification', as suggested by Alister McGrath, that was the primary influence on Newman in the conjugation of faith and works in his conception of a definition of justification.[11] Rather, Newman's own recollections point to his reading of Sumner's modest early editions of the *Apostolic Preaching* as the main literary means by which he crystallized his thinking on the subject of justification.

In letters and diary entries, Newman claimed that the combination of reading Sumner's *Apostolical Preaching* and the raw experience of life as a curate in his first parish incited him to reject his initial evangelical beliefs.[12] This argument is substantiated not only from Newman's autobiographical comments, but, more remarkably, from the influence which Sumner's work clearly exerted on the *Lectures*. Whether that influence was conscious or unconscious, it is particularly evident in just that area where Dessain, for example, was quick to praise Newman's interpretation of the doctrine of justification as both biblical and catholic, that is, the indwelling of the Holy Spirit as the foundation of salvation.[13] This comprehension of the doctrine appears to have resulted, not from Newman's interest in the Eastern Orthodox Church, but from his reading of Sumner. The confusion over the exact nature of the relationship between declarative justification and the experience of habitual sanctification as enshrined in Newman's 'umbrella' definition, can be seen very clearly to have also existed in embryo in Richard Hooker's *Sermon on Justification*. In stressing the need for both faith and works, Newman does not in fact deviate from the ethos of Cranmer's authorized *Homily on Salvation*. Significantly, where Newman does break with Anglican tradition is in his derision of Luther. Newman at no time acknowledged that Luther's doctrine of justification rested on a *fides Christi* approach rather than *sola fide*. Crucially, what Newman failed to realize, was that Luther's doctrine of justification was equally as dependent upon the Trinity as was his own. To that end, the confusion surrounding the historical comprehension of Luther and his teaching in England is reflected in Newman's polemic.

The *Autobiographical Writings* record, 'This book [*Apostolical Preaching*] was successful in the event beyond anything else, in routing out evangelical doctrines from Mr Newman's creed.'[14] Newman himself pondered,

> Lately I have been thinking much on the subject of grace, Regeneration &c and reading Sumner's 'Apostolical Preaching' which Hawkins has given me. Sumner's Book threatens to drive me into either *Calvinism or Baptismal Regeneration*, and I wish to steer clear of both at least in preaching. I am always slow in deciding a question; and last night I was so distressed and low about it, that the thought even struck me I must leave the Church. I have been praying about it, before I rose this morning, and I do not know what will be the end of it. I think I really desire the truth, and would embrace it wherever I found it.[15]

That Newman was genuinely distressed by this topic there is no doubt. That he chose the doctrine of baptismal regeneration history attests.[16] Two further questions need to be answered: (i) what it was about Sumner's work that caused Newman such distress; and (ii) what influenced him to choose baptismal regeneration as opposed to Calvinism, which significantly he later renamed 'Lutheranism'. To seek to answer these questions a number of other questions must first be reflected upon.

What Newman implied or wished to determine by the statement 'as being drawn not from Primitive Christianity but from Scripture' has given rise to much discussion. Dessain, for one, used the phrase to support the ecumenical potential of

Newman's work.[17] By 1874, when Newman republished his *Lectures* as a Roman Catholic, it was certainly possible to read an ecumenical gloss into the text, as illustrated by his revised Advertisement.

> Their drift is to show that there is little difference but what is verbal in the various views on justification, found whether among Catholic or Protestant divines; by Protestant being meant Lutheran, Calvinistic and thirdly that dry anti-evangelical doctrine, which was dominant in the Church of England during the last century, and is best designated by the name Arminianism.[18]

These words were *not* however supported in the text itself, which retained all his personal polemic against Luther. The only alterations to the text of 1838 were made to ensure that his definition of justification ultimately rested on an intrinsic understanding of justification, in conformity to orthodox Roman Catholic teaching.[19] It is indeed proof of the breadth – some might say confusion – of the original text, that Newman was able to republish the work as a Roman Catholic almost as it had stood in 1838. It is clear from correspondence to his sister in 1838 that ecumenism was neither his original aim nor intention in writing the *Lectures*: he confessed, 'I feel certain it is the right way of taking the question – and that it will (at least I trust so) if so taken now introduce the same confusion into their ranks, as an ambush rising up would', the ambush being intended for evangelicals and liberals.[20]

Prior to 1822,[21] Newman had simply accepted the stereotypical view of reformed faith testified to by eighteenth- and nineteenth-century evangelicals in England. It is here suggested that the strength of his objection to Luther expressed in the *Lectures* is rooted in self-criticism, for having once held beliefs that he later came to reject. This might also explain why he directed his polemic against Luther and not Calvin; it sounded less contradictory. Unfortunately, what Newman believed and understood about Luther was little more than a hollow caricature.

The 'influences' that Newman experienced in 1822 were those of the historical and doctrinal heritage of a Christian tradition that was antecedent to the Reformation. Others involved with the Oxford Movement – for example W. F. Hook and, to an extent, Pusey – incorporated the experience of the sixteenth century into an inclusive and unbroken line of continuity with the early church and sacramental practice. It explains why they were able to remain within the perimeter of the Anglican Communion. This was not the case with Newman. Explaining why he came to take such a decision, Newman pointed to the influence of Sumner's *Apostolical Preaching*.

Sumner's work is neither negative nor unjustly critical of evangelicalism. Where there is criticism, it is implied rather than obvious. Overall, Sumner's work exemplifies a particularly irenic approach to Christian faith and practice, itself reflective of Sumner's own understanding of the *via media* character to the Church of England. Circumstantially, the impact of Sumner's *Apostolical Preaching* was amplified by the fact that it coincided with the awakening of Newman's anxiety about the uncertainty of salvation. Newman's realization that he could not, as he had thought, neatly divide the world into two classes 'the one all darkness and the other all light' created a spiritual crisis.[22] Sumner's work was crucial because it highlighted to him that the teaching of St Paul enshrined in Scripture held out intrinsic, and therefore ultimately subjective, proof, and not external or objective confirmation. Newman's trust in an external and historically verifiable tradition was the answer to his own *Anfectung*. Sumner's *Apostolical Preaching* is a work now generally overlooked, and yet it is responsible for polarizing the baptism versus conversion argument for Newman. The decision that Newman made regarding this argument laid the foundation, among more general topics, for his specific rejection of Luther and simultaneously planted the seeds of what became his concept of 'justification by baptism', as articulated in the *Lectures on Justification*. It hardly needs to be mentioned that Newman went from one end of the doctrinal spectrum to the other on the subject of justification.

Sumner's work offers an exposition of the doctrine of grace that is purposively *inclusive* in recognition that the Church of England was representative of the English populace. It is this comprehension of grace that was evidenced in the Gorham

Judgment, under Sumner's primacy at Canterbury, some thirty-five years later. Newman, presented with the same scriptural evidence as Sumner, developed a rigid doctrine of baptismal grace. Curiously, both churchmen stressed the ultimate and enabling role of the Holy Spirit in the act of justification: this was the sole feature which united them as fellow members of the Church of England, both past and present. Sumner's work was obviously congruent with that of other Anglican divines, namely Cranmer and Hooker.

In the *Apostolical Preaching*, Sumner's reading of St Paul led him to conclude that the doctrines of grace and justification by faith sprang immediately from the fact of human corruption; to that end, grace and faith were the God-given remedy for man's helplessness. As a result of man's inherent corruption, the solution, argued Sumner, must originate *exterior* to man. Commenting specifically upon the text of Romans 8:11 and Titus 3:6, Sumner clarified: 'Throughout his [St Paul's] writings, conversion to the Christian faith, perseverance in it, renunciation of sin, and the practice of holiness, are universally ascribed to the influence of divine grace, and the operation of the Holy Spirit.'[23] This belief Sumner saw replicated in Article 11, which likewise makes a case for man's helplessness. In short, Sumner's argument rests on the fact that justification is external to our nature and can be achieved by God alone. He contended, 'faith and holiness are no natural produce of the human heart, but implanted and nourished there by the "Spirit of God"'.[24] Where Newman understood Luther to place the 'miracle' in the act of man's ability to believe, which mechanically effected a legal justification without love or works, Sumner understood the 'miracle' to be just that that made the 'moral' possible by the activity of the Holy Spirit. It was the same sacramental position as that held by Luther. For Newman, this activity was inherent; for Sumner, it can be inferred from his understanding of St Paul and reverence for Luther that this activity remained extrinsic. Sumner explained,

A review of the quotations, I think, must lead to a conviction that the ideas of sanctification and grace were thus habitually associated in the Apostle's mind, so that, it was unnatural to him to remind the churches of the holiness expected of them, without reminding them of the means by which it must be produced, established, strengthened, and preserved. A preacher who should enforce the one without reference to the other would act as a sort of Egyptian taskmaster to his congregation: he issues the order, but denies the means of its accomplishment.[25]

Sumner's own conception of Luther was that of a preacher who taught the need for both 'the miraculous and the moral'. Sumner began the sixth chapter of his *Apostolical Preaching* with a quotation from Luther's *Commentary on Galatians*, 'Faith alone justifies, yet faith is not sufficient': that is precisely the impetus of both Cranmer and Hooker in their works on justification. It is in this context that Sumner spoke of a man being renewed:

This much then is unquestionably certain: St Paul declares grace to be necessary to all 'good works, to faith, and calling upon God.' He affirms this by implication, when he teaches the natural inability of man: he affirms it positively, when he ascribes the ability of the renewed man to 'God, working in him both to will and to do.' On this point there can be no hesitation: and all that appeal to the same authority, ought to agree in the same doctrine.[26]

It is here that Newman appeared to take issue with Sumner's doctrine of justification. In short Newman was much troubled by the lack of authority and certitude in Sumner's definition of grace. Newman, in tandem with Luther, craved salvific assurance. He did not find such assurance in his Calvinism (as he named it), as was underlined by his pastoral work, which proved to him that human nature was a curious and indistinguishable mixture of good and evil. Sumner's work was therefore influential on Newman because it extirpated all notions of visible predestination, which is the bank in which Newman had entrusted his soul up until 1822. Sumner's work unconsciously demonstrated to Newman the ambivalent nature of Scripture as a source of unequivocal authority. Sumner's own intention had been to stress the outward and visible verification of Scripture by highlighting the institution of the sacrament of baptism as the promise of the Word. 'On the other hand, the example of St Paul authorises us to assert, that grace sufficient to salvation is given to all who are dedicated to Christ in baptism.'[27] To that end Sumner must be credited or castigated for teaching Newman where to find assurance. The editor of the *Autobiographical Writings* clarified that Newman read into the *Apostolical Preaching* a different concept of grace from that intended by its author, an emphasis that may have been stimulated by his simultaneous discovery of the potential of ecclesiastical tradition as a source of spiritual authority.

There is, therefore, a fundamental difference between the stress that Sumner placed on baptism and that of Newman. Sumner emphasized the act of baptism because of its inclusiveness, as he understood St Paul to teach that grace is within the reach of all, without reserve or distinction, that the Spirit 'works' in the souls of all, enabling them 'to work out their own salvation'.[28] Newman, on the other hand, stressed baptism – or, more precisely, the preservation of baptismal grace – for its exclusiveness, an assertion corroborated by his preoccupation with post-baptismal sin, a belief in which he was strongly influenced by Pusey. By contrast, Sumner understood grace to be a gift that was freely available to counter the negative effects of post-baptismal transgressions.

For Sumner it will be evident that the 'moral' was dependent upon the 'miraculous': it acted as its mirror, its reflection. Commenting on Romans 2:6ff. and Galatians 3:26, Sumner expressed the heart of his definition of grace to rest on the understanding that:

> With equal clearness he [St Paul] intimates, that the Christians he addresses were thus regenerate: as having 'put off the old man with its deeds'; and having become 'temples of the Holy Ghost' . . . ' For, as many of you as have been baptised unto Christ, have put on Christ.' On the authority of these examples our Church identifies regeneration and baptism.[29]

To clarify, Sumner believed that without the miraculous, that is faith, the moral was empty and likewise without the moral the miraculous remained ineffective.[30] To support this position Sumner quoted, in an extended footnote, from a tract that he attributes to Doddridge:[31]

as Doddridge argues, it too evidently follows, that every one who is baptised is not, of course, born of God, or regenerate: and therefore, that baptism is *not* Scripture regeneration. But if it be interpreted as signifying an exemption from the penalty of Adam's sin by admission into the covenant of Christ, it does take place at baptism: and as this is the sense in which our Church uses the word, it ought not to be lightly departed from. Particularly it should be observed, that this latter is the only sense in which it can be said to take place at a *definite time*. The usage of the word, to imply that gradual change which is produced in the heart of the true believer by the influence of the Holy Spirit, may be just in many respects, but it is liable to mistake. Thus our Church calls 'spiritual regeneration,' in the baptismal service; and in the 27th Art. speaks of baptismal regeneration as a sign of spiritual regeneration. There is a fallacy in arguing from this Article, that baptism cannot be the regeneration intended by our Church, inasmuch as it is here called the 'sign' of it. The question is not, whether regeneration and baptism are synonymous words, which will hardly be contended; but, whether regeneration *takes place* at baptism.[32]

Sumner believed, in conformity with the teaching of Article 13, that man was unable to perform good works before 'the Grace of Christ and the Inspiration of his Spirit'.[33] He continued,

St Paul expressly affirms, that no man can attain any degree of holiness without grace; and no less clearly intimates that all men, under the Gospel, are endued with such grace as may enable them to strive against natural corruption, to seek for the larger influence of the Spirit, and to work acceptably in the sight of God: such grace, as, when it meets with a willing mind is increased 'day by day,' and 'inwardly renews' the Christian; where it is neglected and 'done despite unto, is gradually withdrawn, and the obdurate sinner at last 'given over to a reprobate mind.'[34]

Sumner was anxious to show that belief in a doctrine of declarative righteousness did not deviate from the importance of the sacrament of baptism, for the sacramental character itself is dependent upon an effusion of the Holy Spirit towards the inward renewing of the heart, that the person baptised, who of his own nature could 'do no good thing,' ... – if in effect, I say, of baptism is less than this, what becomes of the distinction under John, 'I indeed baptise with water, but He who comes after me, shall baptise with the Holy Ghost?.[35]

Although Sumner believed that a person could reject grace, he was not convinced of the opposite argument, that a person could 'actively' accept it.[36] It is an interpretation of Luther's belief in the essentially passive nature of salvation, a belief shared by Coleridge, Maurice and Kingsley. For Maurice particularly, it was the basis of his universalistic comprehension of salvation. Like Luther – and Cranmer – Sumner believed that salvation was an ongoing – day-by-day – process, a daily renewal of both the promise and power of baptism.[37]

To summarize, the *Apostolical Preaching* is based on the proposition that the Church of England was restructured at the time of the Reformation. Written fourteen years before the Act of Catholic Emancipation, the work demonstrates that it was both the product of its time in its attitude to Roman Catholics, and also before its time, in linking the names of Cranmer and Luther without reference to the rest of the entourage of the Reformation. '*Thus the doctrine of Luther and Cranmer was rather a restoration than a reformation of the Christian scheme*: and the arguments they used in support of it were the same which St Paul had used to the advocates of the Jewish Law, whether moral or ceremonial, in addressing the Romans and Galatians.'[38]

The fact that Sumner saw the work of Luther as a restoration of Christian truth rather than a reformation was key to an objective understanding of Luther. Both Roman Catholics and ultra-evangelicals believed in a perception of Luther that stressed his break with the past, rather than its purification and renewal. This was also fundamental to Newman's theological objection to Luther. Sumner's work is an excellent example of the way in which Luther was part of the general consciousness – indeed, sub-consciousness – of religious faith in England; underlined by his liberal use of quotations from Luther's *Commentary on Galatians*. It would take the subsequent religious polemics initially aroused by the Oxford Movement to give this general consciousness a more definite shape.

The stress that Newman placed on Sumner's *Apostolical Preaching*, both at the time of his acquiring the work and retrospectively in the *Apologia*, confirms the prejudice of his antagonism to Luther, as he first read the work fourteen years before he published the *Lectures on Justification*. Although it does not directly affect the current discussion, what Sumner's work revealed was a concept of justification and sanctification dependent upon the Holy Spirit that was common to all shades of churchmanship in the Church of England. It is not, therefore, a concept original to Newman or dependent upon his interest in the Eastern Orthodox Church, as argued by C. S. Dessain.

Before concluding, as a general comment it is worth noting that, at best, the ecumenical potential and, at worst, the confusion of Newman's *Lectures* are most clearly evident in the secondary material. The breadth of the *Lectures* has allowed later commentators to see what they want to see; one needs to be constantly on guard to retain a sense of objectivity.

Concerning Newman's personal opinion of the Reformation, and more particularly Luther, he confessed in a private moment:

> It [the doctrine of justification] is a terra incognita in our Church, and I am so afraid not of saying things wrong so much, as queer and crotchety – *and -misunderstanding other writers for really the Lutherans etc. as divines are so shallow and inconsequent, that I can hardly believe my own impressions about them.*[39]

This confession adds weight to the assertion that Newman's portrayal of Luther was founded on bias and personal prejudice. Not surprisingly, in a letter written to Keble in early 1838, Newman appeared agitated, if not desperate, to rid himself of the charge of Romanism.[40] Even after finishing his *Lectures* and relinquishing them to the publisher, Newman could still write to his sister, 'The great difficulty was to avoid *being* difficult – which, on the subject of justification is not a slight one – it is so entangled and mystified by irrelevant and refined questions.'[41] C. S. Dessain recorded that Newman burnt six hundred draft pages of his *Lectures* when he published the book.[42] In spite of the many recent attempts to soften the vehemence of Newman's reproach of Luther, there is little reason to doubt that what he says about Luther in the written *Lectures* is what he wanted to say, especially because he repeated it when the work was republished in 1874.[43]

Conclusion

John Henry Newman's comprehension of justification is best understood as neither moral nor miraculous, and being as much a product of his historical situation as was Luther's association with the doctrine of justification. One could, how-ever, be forgiven for thinking Newman's doctrine of justifica-tion erred on the side of the moral, and likewise Luther's on the side of the miraculous. Sumner, for his part, sought to hold the two positions in creative tension.[44] Both Newman and Luther were misunderstood. Newman identified most closely with a sacramental view of justification, as it is in and through the sacraments that the Holy Trinity comes to dwell in man through the gift of the Holy Spirit; objectively, a doctrine very close to that of Luther's *alien righteousness of Christ*. New-man's unsystematic use of Luther in his *Lectures* continued the Anglican trend of using Luther for its own ends, rather than in a historically critical manner.

Newman's portrayal of Luther in the *Lectures* was, above all, personal and contextual. It was personal, in that the *Lectures* fell within a new temperament in the Oxford Move-ment. (From 1836 onwards, Newman could no longer fit his conception of catholicism into a comprehension of Protestant-ism; as such, the *Lectures* played a determinant role in the presentation of the Movement to the world at a crucial stage in its evolution). In explaining his motives for writing, he con-fessed to having been inspired by the doctrinal seriousness of Pusey. He admitted to feeling a certain, 'intellectual cowardice in not finding a basis in reason for my belief'.[45] It was contextual, because the *Lectures* were essentially produced to defend the ecclesiological opinion of the Oxford Movement rather than being the basis of the Movement. The *Lectures* were very much the product of the 1830s. They confirm the Oxford Movement's primary concern with ecclesiology rather than doctrine. Newman approached Luther with a fixed mind, fixed between 1824 and 1834. At best, one can say that Newman had 'tunnel vision' in approaching Luther by 1837–8. If Newman was defending any individual, apart from his own opinions, it was Pusey. The portrayal of Luther in the English Church is best described as 'pick 'n mix', an approach that was not confined to Newman but was shared by John Foxe, who, for example, although a strong supporter of a forensic doctrine of justification, was embarrassed by Luther's retention of the real presence. Luther was never an obvious person of importance for Newman. Newman's attitude to Luther can be viewed as a waste product of his decision to accept the doctrine of baptismal regeneration.[46]

If one compares the 1838 edition of the *Lectures* with the 1874 edition and the environment in which each was published, Newman's ecumenism in the *Lectures* appears to have been an afterthought, rather than the result of forethought and intention. What prevents his Lectures from being intrinsically ecumenical is their polemic against Luther. The work certainly alienated evangelical support from within the Church of England for the Oxford Movement. A good example of this is the effect which Newman's *Lectures* had on Samuel Wilberforce, who confessed to having a 'a growing suspicion of the unsoundness of Newman's unscriptural emphasis on sanctification as . . . the *fons et origo* of all other tractarian errors'.[47] The *Lectures* also pulled the Movement away from its High Church roots (of which W. F. Hook's attitude is a good example). After 1840, Newman chose to close his mind to the 'painful' subject of justification. As G. S. Faber pointed out, what caused the confusion in the first edition of Newman's *Lectures* was that he does present two systems of justification, neither of which is exclusive. This was something which Newman himself did not deny. In reply to Faber's questioning over this exact point, Newman wrote on 11 April 1838: 'I think you are right in saying that I partly agree with you, partly with Mr. Knox, and partly with neither.' The one thing that

Newman was certain of in his *Lectures* was that Luther's presentation of justification was ecclesiastically erroneous.

Newman and others of the Tractarians failed to acknowledge that the Reformation itself was built on antiquity as well as Scripture. At the end of the day, one is left with little choice but to conclude that Newman's portrayal of Luther and his comprehension of the manner of justification in the Anglican Church were flawed. This conclusion can, sadly, be underlined by the fact that Newman chose to persist in this subjective portrayal of Luther when the work was republished in 1874. Further, his verbal economy in quoting Luther's *Commentary on Galatians* went beyond simple polemicism, and is illustrative of his intention to use Luther to support his own position. One should not, however, dismiss the fact that Newman had to face immense difficulties in attempting to construct a genuinely Anglican doctrine of justification; his choice of Luther as an adversary was partly to make this task more manageable. The fact remains, however, that a mid-Victorian Primate achieved a comprehension of Luther and justification that was true to the one and sustained the much-sought-after *via media* between justification and sanctification of the other. Sumner's position on justification suggests that Newman's own comprehension of justification held within the Church of England – a comprehension that led him to flee the church of his birth, with all the subsequent reverberations – might actually have been unnecessary. To ruminate on such issues is to seek to rewrite history. The lack of importance attached to Sumner's *Apostolical Preaching*, however, compared with the prominence afforded to Newman's *Lectures on Justification*, begs the question: had Newman remained an Anglican, would his voice still be the tolling bell of English theology? Or, is the notoriety attached to his secession, and the polemic it implies, the reason his voice is still heard today?

Notes

1   J F Perry SJ, *unpublished* 'Newman's Treatment of Luther in the

Lectures on the Doctrine of Justification'. Th.M. Thesis, (1976) St. Mary's University, Halifax, Nova Scotia. Perry made the important suggestion that Froude's attack on the Reformation can be attributed to the debate on Luther aroused by Sir William Hamilton.

2   See H. E. Jacobs, *The Lutheran Movement in England*, rev. edn (Philadelphia, 1891), p. 32. 'The great Reformer had so stamped an image of himself upon the Teutonic movement, that similar tendencies in other lands were vaguely named after him.'

3   J. H. Newman, *Apologia Pro Vita Sua*, ed. M. J. Svaglic (Oxford, 1967), p. 74 (hereafter *Apologia*). See P. E. More, *Anglicanism: The Thought and Practice of the Church of England* (London, 1935), p. xxx.

4   See Peter Toon, 'A Critical Review of John Henry Newman's Doctrine of Justification', *Churchman*, 94 (1980), 335–44 and *Evangelical Theology 1833–1856: A Response to Tractarianism* (London, 1979); Fr. Thomas Sheridan, *Newman on Justification* (New York, 1967); Sheridan Gilley, *Newman and his Age* (London, 1990); B. M. G. Reardon, *From Coleridge to Gore: A Century of Religious Thought in Britain* (London, 1971), pp. 116–21; P. Nockles, *The Oxford Movement in Context* (Cambridge, 1994), pp. 228–69; H. Cuncliffe-Jones, 'Newman on Justification', in *Clergy Review* (1969), 117–24; Y. Brilioth, *Anglican Revival* (London, 1925); R. A. Leaver, *The Doctrine of Justification in the Church of England* Latimer Studies, 3 (Latimer House, 1979); David Newsome, 'Justification and sanctification: Newman and the evangelicals', *Journal of Theological Studies* (1964), 32–53; A. E. McGrath, 'John Henry Newman's "Lectures on Justification": the High Church misrepresentation of Luther', *Churchman*, 97 (1983), 112–22; *Iustitia Dei*, 2 vols (Cambridge, 1986), II, section 33, pp. 121–34; H. Chadwick, 'The lectures on justification', in I. Ker and A. G. Hill (ed.), *Newman after One Hundred Years* (Oxford, 1990), p. 295ff; F. L. Cross, *The Oxford Movement and the 17th Century* (London, 1933), 'The thought and practice of the Church of England illustrated from the religious literature of the 17th century', in F. L. Cross and P. E. More (eds), *Anglicanism* (London, 1935) and *John Henry Newman* (London, 1935); C. C. J. Webb, *Religious Thought in the Oxford Movement* (London, 1928); Ian Ker, *The Achievement of John Henry Newman* (London, 1991), pp. 106–9 and *Newman and the Fullness of Christianity* (Edinburgh, 1990), pp. 95–7; C. S. Dessain, 'The biblical basis of Newman's

ecumenical theology'; J. Coulson and A. M. Allchin (eds), *The Rediscovery of Newman: An Oxford Symposium* (London, 1967).

5   *Letters and Diaries of John Henry Newman*, 31 vols (Oxford, 1961–) VI, p. 52 (hereafter *LD*).

6   *Apologia*, p. 74.

7   *LD*– VI, p. 104.

8   Ibid., p. 103.

9   Ibid., p. 104: 'I do not doubt that my correspondence with the Christian Observer has done what I intended it to do – *frighten* our particular brethren … It is remarkable how plans of altering the Liturgy have died away ever since our movement began. We have given them other things to think about … '.

10 Ibid., pp. 253–4, 212, 70–3.

11 In both volumes of the *Iustitia Dei* and a series of individual articles, published in the *Churchman*, Alister McGrath based his critique of Newman's use of Luther on the false assumption of Newman's literary and doctrinal dependence upon Alexander Knox's 'Essay on Justification'. McGrath stated, 'The editor of Knox's *Remains*, John Henry Newman, subsequently delivered a course of lectures at Oxford in which he defended and enlarged upon Knox's essay of 1810' (*Iustitia Dei*, II, p. 122). Newman was not the editor of Knox's *Remains*, rather, Newman spoke of the editor as being the Reverend James J. Hornby, Rector of Winwick, Lancaster. In acknowledgement of Hornby's editorship, Newman chose him, together with the evangelical churchman G. S. Faber (author of *The Primitive Doctrine of Justification Investigated*), to review his published *Lectures on Justification*. Although Newman was not the editor of Knox's *Remains*, the fact that he chose Hornby to review his work implied a certain familiarity with Knox's writings, and there is an indubitable similarity between Knox's perception of the doctrine of justification and that of Newman. I would argue, however, that the resemblance of doctrine between Knox and Newman is parallel rather than sequential. Both Knox and Newman rooted their perception of justification in a Church of England that pre-dated the Reformation. Alexander Knox's 'Essay' (*Remains*, 4 vols (London, 1834–7), I, pp. 256–8) owes its notoriety to its association with Newman's *Lectures* and not vice versa. Knox's essay began as a letter to a D. Parken of Dublin, written 16 April 1810, and is intended to be a response to Milner's portrayal of an exclusive evangelical Lutheran doctrine of justification in *The History of the Church*. Knox

NOTES

tentatively acknowledged that this attitude might well be the
product of the current times rather than Luther's original
intention, although in general his essay is concerned specifically
with tracing the Anglican lineage of the doctrine of justification
to the early church, a lineage he saw reflected in Cranmer's
Homily on Salvation. Knox critically bypassed the continental
Reformation and in conclusion advocated a doctrine of extreme
baptismal regeneration as the orthodox means of justification in
the Church of England (p. 287). Knox's essay is best seen as a
reaction to the prevailing spirit of evangelical fundamentalism,
he concluded; 'All I have said tells you, that I do not follow the
moderns, to the neglect of the ancients; and that I am not
deterred from candidly examining, the countenance of a
doctrine, by seeing its back marked with the terrible word,
Popery.' If the preface to the *Lectures* is to be taken seriously,
Newman there denied any influence from the works of Knox on
the one hand and G. S. Faber on the other.

12 Gilley, *Newman and his Age*, p. 50.
13 Cf. Dessain, 'Biblical basis', pp. 100–22 and 'Cardinal Newman
and the Eastern tradition', *Downside Review*, 94 (1976)
pp. 83–98.
14 *AW*, p. 77.
15 Ibid., p. 78.
16 Ibid. On 13 January 1825, Newman announced, 'I think I must
give up the doctrine of imputed righteousness and that of
regeneration as apart from baptism'.
17 Cf. Dessain, *Rediscovery of Newman*, p. 121.
18 *LJ*, 3rd edn (London, 1874), p. ix.
19 Toon summarized the situation in his article, 'A critical review
of John Henry Newman's doctrine of justification.' pp. 343–4.
'Newman reissued the Lectures in 1874 when he was a
respected Roman Catholic. The material is precisely the same,
except for the addition of a new preface of about a thousand
words and fourteen brief notes placed in square brackets at the
bottom of the appropriate page.'
20 *LD-*, VI, p. 253–4.
21 *Apologia*, p. 20: 'In 1822 I came under very different influences
from those in which I had hitherto been subjected'.
22 *AW*, p. 77.
23 J. B. Sumner, *Apostolical Preaching Considered in an
Examination of St. Paul's Epistles* (London, 1815), p. 123
(hereafter *AP*).
24 Ibid., p. 126.

25 Ibid., pp. 126–7.
26 Ibid., p. 127.
27 Ibid., pp. 128–9.
28 Ibid., p. 129.
29 Ibid., pp. 136–7.
30 Ibid., pp. 137–65.
31 It has not proved possible to trace the exact reference of Sumner's quotation, although Sumner's first sentence appears in Doddridge's 'First Sermon on Regeneration', *Works*, II, p. 394.
32 *AP*, p. 137.
33 Ibid., p. 140.
34 Ibid., p. 144.
35 Ibid., pp. 146–7.
36 Ibid., pp. 152–3.
37 Ibid., pp. 164–5.
38 Ibid., p. 178 (italics mine).
39 LDN, vi, p. 188.
40 Ibid., p. 190.
41 Ibid., p. 221.
42 Dessain, 'Biblical basis', p. 119.
43 Ibid., pp. 121–2; see also Dessain, 'Cardinal Newman and the Eastern tradition', 98.
44 *AP*, p. 160 ff.
45 *Apologia*, p. 66.
46 See A. Mozley, *Letters and Correspondence*, I, p. 120 (13 January 1825).
47 Cited in Newsome, 'Justification and sanctification', 53.

Index